W9-ABP-923

SOLIDARITY AND THE SOVIET WORKER

The Impact of the Polish Events of 1980 on Soviet Internal Politics

Elizabeth Teague

CROOM HELM
London • New York • Sydney

Croom Helm Ltd, Provident House, Burrell Row,
Beckenham, Kent, BR3 1AT
Croom Helm Australia, 44-50 Waterloo Road,
North Ryde, 2113, New South Wales

Published in the USA by
Croom Helm
in association with Methuen, Inc.
29 West 35th Street,
New York, NY 10001

British Library Cataloguing in Publication Data

Teague, Elizabeth
Solidarity and the Soviet worker: the
impact of the Polish events of 1980 on
Soviet internal politics.
1. Soviet Union — Politics and government
— 1953–1982 2. Poland — Politics and
government — 1980–
I. Title
320.9438 DK274

ISBN 0-7099-4350-4

Library of Congress Cataloging-in-Publication Data

Teague, Elizabeth.
Solidarity and the Soviet worker: the impact of the Polish events of 1980 on Soviet internal politics/Elizabeth Teague.
p. cm.
Originally presented as the author's thesis (Ph. D.) — University of Birmingham.
Bibliography: p.
Includes index.
ISBN 0-7099-4350-4
1. Soviet Union — Politics and government — 1982- 2. Labor and laboring classes — Soviet Union. 3. Public opinion — Soviet Union. 4. NSZZ "Solidarność" (Labor organization) 5. Poland — Politics and government — 1980- I. Title.
DK288.T43 1988
947.085'3 — dc 19 87-31036

The camera copy for this book was prepared by the author. The publisher acknowledges that the inverted commas do not appear in the standard form.

Printed and bound in Great Britain by
Biddles Ltd, Guildford and King's Lynn

CONTENTS

ACKNOWLEDGEMENTS

This book began life as a doctoral dissertation, and I wish to thank Professor Philip Hanson and Dr Nicholas Lampert of the Centre for Russian and East European Studies at the University of Birmingham for their support while I was working on it. It was Professor Hanson who first suggested that some of the research reports I was writing for Radio Liberty might be expanded into a thesis, and without his encouragement I should never have seen the project through. I am also grateful to Dr Iain Elliot, the external examiner for the thesis, for his comments on the study at that stage in its evolution. Both he and Dr Lampert made valuable suggestions which have assisted me in turning the thesis into a book.

I owe a great deal to my colleagues at Radio Free Europe/Radio Liberty. I am particularly grateful to Keith Bush, Jon Lodeesen, Sergei Voronitsyn, Lev Roitman, Vladimir Kusin, Bohdan Nahaylo, Kevin Devlin, Mario Corti, Herwig Kraus and Alexander Rahr, to Robert Farrell and the editorial staff, and to the staffs of the Library, Red Archive, Samizdat Archive, Current Information Service, Central News Division, and Computer Center. I also wish to thank Abraham Brumberg for his encouragement, and to express my gratitude for the valuable discussions I have had with Professor Ernst Kux.

I am deeply grateful to Professor B.P. Pockney and his colleagues in the Department of Linguistic and International Studies at the University of Surrey, and to my friends Rosemary Graham, Rosemary Davidson, Anne Kelly, Mark Cohen and Mara Cooper for their encouragement when I first began my studies.

Finally, this book is dedicated, with love and gratitude, to my parents, my aunts, and my friend.

QUESTION: What does "Solidarity" mean?

ANSWER: "Solidarity" means that when the Russians have no meat, the Poles go on strike.

(Joke current in the USSR, 1980-81)

Chapter 1

INTRODUCTION: "THE LEADERS AND THE LED"

Poland in the summer of 1980 saw the eruption of labour unrest on an unprecedented scale. Faced with nationwide strikes, the leadership of the ruling Communist Party, the Polish United Workers' Party (PUWP), was forced to come to terms with the striking workers and to sanction, for the first time in a socialist country, the creation of independent, self-governing trade unions, free of Communist Party and government control. The rise of Solidarity--as the autonomous trade union movement was called--led to the near collapse of communist rule in Poland. This unique attempt to make a non-violent workers' revolution was brought to an abrupt end with the declaration of martial law on 13 December 1981.

The emergence of Solidarity challenged more than the right of the Polish Communist Party to its self-proclaimed leading role. The events in Poland were also viewed with acute anxiety by the country's socialist allies and, in particular, by the Union of Soviet Socialist Republics (USSR). Poland is, first of all, the largest and strategically the most important of the Soviet Union's western neighbours. Occupying the corridor along which invading European armies have traditionally attacked the Russian heartland, Poland both joins the USSR to and separates it from Germany. Any change in Poland's system of government might remove this buffer and leave both the USSR and the German Democratic Republic (GDR) exposed. Maverick Polish behaviour might also encourage centrifugal forces in Eastern Europe and threaten Soviet hegemony in areas of vital concern to the USSR: the Warsaw Treaty Organisation and the Council for Mutual Economic Assistance (the Soviet-led trading bloc).

Finally, there was in the eyes of the leaders of both the USSR and its East European allies a danger that Poland's labour unrest might inspire protests by workers in other countries of the socialist bloc. This anxiety was heightened by the serious economic and social problems troubling the countries of the socialist community as the 1980s began. The USSR, in particular, faced not only stagnation in economic growth but also, as the long years of the leadership of Leonid Brezhnev drew to a close, a generational change in the ruling elite. These factors added to the Kremlin's unease as the events in Poland unfolded.[1]

This book examines Soviet domestic policies in the period following the birth of Solidarity and the measures the leadership took to prevent the spread of the "Polish virus" to the Soviet population. Its aim is to discover how the Soviet leaders of the early 1980s perceived--and managed--their relations with the general population. So, to begin with, what do we mean by the "leaders" of the USSR?

When the Bolsheviks came to power in Russia in 1917 they set up a government entitled the Council of People's Commissars. Known today as the Council of Ministers, the Soviet government is in theory appointed by and responsible to a bicameral national parliament, the USSR Supreme Soviet, elected every five years by universal adult suffrage.

Of course, that is only half the story. The Soviet political system is split in two and, at every level of the hierarchy, there exists a parallel Party structure that supervises the work of state and government bodies. The key to the influence of the Communist Party lies in the system known as the *nomenklatura*, that is, the control the Party exercises over recruitment and appointment to all offices with decision-making powers. This is as true of a post at the lowest rung of Soviet local government as of one in the Council of Ministers.

From the earliest days of Soviet power, the real centre of decision-making has been not the government, but the topmost levels of the Bolshevik Party, known since 1952 as the Communist Party of the Soviet Union (CPSU). The CPSU is not a political party in the way that concept is normally understood in Western democracies; the only legal political party in the country, it is described in the Soviet constitution of 1977 as "the leading and guiding force of Soviet society and the nucleus of its political system, of all state and public organisations."

The Party is hierarchically structured. Power flows downward from its inner cabinet, or Politburo, which includes among its members not only those who hold the top posts in the Party leadership, but also representatives of key interest groups such as the prime minister, the foreign minister, and the head of the secret police (KGB). In theory, the Politburo is responsible to the Party's Central Committee, by which its members are elected. In practice, it is the real power centre of the CPSU, and therefore of the USSR. The Central Committee meets, as a general rule, every six months, whereas the Politburo meets weekly and is supported by the staff of the Central Committee Secretariat. The Secretariat briefs the Politburo and relays its decisions to lower Party, state and government organs.

In this study, the term "Soviet leadership" denotes a very small group: those belonging to the Politburo and Secretariat and, to a lesser extent, those upon whom they call for advice: the staff of the Central Committee apparatus, government ministers, secret police and foreign ministry officials, members of the Party's ideological apparatus, Party and government leaders in the fifteen Soviet republics and, finally, leaders of the Soviet Union's mass organisations (trade unions, youth organisations, and so on).

What is the relationship of this group to the society it leads? The Polish events of 1980-81 raised the selfsame question, albeit in the Polish context and in an unusually acute form. Pressure for change came from outside the Party, from workers, intellectuals, peasants, and students. At issue was the fundamental principle of the communist system: the primacy of the Party. As one writer puts it, "what shipyard workers in Gdansk and miners in Katowice demanded was Poland's right to organize itself."[2]

Relations between the Soviet regime and the people it governs have always, it may be argued, been problematic. Indeed, this is a phenomenon with roots in the tsarist era, dating back long before the Revolution of October 1917. Michael Binyon, former Moscow correspondent of the London *Times*, asserts that Russian leaders, struggling to enforce their authority over their far-flung empire, "have always lived with insecurity, seeing threats to their authority in the slightest expression of opposition or nonconformity." This fear, Binyon suggests, was only increased by the October Revolution for, "if one revolution could begin with a small group of dedicated conspirators, so perhaps could another."[3]

It seems possible and even likely that the Soviet leaders have seldom felt confident that they enjoyed much popular support. There may even have been times when they feared a popular revolt.

This proposition cannot be easily tested. A brief recital of some familiar events from Soviet history shows, however, that it is not implausible. In the elections for the Constituent Assembly held in November 1917, for example, the Bolsheviks won less than 25 percent of the vote.[4] Having lost one election, they ensured that their popular support would never again be put to the test in multiparty elections. The elections of November 1917 were the last free elections ever held in Russia, just as the Constituent Assembly was the last freely-elected, representative body in Russian history. When it met in January 1918 and proved hostile to the Bolsheviks' programme, it was unceremoniously dispersed by force.

Bolshevik control of the infant Soviet republic was secured only after the defeat of foreign intervention and the waging of a long and bloody civil war. The climax of anticommunist revolt--involving, as the leader of the Bolshevik Party, Vladimir Lenin, admitted, "discontent not only among a considerable part of the peasantry but among the workers as well"[5]--came with the Kronstadt uprising of March 1921. Lenin was well aware that the revolt at the great naval base, which had in 1917 been one of the strongest bulwarks of the Bolshevik cause, was not an isolated event but an expression of widespread popular dissatisfaction. "We have failed," he said, "to convince the broad masses."[6] It was a warning of the precarious nature of the new government's hold on power, and it prompted a sharp turnabout in economic strategy: the adoption of the New Economic Policy (NEP), which permitted the temporary revival of small-scale private enterprise.

But the next major change in national economic and political strategy--the collectivisation of agriculture and the launching of the industrialisation drive by Josef Stalin--had no such implicit popular mandate. Party leaders and government officials cannot have been unaware of the hostility that forced collectivisation aroused among the peasantry. The number of unnatural deaths in the USSR in the period 1926 to 1937--years that witnessed the collectivisation famines--has been estimated by the British historian Robert Conquest to be some 14 million men, women and children.[7] Conquest believes that between five and seven million people died in the Great Ukrainian Famine alone,[8] while the Soviet physicist and human rights activist Andrei Sakharov has estimated that more than 1.2 million Party members alone were arrested during the "Great Purge" that followed collectivisation, that 600,000 of them were executed, and that of the others only 50,000 ever came out of prison.[9]

These figures are contentious, and considered to be too high by some Western experts. Stephen Wheatcroft argues, for example, that "there is no demographic evidence to indicate a population loss of more than six million between 1926 and 1939 or more than 3 or 4 million in the famine."[10] Other scholars assert, too, that the accelerated rates of upward social mobility that characterised Soviet society during the Stalin period acted as a powerful agent to bind many citizens to the new order.[11] It is universally acknowledged, nonetheless, that Stalin's victims ran into the millions and it seems unlikely, in the final analysis, that his methods of government increased the trust of subsequent generations of Soviet citizens in their leaders.

Indeed, the existence of some popular antipathy to Communist Party rule was demonstrated by the initial enthusiasm with which the invading German armies were greeted in 1941 in the USSR's border areas. Far from rallying to the defence of the motherland, many Ukrainians, Belorussians and Balts looked initially to the Germans to bring them liberation from "Russian Bolshevism." In the Baltic areas and Western Ukraine, attempts were made to establish independent statehood.[12]

Many collective farms in areas overrun by the *Wehrmacht* were spontaneously dissolved by the peasants themselves.[13] In Smolensk, the city soviet (local council) petitioned the German authorities for permission to form a "free Russia" government and an anticommunist army. The author Aleksandr Solzhenitsyn records that "the Germans were met with bread and salt in the villages on the Don."[14]

Thousands of Soviet prisoners-of-war agreed, moreover, to help the Nazis fight Stalin. By the end of 1941, between three and four million Soviet soldiers had been captured or had deserted. According to Solzhenitsyn, "nothing could possibly be more convincing than the way these men, soldiers in their prime, voted with their feet."[15]

The Great Patriotic War, as the Soviet Union's four-year struggle with Nazi Germany is known, was the greatest challenge the USSR has ever had to face. National loyalty, together with the brutality with which the German invaders treated the Soviet population in the occupied areas, had by 1942 united people and rulers against their common enemy. This was almost certainly a time when the leadership could feel confident of popular support. To this day, the shared experiences of the war years provide a wellspring of popular enthusiasm upon which Soviet leaders are able to draw. In recent years, in fact, the authorities appear to have relied increasingly upon this resource as a means of mobilising support for policies--such as the maintenance of a large standing army and compulsory military service--that might otherwise be unpopular.

During the war years, according to the former Yugoslav communist Milovan Djilas, many Soviet citizens hoped that the unity of Party and people that characterised the period might lead to a relaxation of terror and an easing of social controls once the war was over.[16] Relaxation came, however, only after Stalin's death in 1953 and, even when the process of destalinisation was completed, the Party retained its monopoly of political and economic organisation and of public communication.

Members of the Soviet elite have traditonally behaved as if they feared assassination or popular uprising. Bullet-proof cars; secret police informers; bizarre incidents such as the placing of a ring of troops around Moscow's Novodevich'e cemetry during the funeral of the disgraced leader Nikita Khrushchev[17]--such conduct suggests that Soviet leaders put little trust in their own popularity and constantly, therefore, anticipate trouble. In a country whose citizens have little opportunity--by international standards--for armed revolt, such precautions are striking.

At the same time, the true nature of Soviet popular perceptions of the political elite, and of the institutions upon which that elite bases its power, can be a matter only of speculation. The process by which the Soviet leadership attempts to construct and maintain its legitimacy in the eyes of the population is one in which the inputs are more visible than the outputs. The tendency to build a "cult of personality" around each new leader is, for example, a widely recognised phenomenon of the Soviet political system. Democratic societies encourage the dissemination of information concerning the range, distribution and intensity of popular sentiment about individual political leaders, parties and policies, as well as about existing social and political institutions and processes. Little public discussion of such topics is tolerated within the USSR, and there exists no freedom of the press. (This is not to say that data concerning public attitudes and opinions are not collected in the USSR; only that their collection is permitted exclusively under official auspices and that the results of public opinion sampling, when they are published at all, appear in highly selective form.)

It is therefore possible for Western students of Soviet politics to put forward diametrically opposed views of the nature of the relationship between regime and population. There are those, for example, who have portrayed Soviet society as on the verge of crisis and disintegration. Economic difficulties and hardships will, according to the proponents of this view, exacerbate smouldering national and social tensions and erupt, eventually, into open conflict between leaders and led. On the other hand there are those who stress the existence of elements of pluralism in the post-Stalin Soviet Union and argue the possibility for the articulation and aggregation of conflicting interests within Soviet society.[18]

The debate began soon after Khrushchev's ouster in 1964 and remains pertinent today. At issue was the question of "evolution or revolution," "adaptation or disintegration" for the Soviet system. As Soviet society became more complex and sophisticated, it was argued, the methods of overt terror employed during Stalin's rule became increasingly dysfunctional; a complex modern society requires a free rein for individual initiative and for the expression of the particular interests of various social groups.

Writing in 1966, the American scholar Zbigniew Brzezinski argued that the Soviet political system, primarily designed for the conduct and consolidation of the revolution, was ill adapted to the needs of a modernising society. The CPSU, he asserted, had grown so rigidly centralised and hierarchical, so "corrupted by years of unchallenged power," that it was "inimical to talent" and "hostile to political innovation." Brzezinski expressed doubt whether the system had the will or the capacity to accommodate new social and intellectual forces. In such circumstances, he argued, "decay is bound to set in."[19]

Brzezinski was supported by Robert Conquest, who described the Soviet political system as "radically and dangerously inappropriate to its social and economic dynamics." Conquest saw the system as "strong and experienced but with little 'give,' at present sufficient to contain the social and economic forces, but not designed to cope with the unexpected."[20]

Other scholars saw the Soviet system as able to

evolve and to transform itself. Merle Fainsod, for example, sided with those who predicted that the regime would "continue to muddle along, patching up compromises and adjustments, and responding sufficiently to the aspirations of its people to avoid total collapse."[21] Hans Morgenthau was another who argued that the system had a good chance of survival, for while "ideological dissatisfaction may lead to grumbling and indifference,... it will not lead to political action as long as the government is able to satisfy the basic aspirations of the population at large."[22]

Many Western commentators have argued that Nikita Khrushchev's abandonment of the use of terror constituted a major transformation of the Soviet system. In Fainsod's words, "By abandoning mass terror and placing greater reliance on incentives and amenities, [the post-Stalin leadership] has sought to narrow the gap between rulers and ruled and to broaden its base of popular support."[23]

In a series of controversial articles, the American political scientist Jerry Hough challenged the idea, put forward by some Western scholars, that there was a widening gulf between the regime and the Soviet people.[24] In particular, Hough drew attention to the steps taken by the post-Khrushchev leadership toward greater egalitarianism, steps that amounted, in his view, to "a veritable war on poverty affecting millions of low-income citizens."[25] Under the leadership of Leonid Brezhnev, Hough asserted, the Soviet system demonstrated its adaptability by allowing increased participation in the political process by a number of social groups. To the image of the Soviet Union as a monolithic, "command-directed" system in which power flows from the top down, Hough counterposed a model which he named "institutional pluralism." Since the days of Stalin, Hough said, there had taken place a diffusion of power from the apex to other levels of society, with the result that ideas and power could now flow up as well as down the administrative hierarchy.[26] The post-Stalin leadership had shown itself increasingly willing "to listen to policy advice from 'society' and to permit far-reaching public discussion of policy questions."[27]

Hough depicted the Party of the second half of the twentieth century as a kind of "political broker" or mediator between different and competing interest groups.[28] This image of the CPSU was a far cry from the concept of a single, hierarchically organised mass party, exercising all the prerogatives of political power, that is a key component of the traditional totalitarian model of the Soviet system.[29] Hough cited evidence of incrementalism in policy change to support his contention that the Soviet system was well capable of adapting to fresh challenges:

> Whereas Stalin in his last years basically ignored the policy suggestions of the institutional centers of power, and whereas Khrushchev challenged the basic interests of almost every one of these centers..., the present leadership has not done battle with any important segment of the establishment and seems, on the contrary, to have acceded to the most central desires of each.[30]
>
> ...Not only are more people participating in decision-making, but a real de facto (if perhaps temporary) diffusion of power has occurred in the Brezhnev years. The Politburo retains the power to take any decision and to impose its will on any group, but the pattern of decisions clearly shows that the political leadership has intervened much less frequently to over-

> ride the judgements reached by the major participants (first of all, institutional ones) in each specialized policy area.[31]

Like Hough, the American historian Stephen Cohen has rejected the "persistent notion" that the CPSU is remote and isolated from the people. Such a conception, Cohen has written, "makes no sense in a country where the state employs almost every adult citizen and the Party has 18 million adult members." In fact, Cohen goes on, "there is reason to think that virtually all the diverse trends in society, ... including those expressed by dissidents, also exist inside the political officialdom, however subterraneanly." As a result, he argues, the Soviet system has far more popular support than Western scholars generally concede. Indeed, Cohen goes further and asserts that the "profound conservatism" of the mass of the Soviet population is not only the main source of the regime's stability but also the "main obstacle to change" in the USSR.[32]

Another viewpoint is expressed by the concept of an implicit "social contract" between leaders and led. The Soviet-born academic Dimitri Simes, for example, argues that throughout history an unwritten contract existed between the Russian government and the people, whereby the tsar provided protection in exchange for the people's obedience and service to the state. Upheavals resulted whenever the government failed to keep its side of the bargain.[33]

The British academic Alex Pravda has analysed this "social contract" at length, arguing that the mature Soviet system guarantees the population security of employment and continuing growth of real incomes, while permitting lax supervision and low labour discipline. In return, the vast majority of the population are content to remain socially and politically quiescent.[34] The former Moscow correspondent of the *Washington Post*, Robert Kaiser, has described just such an attitude, as expressed to him in Moscow by "a senior Communist Party official":

> "I think if you put the question to a referendum, and asked our people if they want the current system, with some shortages and problems, but also guaranteed access to the necessities of life, or do you want another arrangement in which much more is available, but in which you might get fired if you don't really work hard, I have a feeling that our people would vote to keep things the way they are. Every society has to make a choice, according to its own values."[35]

According to this interpretation, however, any faltering of economic performance would automatically put the social compact at risk. Prognoses about the stability of the regime have generally, after all, been based on the assumption that the state could and would continue to ensure a steady, if slow, improvement in popular living standards. If Soviet leaders failed to keep their side of bargain, what would be the result? Could the regime continue to mobilise the population without slipping back into reliance upon the methods of terror employed for that purpose by Stalin?

It was, indeed, after economic setbacks that Solidarity had its birth in Poland. And, if there was one development that distinguished the last years of the Brezhnev era from the earlier ones, it was the fact that, for the first time since the Stalin period, a decline in popular living standards seemed a real possibility.

The Soviet economy grew rapidly, by international standards, in the 1950s, but thereafter its growth gradually slowed. Between 1960 and 1970 annual economic growth was close to 5.0 percent;

between 1970 and 1975 it was slightly over 4.0 percent; between 1975 and 1980 it was just above 3.0 percent; it hovered thereafter at around 2.0 percent. Some scholars even argued that subsequent years saw no increase in net material product, and asked whether the Soviet economy had not stopped growing altogether.[36] This introduced a new element of uncertainty into the equation. What might be the reaction of the population in such circumstances?

As mentioned above, some scholars drew pessimistic conclusions from such trends and suggested that the Soviet system was facing disintegration and even eventual collapse. Others portrayed the system as highly repressive, but successfully so: even a sharp deterioration in living standards would produce no upheaval because the Russian cultural heritage combines with the Party-state dictatorship to make Soviet citizens malleable and docile.[37] Harvard historian Richard Pipes for example argued that, although "a violent collapse of the Soviet regime cannot be precluded, its likelihood appears low.... Russia has had her share of revolutions and Russians no longer believe that radical and violent change brings improvement."[38] Soviet Communism, in Pipes' view, was the natural outgrowth of Russian traditions; throughout their history, the Russian people had never proved capable of restraining the absolute and arbitrary power of their rulers. Seweryn Bialer of Columbia University distinguished between what he called a crisis of survival and a crisis of efficiency. The Soviet system, Bialer argued, was not in danger of collapsing; it was merely failing to perform. Economic and social problems notwithstanding, the sources of stability within Soviet society were strong enough, in Bialer's view, to rule out any immediate danger of systemic collapse.[39]

Another distinguished American specialist, Walter Laqueur, argued that in the USSR bad harvests, long queues and stagnating living standards were politically "not very significant, certainly not in the short run. The Soviet economy has never functioned well, there have always been shortages and queues, and Soviet citizens have learned to live with them." A modern dictatorship, Laqueur wrote,

> has powerful instruments with which to assuage, to suppress protest, to postpone the day of reckoning for a very long time. A sizable part of the population has a vested interest in the perpetuation of the system. The majority, whatever its discontents, is apathetic and incapable of organizing.[40]

One original and systematically-developed analysis of Soviet society, by the philosopher and novelist Alexander Zinoviev, arrives at a similar conclusion by means of different reasoning. Zinoviev argues that support for the Soviet system is deeply embedded in Soviet society, and has its roots in the innumerable workplace collectives. These collectives Zinoviev views as microcosms of society as a whole. Within them, competition among individuals for security and short-term material advantage creates a mass of vested interests tied to the structure of official positions. The "regime" is, in his view, a true expression of popular power; it is misleading to envisage it merely as a system whereby a small number of people "at the top" manages to hold down a vast number of people who consider themselves to be oppressed.[41]

These widely-differing perspectives are outlined simply to bring out their divergence. To establish which approximates most closely to the true relationship between the Soviet political leadership and the population is beyond the scope of this study, whose aim is the more modest one of deducing, on the evidence of Soviet internal policies pursued in the period following the emergence of Solidarity, what view the Soviet leaders themselves took of the risks of popular discontent. What balance, in other words, did the Soviet leaders of the early 1980s think they should strike between discipline and control, on the one hand, and the positive inducements of improved material well-being and (perhaps) increased popular participation, on the other?

To consider the whole range of Soviet policies on welfare, consumption and labour relations would be beyond the scope of this study. Instead, attention is chiefly focussed on policy relating to the workforce. The bulk of the source material is drawn from official Soviet newspapers and journals, and from monitored reports of Soviet radio and television broadcasts; use has also been made, wherever possible, of unofficial source materials such as *samizdat* (privately circulated typescript), and opinion polls carried out among Soviet visitors to the West.

The source material dates mainly from 1980-83, that is, before Mikhail Gorbachev's policy of *glasnost'* (openness) relaxed restrictions on the official media. The fact that in the period under review Soviet press materials were subject to rigorous prepublication censorship places obvious limitations on a study based on such sources. The Soviet press has always contained much that is not intended to be anything other than propaganda, as well as much that is written in Aesopian language. So far from invalidating its use, however, the fact that the Soviet press is used by the authorities as a means of communication with the general population makes it especially valuable for a study such as this that focusses on relations between the leaders and the led. Moreover, the Soviet media have regularly served as a means of intra-elite communication. Used with caution, the official press can be a goldmine of information about relationships between the various strata of Soviet society.

To find out why the Soviet leaders were so anxious that Poland's labour unrest might spread to the Soviet population, this book begins with a description of the role of the USSR's official trade unions, the forms taken by workers' protests in the Soviet Union, and the fate of past attempts to set up unofficial trade unions there (Chapters 2 and 3). Attention then turns to the immediate steps taken by the Soviet authorities in their attempt to ward off the "Polish infection" as regards the official trade unions (Chapter 4), public opinion (Chapters 5 and 6), and changes in plan priorities (Chapter 7). Next comes a review of evidence from non-official sources as to the impact of the Polish events on the general Soviet population (Chapters 8 and 9).

The book goes on to examine the toughening-up that occurred in Soviet internal policies in mid- to late-1981, and to trace its relation to the Kremlin succession struggle under way at that time (Chapters 10-13). Chapter 14 examines the ideological debates sparked in the Soviet press by the Polish events. Finally, Chapter 15 summarises the findings, and considers their implications for the leadership of Mikhail Gorbachev.

FOOTNOTES TO CHAPTER 1

1. For details of the Polish events of 1980-81, the reader is referred to the following studies: Neal Ascherson, *The Polish August*, Harmondsworth, 1981; Abraham Brumberg (ed), *Poland: Genesis of a Revolution*, New York, 1983; Timothy Garton Ash, *The Polish Revolution*, London, 1985; F. Stephen Larrabee, "Instability and Change in Eastern Europe," *International Security*, Winter 1981-82, pp. 39-65;

idem, "Soviet Crisis Management in Eastern Europe," in David Holloway and Jane M.O. Sharp (eds), *The Warsaw Pact: Alliance in Transition*, Ithaca, NY, 1984, pp. 111-38; Edwina Moreton, "The Soviet Union and Poland's Struggle for Self-Control," *International Security*, Summer 1982, pp. 86-104; Andrew Nagorski, *Reluctant Farewell*, New York, 1985; Radio Free Europe (hereafter RFE) Research, *The Strikes in Poland*, Munich, 1980; Jan B. de Weydenthal, Bruce D. Porter and Kevin Devlin, *The Polish Drama: 1980-1982*, Lexington, Mass., 1983.

2. Jack Bielasiak, "The Party: Permanent Crisis," in Brumberg (ed), *op. cit.*, pp. 10-25.

3. Michael Binyon, *Life in Russia*, London, 1985, p. 363.

4. Oliver Henry Radkey, *The Election to the Russian Constituent Assembly of 1917*, Cambridge, Mass., 1950, pp. 16-17.

5. Quoted in Donald W. Treadgold, *Twentieth Century Russia*, fourth edition, Chicago, 1976, p. 197.

6. Quoted in Robert Conquest, *Lenin*, London, 1972, p. 105.

7. Robert Conquest, "Moscow Silences the Voices of Delusion," *International Herald Tribune*, 3 September 1983.

8. Conquest is the author of the first comprehensive study of the Ukrainian Famine of 1932-33: *The Harvest of Sorrow: Soviet Collectivization and the Terror-Famine*, London, 1986.

9. Quoted in Robert Conquest, "*The Great Terror* Revised," *Survey*, Winter 1971, pp. 92-98 at p. 93. Conquest's *The Great Terror*, New York, 1968, is the classic work on the period.

10. The reader is referred to the continuing debate in Western academic journals, in particular, the articles by Stephen G. Wheatcroft in *Soviet Studies*, April 1981, April 1983 and April 1984, and *Slavic Review*, Fall 1985; and those by Steven

Rosefielde in *Soviet Studies*, July 1983, and *Slavic Review*, Spring 1984 and Fall 1985. The words quoted here are taken from Wheatcroft, "New Demographic Evidence on Excessive Collectivization Deaths: Yet Another *Kliukva* from Steven Rosefielde?" *Slavic Review*, Fall 1985, pp. 505-8, at p. 508.

11. See the interviews with Alexander Zinoviev by George Urban, "A Dissenter as a Soviet Man," Parts I and II, in *Encounter*, April and May 1984; and by Georges Nivat in *L'Express*, 12 April 1985. See also Sheila Fitzpatrick, *Education and Social Mobility in the Soviet Union, 1921-1934*, Cambridge, 1979.

12. A useful overview is provided by Bohdan Nahaylo, "World War II: Moscow's Selective Memory," *Wall Street Journal*, 8 May 1985. See also Chapter 4 in Nahaylo, *Opposition and Dissent in the USSR: A Chronicle of Resistance*, forthcoming.

13. Treadgold, *op. cit.*, p. 363.

14. Aleksandr I. Solzhenitsyn, *The Gulag Archipelago III*, New York, 1976, p. 30.

15. *Idem*, *The Mortal Danger: How Misconceptions about Russia Imperil the West*, London, 1980, pp. 39-40. Note, however, that many prisoners of war did not "volunteer" willingly but as the result of starvation and duress; this point is stressed by Aleksandr M. Nekrich in his study of the wartime fate of the Soviet minorities, *The Punished Peoples*, New York, 1978.

16. Milovan Djilas, *Conversations with Stalin*, Harmondsworth, 1963, p. 40.

17. See *AFP*, 13 September 1971; *The Times* and the *International Herald Tribune*, 14 September 1971.

18. This subject is skillfully discussed by Terry McNeill in "Images of the Soviet Future: The Western Scholarly Debate," paper presented at the Second International Congress of Professors World Peace Academy, Geneva, August 1985.

19. Zbigniew Brzezinski, "The Soviet Political

System: Transformation or Degeneration?" *Problems of Communism*, January-February 1966, pp. 1-15.

20. Robert Conquest, "Immobilism and Decay," *Problems of Communism*, September-October 1966, pp. 35-37.

21. Merle Fainsod, "Roads to the Future," *Problems of Communism*, July-August 1967, pp. 21-23.

22. Hans J. Morgenthau, "Alternatives to Change," *Problems of Communism*, September-October 1966, pp. 38-40 at p. 39.

23. Fainsod, *op. cit.*, p. 22.

24. Jerry F. Hough, "The Soviet System: Petrification or Pluralism?" *Problems of Communism*, March-April 1972, pp. 25-45; *idem*, "Political Participation in the Soviet Union," *Soviet Studies*, January 1976, pp. 3-20; *idem*, "Pluralism, Corporatism and the Soviet Union," in Susan Gross Solomon (ed), *Pluralism in the Soviet Union*, London, 1983.

25. Hough, *Problems of Communism*, *op. cit.*, p. 39.

26. *Ibid.*, p. 27.

27. *Ibid.*, p. 30.

28. *Ibid.*, p. 34.

29. A summary of the development of the totalitarian model and a bibliography are to be found in Leonard Schapiro, *Totalitarianism*, London, 1972.

30. Hough, *Problems of Communism*, *op. cit.*, p. 32.

31. Jerry F. Hough, "Soviet Succession - Challenge for Kremlin and the U.S.," *Guardian Weekly*, 1 May 1977.

32. Stephen F. Cohen, *Rethinking the Soviet Experience: Politics and History since 1917*, Oxford, 1984, pp. 132-3.

33. Cited by *AP*, 2 May 1986.

34. Alex Pravda, "East-West Interdependence and the Social Compact in Eastern Europe," in M. Bornstein, Z. Gitelman and W. Zimmerman (eds),

East-West Relations and the Future of Eastern Europe, London, 1981, pp. 162-91.

35. Robert G. Kaiser, "The Soviet Union: A Time of Failure," *International Herald Tribune*, 26 September 1984.

36. Michael Ellman, "Did Soviet Economic Growth End in 1978?" in Jan Drewnowski (ed), *Crisis in the East European Economy: The Spread of the Polish Disease*, New York, 1982, pp. 131-42; and Alec Nove, "Has Soviet Growth Ceased?" Manchester Statistical Sciety, 1983.

37. This view is vividly expressed, with many examples of Russian passivity toward authority, by Hedrick Smith in *The Russians*, London, 1976, pp. 296-333. Smith also stresses the ingrained belief of many Russians that disorder is an ever-present danger requiring constant countermeasures.

38. Richard Pipes, "The Soviet Union in Crisis," mimeo, 1982. See also *idem*, *Survival Is Not Enough*, New York, 1984, p. 200.

39. Seweryn Bialer, *The Soviet Paradox: External Expansion, Internal Decline*, New York, 1986.

40. Walter Laqueur, "What We Know About the Soviet Union," *Commentary*, February 1983, pp. 13-21 at p. 16.

41. This is a simplified summary of arguments set out in Zinoviev's most systematic work of social analysis to date, *Kommunizm kak real'nost'*, Lausanne, 1981. For an assessment of Zinoviev's views, see Philip Hanson, "Alexander Zinoviev: Totalitarianism from Below," *Survey*, Winter 1982, pp. 22-49.

Chapter 2

TRADE UNIONS UNDER SOCIALISM: THEORY AND PRACTICE

"We organised the strike without the unions, because they do not represent or defend our interests."[1] These words were used by a Lublin strike-leader in the summer of 1980 to explain why millions of Polish workers abandoned their officially-approved trade unions and demanded the right to set up independent organisations, free of state and Party control.

The official trade unions operating in Poland in 1980 were carbon-copies of those in the USSR, and what the Polish workers were turning their backs on was the Soviet model. The words of the Lublin strike-leader go some way toward explaining why, when Poland's labour unrest erupted in 1980, the Soviet authorities feared the Polish example might also prove attractive to the workers of the world's first workers' state.

Soviet-style unions bear only a superficial resemblance to their counterparts in the West, where trade unions are understood to be autonomous associations of workers formed for the sole purpose of protecting the rights and interests of their members. The characteristic activity of Western trade unions is collective bargaining, carried out with the employers by representatives acting on behalf of the union as a whole; the workers' demands have force because they are backed up by the threat or use of strike action.

Soviet trade unions lack the collective bargaining function of Western unions, and they have no recourse to the strike weapon (though, as will be seen in the next chapter, this does not mean that no strikes occur in the USSR). Nor is their role an adversarial one: there can be no question of their advancing the interests of the workers against those of the state.

Instead, Soviet theory decrees a dual function for trade unions in socialist society.[2] Their primary task is to boost labour productivity; their second is to defend the rights of the workers from abuse. Although the simultaneous pursuit of higher production and worker protection may appear contradictory, Soviet theory denies that the two goals are incompatible. Under socialism, the argument runs, workers who produce more are producing more for themselves. Increased productivity is in the common interest of both workers and state.

Soviet ideology maintains that there is no real conflict of interest between the various social strata in a socialist system. Workers' interests are not viewed as different from those of other social groups, and unions are organised on the assumption that society is politically homogeneous.[3] In fact, conflicts of interest do occur in the workplace; when that happens, the unions' role is to resolve disputes by mediating between management and labour.

The concept of dual-functioning trade unions dates back to the early years of the Soviet state, which found the leaders of the Bolshevik Party divided over what role the unions should play in the new society. The dispute came to a head at the Party's Tenth Congress in March 1921. On one wing of the Party, Leon Trotsky and Nikolai Bukharin called for "militarisation" of the unions; they were to be wholly absorbed into the government and would merely transfer the Party's orders to the workers as if to soldiers at the battlefront. At the other extreme was the syndicalist "Workers' Opposition," whose members advocated the transfer of total control of industrial production to the unions.[4]

Lenin, backed by Stalin, proposed a compromise: the unions would be non-governmental bodies collaborating with both state and management; they would act as "transmission belts" of Party policy to the masses, and at the same time they would protect the rights of working people and defend them against high-handed bureaucrats and negligent managers. Lenin's formulation carried the day, and has determined the role of Soviet trade unions ever since.

The trade unions are by far the largest public organisation in the USSR. In 1980 they numbered 127 million members, that is, 98 percent of the working population.[5] Membership is voluntary and open to all workers--white-collar as well as blue, agricultural as well as industrial. Most workers join because, in return for modest dues (one percent of the worker's monthly pay), members are eligible to receive welfare benefits at greatly enhanced rates.

A characteristic feature of the Soviet trade union system is that it is organised along "branch" or industrial lines, and that membership is determined by the "production principle." This means that manual and non-manual workers within an enterprise belong to one and the same union; the actual jobs they do are irrelevant. An electrician will belong to the coal-mining union if he works in a coal mine, and to the railway union if he works on the railways. According to this principle, both rank-and-file workers and their managers belong to one and the same union.

The unions are organised hierarchically. Primary trade union organisations are formed at the workplace and elect factory and local committees (*fabzavmestkomy*). These are subordinated to inter-union councils operating at the regional, republican, and all-Union levels.

THE UNIONS AT NATIONAL LEVEL

At the apex of the hierarchy is the All-Union Central Council of Trade Unions (AUCCTU). Elected every five years by a national congress of trade unions, the AUCCTU is the unions' executive body. It acts as advisor to the state on labour matters, participating in the drafting of economic plans and legislation regarding working hours, vacations, work norms and safety measures. National wage scales are decided by the central planners in Moscow; the AUCCTU has a consultative role in this process, but it does not have the deciding voice.

At both national and local level, unions oversee the distribution of social welfare benefits: sickness, maternity, industrial injury and family allowances, as well as old-age pensions and medical treatment benefits. This gives the unions a quasi-governmental character; in many other countries, this role is played by a government ministry. In addition, Soviet trade unions run holiday and rest home facilities; they build palaces of culture and they organise sports events.

THE UNIONS AT LOCAL LEVEL

At local level, the unions' chief task is to mobilise the workforce to work harder and produce more. Indeed, trade union officials bear joint responsibility with management and the enterprise Party committee for seeing that the enterprise meets its planned production targets. To this end, the enterprise union committee (*fabkom*) organises "socialist competition," the scheme whereby bonus payments and other prizes are awarded to workers, teams, and enterprises that perform well.

An important union activity at enterprise level is the regulation of conflicts between management and individual workers. Such disputes are referred to an enterprise investigatory commission, made up of equal numbers of union and management representatives. If the commission fails to give satisfaction to the worker, he or she can appeal to the union committee. According to the British scholar Mary McAuley, the vast majority of management-worker disputes are settled quickly at enterprise level.[6] The union committee must be consulted by management whenever disciplinary measures are to be taken against a worker who has infringed work regulations (for instance, by turning up for work late or in a drunken state). Management must also seek union permission before dismissing a worker. (Evidence suggests, however, that in a significant number of cases managers bypass the *fabkom* when sacking troublesome employees.[7])

The *fabkom* is also responsible for negotiating with the management over the terms of the enterprise's "collective agreement." This document is drawn up annually between the union (acting on behalf of the workforce) and the management, and sets out the mutual obligations accepted by each side for the coming year. Since wage scales and certain other conditions of employment are decided nationally within the framework of the government's overall economic plans, they fall outside the scope of the collective agreement and are not amenable to bargaining between union and management. Within these predetermined national guidelines, however, the collective agreement lays down local working hours, vacation periods, bonus distribution rates, and enterprise housing construction plans for the coming year. The union is responsible for monitoring the management's adherence to the provisions of the agreement.

Finally, union officials oversee the distribution of welfare benefits within the enterprise and administer the various catering, housing, education, sports and leisure services attached to it. The *fabkom* is also responsible for enforcing health and safety regulations in the work-place, and has the power to shut a plant down if they are infringed.

ON THE SIDE OF WORKERS OR MANAGEMENT?

Despite their considerable powers, it appears that local union committees not infrequently fail in their protective role. The evidence of *samizdat* writings, as well as of the official media, is insistent on this point. According to *Trud*, the unions' daily newspaper:

> Sometimes, trade union committees, anxious not to spoil relations with management, consent to the dismissal of workers without checking the circumstances of the case.... As a result, people are illegally dismissed and later have to be reinstated by the courts.[8]

> ...In order not to spoil their relations with the management, trade union committees often compromise when labour laws are flouted.[9]

And according to a report published in the official newspaper of the Soviet Communist Party, *Pravda*:

> It is still not unusual to find factories where trade union organs have become mere adjuncts of management, with no character of their own.[10]

Why are local union officials so often accused of ignoring the needs of the workers? In the first place, the unions are not independent bodies but, like all organisations in the Soviet political system, perform their functions under the direction of the Communist Party.[11] This alone means that union officials are accountable not to their members but to the Party and the state--over which the Party also exercises a leading role.

The Party exercises this control both through Party members active within the trade unions and through the nomination of its own candidates to responsible posts. Top-level union positions fall within the Party's *nomenklatura*, that is, they are among the (nominally elective) posts to which, in reality, the Party maintains exclusive rights of appointment. The chairman of the AUCCTU, for example, has always been a Party appointee, often with little or no previous experience of union work.[12]

Even at enterprise level, where union officials are supposedly elected by the workers, reports of election-rigging abound.[13] *Samizdat* materials, and even some reports in the official media, make it clear that candidates for election must have the prior sanction both of the management and of the enterprise Party organisation, and that workers are called upon merely to vote in accordance with a pre-approved list. Union officials therefore find themselves beholden to the enterprise director and the secretary of its Party organisation for posts that carry numerous privileges and career advantages.

In 1979, an open letter entitled "Appeal to Nowhere" reached the West. Signed by a group of workers at a dairy in the city of Tol'yatti, the letter described how union officials were elected at the enterprise. The union chairman had been replaced, without explanation, by order of the management; the workers were then required to vote for a single unopposed candidate--a woman nominated by the director. "All we had to do was raise our hands in approval. And, accustomed to our position as robots, we did just that," the document stated.[14]

The letter lamented that Soviet workers were "voiceless, depersonalised creatures, living appendages of machinery and equipment, robots who are allowed no opinion of their own." It went on to describe how the new trade union chairwoman, working hand in glove with the dairy director and its Party committee, started to demand bribes for allocation of housing and places for workers' children in the kindergarten. The point, the writers stressed, was not that they had a bad trade union chairwoman. It was that *any* union official would behave in the same way, given that he or she was selected not by the workers, but by the enterprise director and the local Party committee.

The same point was made by a Moscow worker, Oleg Alifanov, in a *samizdat* "Letter to the CPSU Central Committee," dated May 1985. "One might have thought," Alifanov wrote, "that the trade union would defend the rights of the worker,"

> But there is no sign of this in real life. ... The reason is that union posts are held not by those elected by the workers, but by those appointed by the Party.[15]

It is inevitable, too, that the unions' primary task of boosting production sometimes comes into direct conflict with their secondary task, that of protecting workers' rights. Toward the end of the month, when an enterprise is rushing to meet production targets, workers are often required to put in overtime regardless of whether they wish to or not. It is unlikely that at such a moment any enterprise director would look kindly on union objections either about compulsory overtime or about violations of safety regulations. A union official will be judged not on how well he or she stands up for the workers but on whether or not, when the heat is on, he can mobilise them to fulfill the plan.

The unions' production orientation means officials share more interests with the management than with their members. The American specialist Michael Urban suggests that this may be more than a simple case of the state using the unions as a tool with which to control the workforce. Pointing to a "third set of interests, the interests of officialdom," Urban comments:

> If ... we find union officials colluding

> with management to violate *state* regulations in the area of industrial safety, we can count such behavior as a defense of neither workers nor the state. It looks more like officials cutting deals among themselves.[16]

Some Western scholars, such as the American political scientist Blair Ruble, author of a major study of the Soviet trade unions, maintain that, within certain narrowly defined limits, the unions have in recent years done much to enhance workers' living and working conditions.[17] Ruble argues that productivity increases and the defence of workers' rights need not be incompatible goals if unions reject harsh coercive and punitive sanctions and show--as he says they do--an awareness that improvements in workers' living and working conditions are a more effective way of raising productivity.

Ruble goes on to argue that it is often in the interests of union leaders to promote the welfare of their members because, in so doing, union officials construct a power base upon which to enhance their own standing in the elite. Improvements in the living and working conditions of the workers may, Ruble suggests, reflect no more than the fact that union leaders are ambitious and have resources that they can trade with other members of the elite, but they are real improvements none the less.

Ruble's arguments are persuasive and there is little doubt that, on the national level, Soviet unions constitute a powerful bureaucracy. (Indeed, they are commonly believed to be a major force for conservatism and bulwark against reform of the Soviet social and economic system.) The mere fact, however, that the unions are powerful does not automatically mean either that they derive their importance from the massed might of their millions of members, or that they will use their power to forward the interests of the workers. The influence of the unions, in short, does not necessarily translate into power for Soviet workers; nor does it guarantee the working class an independent voice.

A harrowing picture of the living and working conditions of some Soviet men and women has been painted by the American journalist Kevin Klose. Late in 1980--when worker unrest in Poland was at its height--Klose travelled with a fellow journalist, David Satter, to the coal-mining region of the Donbass, the most heavily industrialised area of Ukraine. They were the guests of Aleksei Nikitin, an engineer sacked from his job ten years earlier for speaking out about safety hazards in the mines.[18]

The impression Klose and Satter gained was of miners living on low incomes and working long hours under harsh conditions. They reported that, in the miners' opinion, the conditions that led to the Polish strikes existed in even more extreme form in the USSR. But the Soviet workers were deprived of any possibility to band together in order to improve their lot. The miners trusted neither their managers nor their union leaders, tending, Klose wrote, "to lump [them] together." "The official union," the miners told him, "is worthless." Describing how Party bosses, enterprise managers and trade union officials acted as moral watchdogs over the workforce, Klose wrote:

> This interlocking official power leaves workers divided and feeling powerless to redress their grievances.[19]

CONCLUSION

Soviet trade unions have important functions. However, they are not authentic workers' organisations but quasi-governmental institutions viewed by the state as instruments to mobilise workers behind its goals. Even their secondary role of defending the workers from exploitation by unscrupulous managers is not viewed as an end in itself but is based on the idea that workers' productivity will be higher if they are well cared for. According to one Western observer, "These organizations are so fundamentally different from the independent trade unions in democratic countries that the term *trade union* is really inappropriate to describe them."[20] The American scholar David Granick has suggested that, by virtue of the way they interact with enterprise directors, Soviet trade union officials can more usefully be seen as the counterparts of personnel managers in capitalist corporations than as representatives of the workers.[21]

Their unions' anomalous nature deprives Soviet workers of an independent voice and of the ability adequately to defend their interests. From time to time, as will be seen in the next chapter, worker discontent boils over into spontaneous outbursts of unrest. By and large, however, Soviet workers are divided and powerless. Small wonder that when, in the summer of 1980, Polish workers decisively rejected the Soviet model of "dual-functioning" unions, Kremlin leaders reacted with alarm lest Soviet workers should seek to follow their example.

FOOTNOTES TO CHAPTER 2

1. *Reuters*, 22 July 1980.
2. This account is based on the following sources: Joseph Godson, "The Role of the Trade Unions," in Leonard Schapiro and Joseph Godson (eds), *The Soviet Worker: Illusions and Realities*, London, 1981, pp. 106-29; Viktor Haynes and Olga Semyonova (eds), *Workers Against the Gulag*, London, 1979; Arcadius Kahan and Blair Ruble (eds), *Industrial Labor in the U.S.S.R.*, New York, 1979; Adrian Karatnycky, Alexander J. Motyl and Adolph

Sturmthal (eds), *Workers' Rights, East and West*, New Brunswick, 1980; Mary McAuley, *Labour Disputes in Soviet Russia: 1957-65*, Oxford, 1969; Alex Pravda, "The Trade Unions," in Archie Brown *et al.* (eds), *The Cambridge Encyclopedia of Russia and the Soviet Union*, Cambridge, 1982, pp. 386-89; Blair A. Ruble, *Soviet Trade Unions: Their Development in the 1970s*, Cambridge, 1981; *idem*, "Labor Relations in a Period of Economic Constraints," mimeo, 1981; *idem*, "Industrial Trade Unions in the USSR: The Soviet Model of Dual Functioning Trade Unions," mimeo, 1983; *idem*, "Soviet Trade Unions and Labor Relations after 'Solidarity,'" in US Congress Joint Economic Committee, *The Soviet Economy in the 1980s: Problems and Perspectives*, Part 2, Washington DC, 1983, pp. 349-66; *Spravochnik profsoyuznogo rabotnika*, Moscow, 1983; *Sotsializm i trud: slovar'-spravochnik*, Moscow, 1985.

3. David Lane, *Soviet Economy and Society*, Oxford, 1985, p. 43.

4. See E.H. Carr, *The Bolshevik Revolution: 1917-1923*, Volume 2, Harmondsworth, 1966, pp. 220-29; Pravda in Brown *et al.*, *op. cit.*, p. 386; Robert V. Daniels in *The New Encylopaedia Britannica*, fifteenth edition, Chicago, 1985, p. 1000.

5. *TASS*, 18 September 1980.

6. McAuley, *op. cit.*, p. 250.

7. On this question, see Nick Lampert, "Job Security and the Law in the USSR," in David Lane (ed), *Labour and Employment in the USSR*, Brighton, 1986, pp. 256-77. *Sovetskaya Kirgiziya* reported on 10 November 1981 that, during the previous year, 62 percent of the workers who appealed in the republic of Kirgizia against dismissal were reinstated in their jobs by the courts. The newspaper said a "significant proportion" were sacked without union permission, and added that unions were showing "unscrupulousness and liberalism" toward managers who acted incorrectly.

8. *Trud*, 12 December 1973.

9. *Ibid.*, 18 August 1979.

10. *Pravda*, 9 March 1982.

11. Article 6 of the 1977 constitution of the USSR describes the CPSU as "the leading and guiding force of Soviet society and the nucleus of its political system, of *all state and public organisations*" (emphasis added). Similarly, the preamble to the Rules of the Soviet trade unions states that "The trade unions do all their work under the direction of the CPSU, the leading and guiding force of Soviet society...."

12. Only two chairmen had had previous union experience: Mikhail Tomsky, ousted from his post by Stalin in 1929, and Stepan Shalaev, appointed in 1982 when his predecessor, Aleksei Shibaev, was implicated in a corruption scandal.

13. At their congress in February 1987, however, the Soviet trade unions adopted new Rules calling for the introduction of multiple candidacy in elections to union posts.

14. *Russkaya mysl'*, 2 August 1979; see also *Soviet Analyst*, 8 August 1979.

15. *Russkaya mysl'*, 6 September 1985; see also *Soviet Analyst*, 23 October and 6 November 1985.

16. *American Political Science Review*, No 3, 1983, p. 789-91.

17. See Blair A. Ruble, "Factory Unions and Workers' Rights," in Kahan and Ruble, *op. cit.*, pp. 59-84.

18. Nikitin spent some thirteen years in prison and mental hospital for his defence of workers' rights, his advocacy of independent trade unions, and his exposure of dangerous working conditions in the mines of the Donbass. While in detention, he was injected with hallucinatory drugs. His health was seriously undermined and he died in 1984 at the age of 47. See Chapters 2 and 3 of Kevin Klose, *Russia and the Russians: Inside the*

Closed Society, New York, 1984, pp. 53-91; for an obituary of Nikitin, see the *Washington Post*, 19 April 1984.

19. Klose, *op. cit.*, Chapter 1, pp. 29-51. See also the articles by Klose in the *Washington Post*, 30 January and 1 February 1981, and by David Satter in the *Financial Times*, 9 and 14 January and 1 February 1981.

20. Arch Puddington in Karatnycky *et al.*, *op. cit.*, p. 7.

21. *Slavic Review*, Spring 1983, pp. 125-26.

Chapter 3

WORKERS' PROTESTS IN THE USSR

Dissatisfaction on the part of Soviet workers with their living and working conditions occasionally boils over into open protest. Alex Pravda has distinguished four main types of spontaneous activity which reflect, to varying degrees, Soviet workers' discontent: frequent job changing; labour discipline infractions; the writing of critical letters to the authorities; and collective protests such as strikes and mass riots.[1] Pravda found the number of Soviet workers involved in such actions to be considerable, and estimated that as many as one in every five or six may undertake some form of spontaneous activity in the course of any one year.

This chapter looks at one of the more extreme forms of protest practised by Soviet workers--work stoppages--and asks why it is that, unlike the demands made by Polish workers in 1980, those of Soviet workers have not been known to pass from the economic to the political. It goes on to recall the few known attempts made by Soviet workers in recent years to set up independent trade unions.

WORK STOPPAGES

Soviet law neither denies nor specifically grants the right to strike. The official explanation is that since in the USSR power belongs to the people, it would make no sense for the workers to strike against themselves. This does not mean that no strikes occur in the USSR, but the non-recognition of the right to strike does mean that strikers and strike leaders can, when the authorities choose, be severely punished for their activities.

It is very unusual, but not unknown, for accounts of strikes to appear in the official Soviet media. In 1972, for example, the youth newspaper *Komsomol'skaya pravda* published an account of a strike by young women tractor drivers on a state farm in Moldavia who were upset that they were being neither paid adequately nor employed in the job for which they had been trained.[2] More recently, the government paper *Izvestia* in 1983 published an account of a strike called by bus drivers in the Estonian city of Narva to protest against the introduction of a more onerous work schedule.[3] In 1984, a report appeared in a Georgian newspaper which revealed that disgruntled teachers in a village kindergarten had walked off the job and locked the school for 28 days; as a result, many parents had to stay away from work to take care of their children.[4]

Such gleanings apart, information on strikes is hard to find in the official Soviet media, and the evidence available to outsiders is mostly anecdotal or drawn from *samizdat* sources. The Soviet dissident Vladimir Borisov claims that strikes occur often in the USSR but adds that, "in my own personal view, no more than ten percent of major strikes, let alone minor ones, become known."[5]

The available evidence suggests that the strike weapon is used by Soviet workers as a protest of last resort, and that the strikes that break out in the USSR are localised, spontaneous, and unorganised. No tendency has been observed among Soviet strikers to progress from expressing economic grievances to making political demands, e.g., for democratic freedoms, such as those called for by the workers in Gdansk in the summer of 1980. When strikes break out, however, the Soviet authorities seem to display considerable nervousness lest they should spread; for this reason, apparently, the authorities often make more or less immediate concessions to the strikers' demands.

The reaction of the authorities seems to follow

a standard pattern: responding quickly to meet workers' demands and defuse the situation and, at the same time, isolating the incident by imposing an information blackout that prevents unrest from spreading to workers in other factories. Some time after the strike the organisers are rounded up and either arrested or transferred to other plants.

The scarcity of reliable information makes it difficult to state with certainty whether strike activity in the USSR has increased or decreased in recent years, or whether the example of the events in Poland had any real influence on Soviet workers' protests. The most comprehensive data available are to be found in a study entitled "Public Unrest in the USSR," compiled by Lyudmila Alekseeva and Valerii Chalidze in 1985.[6] The authors present information on 75 strikes, as well as on other incidents of public unrest, that occurred in the USSR in the period 1953-83.

Since the 1950s a steady trickle of strike reports has reached the West. Strikes and workers' unrest began, in the post-Stalin period, considerably earlier than the human rights movement (which was mainly confined to intellectuals). The late 1950s and early 1960s saw the first work stoppages, strikes, riots and street demonstrations known to have occurred in the USSR since the 1920s.

During Khrushchev's period as Party leader (1953-64), the rate of increase in basic wages was slow, and piece-work rates were reduced. Following a nationwide rise in prices for meat and dairy products, the early 1960s saw a wave of particularly acute workers' protests in many Soviet cities.[7]

Largest and best known of these was the riot that took place in Novocherkassk in Rostov oblast (region) in the summer of 1962; it was triggered by food price rises coupled with a reduction in rates of pay. For three days the town was under workers' control, and the authorities used tanks and troops to disperse the demonstrators. It is estimated that as many as 80 persons may have been killed.[8]

As far as is known, no riots on a comparable scale have occurred anywhere in the USSR since then. The Brezhnev leadership, which came to power in 1964, took care to be more generous to the workers on the matter of wages than Khrushchev had been. Since the early 1970s, however, reports of strikes by Soviet workers have increased. Data collected by Alekseeva and Chalidze suggest that protests tended to become more frequent over time, with the majority (67 percent) falling into the last third (that is, 1975-83) of the 30-year period examined in their study.[9]

It must be stressed that, even if the number of strikes appears to have been increasing, the number of workers involved is still small and strikes seem to remain a rare phenomenon. The vast majority are wildcat or lightning strikes lasting only a few hours, or at most a day or two. They tend to be called over purely local grievances such as poor working conditions, management's failure to observe safety regulations, or the raising of work norms, and they are settled quickly and on the spot. They are poorly organised and, largely because of the immensity of the country and the low quality of the communications system, the general Soviet public remains unaware that they have taken place.

For these reasons, strikes are fairly easily dealt with by the authorities who seem, over the years, to have developed a response that is highly effective. While officially denying that strikes take place, the authorities in reality make every effort to end them by meeting the workers' demands. (Alekseeva and Chalidze found only six strikes known to have ended in defeat for the workers; this explains why the majority of strikes are over within a few days.) Strike organisers receive short shrift, however. According to Borisov:

> The Soviet authorities are very much afraid of organized workers' movements. In general they give in immediately and, if it is a movement of some magnitude, it often happens that a Politburo member comes straight to the spot to satisfy the demands--at which point the movement stops. Afterward...they begin to hit out at the organizers. The latter are arrested or at least laid off work and, as it is illegal not to work, that comes to the same thing in the end.[10]

Police repression against strike organisers seems to be one of the reasons why workers in the Soviet Union have recourse to the strike weapon only in extreme circumstances. According to the former Soviet industrial journalist, Vadim Belotserkovsky, fear of reprisals by the authorities prompts workers to undertake work slowdowns in preference to outright strikes:

> A more common variant is the so-called "Italian strike," in which workers turn up at the factory but in practice do no work. I know about this tactic both from my own experience and from samizdat. As a rule, once a strike breaks out, the workers' demands are satisfied. But for that very reason, they are soon followed by repression against the organisers. And since most workers live in the provinces, they lack one vital means of defence--access to world opinion through contact with foreign correspondents. So strike organisers often simply disappear into mental hospitals without a trial, or else provocateurs are used in order to charge them with assault or hooliganism.[11]

It is important to note that, at around the same time as the outbreak of worker unrest in Poland, reports were being received of strikes in a number of Soviet cities also. There is no evidence to suggest that these strikes were influenced by those in Poland, and they seem to have followed the established pattern, for the workers' demands remained economic, not political. By all accounts the authorities, too, dealt with these strikes in accordance with the routine described above. But it seems likely that the more or less simultaneous outbreak of labour unrest in both Poland and (of course on a lesser scale) the USSR caused the Soviet leaders some alarm.

The best publicised of the Soviet strikes occurred in the huge car factories in the industrial centres of Tol'yatti and Gor'ky, and predated the outbreak of strikes in Poland. The Tol'yatti plant is said to have been hit by labour unrest on 6 May 1980, when a walkout was staged in protest against inadequate supplies of meat and dairy products. The walkout, believed to be the largest in recent Soviet history and to have been supported by thousands of workers, is said to have closed down the Tol'yatti plant and to have idled more than 170,000 workers. Sources informed Western correspondents that the strike was called off only after the authorities ensured that Tol'yatti received large food deliveries.[12]

Another strike--also sparked by workers' dissatisfaction over food supplies--was reported to have occurred at the Gor'ky car and truck plant within days of that in Tol'yatti. Soviet officials indignantly denied that any strikes had occurred, but officials in Tol'yatti later admitted to visiting Western journalists that "a group of spray-painters had held on-the-job 'discussions' about working conditions."[13]

In June 1980, reports were received in the West

that workers at the giant Kama truck factory in Bashkiria had stopped work for some four hours earlier in the month, again in protest over food shortages.[14] Soviet officials denied the rumours. Radio Moscow later reported, however, that a Party meeting at the Kama plant had discussed ways of improving labour discipline. "The number of infringements is worrying us greatly," a Party official told Radio Moscow, and he complained about "the great number of working hours lost."[15]

About a thousand workers at a tractor factory in the Estonian city of Tartu were said to have staged a two-day walkout in October 1980. Dissident sources claimed the protest was inspired by events in Poland, but the concrete reason for the strike was believed to be the workers' demand that production norms be reduced and that chronic shortages of essential working materials be eliminated, so the strike appears to have conformed to the regular pattern. The workers were said to have returned to their duties when the management agreed to their demands.[16]

Samizdat documents describe a number of strikes that reportedly took place in 1981 in Ukraine. These include three strikes said to have occurred in Kiev at the end of March and beginning of April that year. Two were staged in connexion with increased production norms; the third was organised to protest against the lack of a water supply.[17] *Samizdat* sources also reported that workers at the Kiev motorcycle plant--one of the largest of its kind in the USSR--conducted a one-to-two-day strike at the end of August 1981 to protest against cuts in piecework rates and bonuses.[18] All these strikes were said to have ended when the authorities gave in to the workers' demands.

What was particularly interesting was that at least one of these strikes was reported to have been organised by the factory's Party and trade union committees. The factory manager was reportedly dismissed, while the personnel of the trade union and Party committees was changed.[19] Further details are not however available.

Another interesting incident was described in a *samizdat* account of strikes that took place in 1981 and 1982 at a bus factory in the town of Pavlovo, in central Russia's Gor'ky oblast. The document alleges that, in May 1982, secret workers' meetings circulated the slogan, "If the [production] norms are raised, we'll do the same as in Poland!"[20]

This incident apart, it can of course only be speculated whether the strikes in Ukraine and the Baltic area or those in other parts of the USSR were in any way influenced by those in Poland in 1980-81, or whether they resulted solely from deteriorating economic conditions inside the USSR. In any case the Polish strikers, though they began by protesting against the raising of meat prices, soon adopted demands that were purely political. Nothing of this sort appears to have happened on any scale in the USSR. The predominantly "bread-and-butter" nature of Soviet worker action is further underlined by the fact that calls made by Estonian dissidents toward the end of 1981 for token strikes to protest against food shortages, Soviet policy toward Afghanistan and Poland, and restrictions on the development of national culture, went almost totally unheeded by the general population of the republic. (The incident is discussed in Chapter 9.) However, there were reports in winter 1981 that food shortages had led to scattered demonstrations and the circulation of leaflets in several Soviet cities.[21]

FORMATION OF FREE TRADE UNIONS

The right of Soviet citizens "to associate in public organisations" is guaranteed by article 51 of the 1977 constitution of the USSR, but the inclusion of the phrase "in accordance with the goals of communist construction" may be interpreted as restricting the manner in which the citizens' implied right to form trade unions can be exercised.

There have been several recent attempts to set up independent trade unions in the Soviet Union, but none met with adequate support from workers. It has not therefore been hard for the KGB to crush such efforts as have been made, using a combination of harassment, imprisonment, and detention in psychiatric hospitals against leading activists. The treatment such people have received at the hands of the secret police indicates that the constitutional right "to associate in public organisations" is not a reality in the USSR.

The first known attempt occurred at the end of 1977, when the Ukrainian Vladimir Klebanov, who had formerly been a foreman at a coal-mine in Donetsk, announced in Moscow that a group of disaffected workers intended to form an independent trade union. This organisation, the "Association of Free Trade Unions of Workers in the Soviet Union," also became known as "the union of the unemployed," since all those involved were workers or supervisory personnel who had lost their jobs for criticising the management of their respective enterprises. Its aim was to protect workers' rights against managerial abuse, a task which, Klebanov claimed, was neglected by the official trade unions.[22]

By the end of 1978 Klebanov had been put in a mental hospital, and so many members of the organisation had been arrested that it effectively ceased to exist. As far as was known, Klebanov was still being kept in hospital in 1987.

Alekseeva, a leading member of the Soviet human rights movement who now lives in the USA, recalls that Klebanov's group publicly distanced themselves from any form of contact with the dissident movement, emphasising that they "had nothing in common with dissidents" and that their goal was "to help in the successful construction of communism and to combat bureaucracy and red tape." Alekseeva suggests that this was, to some extent, "a naive attempt [on the part of the workers] to protect themselves from persecution, which, as they knew, awaited 'dissidents.'"[23] The American journalist David Shipler, on the other hand, records that when Klebanov approached leading Soviet human rights activists for support, he was disgusted by their haughty attitude to the problems of the workers.[24] Wherever the truth lies, there appears to be a lack of mutual understanding between Soviet dissident intellectuals and members of the working class which, in Shipler's words, "cuts away at any prospective Soviet alliance, along Polish lines, of workers and intellectuals who might struggle jointly to improve job conditions and political liberties simultaneously."[25]

In April 1978, however, another move was made to found an independent trade union, and this time its protagonists were human rights activists. Their attempt to found the "Independent Trade Union of Workers in the USSR" came to nothing,[26] but heated discussions within the human rights movement led, in October 1978, to the foundation in Moscow of the "Free Interprofessional Association of Workers" (SMOT). SMOT was not a union in the true sense; rather, it was an initiative group set up with the aim of inspiring the eventual creation of a free trade union movement. Unlike Klebanov's union, SMOT made public the names of only a few of its members. It consisted of a number of autonomous groups; originally there were said to be eight such groups with a total membership of around 100 people.[27]

SMOT published a series of *samizdat* bulletins, many of which reached the West. The organisation was ruthlessly suppressed by the authorities and, with the arrest or banishment of its leaders, may have ceased to exist.

According to *samizdat* sources, there have been other unsuccessful attempts to create independent trade unions in the USSR.[28] In April 1980, for instance, a previously unknown organisation calling itself the Ukrainian Patriotic Movement issued an appeal in support of Klebanov and urged Ukrainians to organise independent trade unions at their places of work.[29] According to another, unconfirmed report, an attempt was also made in June 1980 to found an independent trade union known as "Unity" in the Ukrainian city of Vinnitsa.[30]

CONCLUSIONS

Given that Soviet workers suffer many, if not all, of the difficulties that beset their Polish counterparts, why is it that in the USSR strikes over economic grievances have shown no sign of developing into strikes for political demands as they did in Poland in 1980? And why have Soviet workers shown so little interest in the various attempts that have been made to create independent workers' organisations?

This question is raised in several of the *samizdat* documents that form the basis of Chapter 9. The consensus is that the explanation lies in differences between the histories and political cultures of Poland and the Soviet Union. Virtually no-one in the USSR today, for example, has had experience of living under anything other than a one-party system; nor did Russia's tsarist Empire have any tradition of political pluralism. Poland, on the other hand, was operating under a capitalist economy until the outbreak of the Second World War and, to this day, some three-quarters of Poland's farms remain in private hands. All this, together with the immense pride Polish people feel in their national heritage and Roman Catholic faith, adds up to make Poland the most stubbornly pluralistic of the Soviet Union's East European neighbours.

Kevin Klose stresses the difference between the Polish and Soviet situations:

> Unlike the Poles, who have drawn strength, and at times even protection, from the Roman Catholic Church, Soviet workers have no recourse to any center of moral leadership outside the Party or Party-run unions.[31]

The prominent Soviet dissident Andrei Amal'rik discussed this question shortly before his death in 1980, stating that:

> Soviet citizens are accustomed to distrust one another and have no experience of working together, except on the initiative of the Party or the State, and this makes it very difficult to establish workers' strike committees, or links between factories and works.[32]

Another particularly important difference between the Soviet and Polish cases is the fact that, unlike the Polish case, contacts between workers and dissident intellectuals have in the Soviet Union been few and far between, and the Soviet dissident movement has made almost no headway among the general mass of the population. Roy Medvedev, a dissident Marxist historian living in Moscow, has also stressed the logistical difficulties facing Soviet workers:

> The Polish workers made political demands, ...and the granting of them has made the Polish movement a serious example for others. But it is not easy to see a similar movement being started from below by Soviet workers. The Soviet working

> class is too nationally mixed, too heterogeneous, and the country too large for strike action.[33]

Alekseeva and Chalidze note that, despite a marked increase in the number of strikes in the USSR in the period 1975-83 as compared to the preceding twenty years, there was no perceptible development in the level of organisation of the participants. On the contrary, they say, the largest and best organised protest for economic motives ever known in the USSR was the general strike and mass demonstration in Novocherkassk in 1962. In the intervening twenty years, Alekseeva and Chalidze found not one repetition of an incident of this kind, and concluded that economic protests in the USSR are confined to isolated, spontaneous strikes, unconnected in either time or place.[34]

Nor is there evidence that, during the period of Solidarity's legal existence, any attempt was made to organise independent workers' movements in the Soviet Union. In short, Solidarity's example cannot be shown to have had any real impact on the majority of the Soviet workforce, who seem to have remained more or less impervious to influences from outside the country.

FOOTNOTES TO CHAPTER 3

1. Alex Pravda, "Spontaneous Workers' Activities in the Soviet Union," in Arcadius Kahan and Blair Ruble (eds), *Industrial Labor in the U.S.S.R.*, New York, 1979, pp. 333-66.

2. *Komsomol'skaya pravda*, 5 September 1972.

3. *Izvestia*, 11 July 1983; and Radio Liberty Research Bulletin (hereafter RL) 266/83, "Labor Dispute in Narva Bus Depot," by Ann Sheehy, 15 July 1983.

4. *Komunisti*, 20 November 1984.

5. Interview with Vladimir Borisov, a founder member of SMOT who was expelled from the USSR in 1980, broadcast by Radio Liberty on 17 January 1981.

6. Lyudmila Alekseeva and Valerii Chalidze, *Public Unrest in the USSR*, report prepared for the Foundation for Soviet Studies, Silver Spring, Maryland, 1985. See also RL 296/85, "Public Unrest in the USSR," by Lyudmila Alekseeva, 9 September 1985. For earlier surveys of strikes in the USSR, see Albert Boiter, "When the Kettle Boils Over...," *Problems of Communism*, January-February 1964, pp. 33-43; Vadim Belotserkovsky, "Workers' Struggles in the USSR in the Early Sixties," *Critique*, Nos 10-11, 1979, pp. 37-50; and Betsy Gidwitz, "Labor Unrest in the Soviet Union," *Problems of Communism*, November-December 1982, pp. 25-42.

7. Belotserkovsky, *op. cit.*

8. The most detailed account of the Novocherkassk riots is in Aleksandr I. Solzhenitsyn, *The Gulag Archipelago III*, New York, 1976, pp. 507-14. For a *samizdat* account dating from 1977, see Radio Liberty's Samizdat Archive (hereafter AS) 3046.

9. Alekseeva and Chalidze, *op. cit.* It is of course possible that more reports of protest actions have reached the West simply because the flow of information in general from East to West increased in the 1970s.

10. An interview published in *Le Monde*, 26 June 1980.

11. *Labour Focus on Eastern Europe*, May-June 1978, quoted in Viktor Haynes and Olga Semyonova (eds), *Workers against the Gulag: The New Opposition in the Soviet Union*, London, 1979, p. 75.

12. *Financial Times*, 13 June 1980.

13. *AP*, *Reuters*, 17 November 1981.

14. *Financial Times*, 23 June 1980.

15. *Radio Moscow*, 10 September 1980.

16. *AP*, *UPI*, 22 October 1980.

17. AS 4354; see also RL 267/81, "*Samizdat* Report on Strikes in Kiev," by Roman Solchanyk, 6 July 1981.

18. AS 4496; see also RL 477/81, "*Samizdat* Report on Strike in Kiev and Food Supply Problems," by Roman Solchanyk, 1 December 1981.

19. Alekseeva and Chalidze, *op. cit.*

20. AS 4985.

21. Cited by Roman Solchanyk in "Nervous Neighbors: The Soviets and Solidarity," *Workers under Communism*, No 1, 1982, p. 17.

22. The fullest accounts of attempts to set up independent trade unions in the USSR are to be found in RL 304/79, "The Independent Trade-Union Movement in the Soviet Union," by John C. Michael, 11 October 1979; and Chapter 18 of Ludmilla Alexeyeva, *Soviet Dissent: Contemporary Movements for National, Religious and Human Rights*, Middletown, Conn., 1985.

23. Alexeyeva, *op. cit.*, p. 407.

24. David K. Shipler, *Russia: Broken Idols, Solemn Dreams*, New York, 1983, pp. 207-8. Andrei Sakharov subsequently told a Western journalist: "As far as the illegal trade unions were concerned, I did not like everything. For instance, how it was presented. It was exaggerated. There were no similarities to the Polish trade union Solidarity"; *Der Spiegel*, 5 January 1987.

25. Shipler, *op. cit.*, p. 203.

26. Alexeyeva, *op. cit.*, p. 408.

27. Michael, *op. cit.*

28. AS 5321.

29. See AS 4130, pp. 2-4

30. AS 4071.

31. *Posev*, No 3, 1981, p. 6.

32. *Washington Post*, 30 January 1981.

33. *Daily Telegraph*, 23 October 1980.

34. *Observer*, 16 November 1980.

35. RL 296/85.

Chapter 4

SPRUCING UP THE IMAGE OF THE OFFICIAL TRADE UNIONS

As was seen in Chapter 2, Soviet trade unions are supposed to play a dual role: first, to help raise productivity and boost production, and second to defend the rights of the workers from abuse by management. Soviet theory denies any contradiction between the two functions. However, greater stress has traditionally been placed on the first, and the obligation to meet production targets can lead union officials to turn a blind eye when health or safety regulations are infringed in the workplace, or when workers are required to put in long hours of compulsory overtime.

It is nonetheless possible for the second function to be highlighted on occasion and for the unions to be enjoined to increase their attention to the workers' living and working conditions. Just such a trend could be observed during the autumn of 1980 and the first half of 1981 when, in the wake of Poland's labour unrest, a concerted campaign was launched by the Soviet authorities to spruce up the image of the officially-controlled trade unions.

First, the Soviet media began to publish a series of articles denying that workers in socialist countries had any need of independent trade unions to defend their interests. Statements designed for mass--including foreign--consumption maintained an air of optimism, admitting to a formal and rather cursory list of shortcomings on the part of the official unions but confidently implying that the situation was under control and that all mistakes were being rectified.

Secondly, the Soviet authorities took urgent steps to preempt grassroots discontent by prodding the official unions into activity. Statements made for specialised audiences--consisting predominantly of union officials and activists--were vehicles for far more candid and extensive criticism, and made no claim that solutions had been found to the trade unions' various shortcomings.

CONFIDENCE AND ASSURANCE FOR MASS AUDIENCES

Within weeks of the outbreak of labour unrest in Poland, articles began to appear in the Soviet press examining the role of trade unions in socialist (that is, Soviet-style) society. The purpose of these articles appeared to be to boost the credibility of the state-controlled trade unions as worthy defenders of working people's interests.

On 16 August 1980--before the Soviet press had so much as mentioned the upheavals in Poland--*Pravda* published a front-page editorial entitled "Raising the Role of the Trade Unions." "Our unions," *Pravda* wrote, "have been given wide powers. They make an important contribution to the development of the economy ... and to the improvement of people's working, living, and leisure conditions." "Recently," the editorial went on, "many local Party committees have significantly increased the amount of attention they pay to such questions." Lamenting that cases of "apathy, bureaucratism and red-tape" were still to be found, the editorial called for "attentive concern" for working people's needs.

On 18 September--barely two weeks after the signing of the Gdansk Accords whereby the Polish government gave in to the strikers' demands for free trade unions--the official Soviet news agency TASS carried an interview with Vasilii Prokhorov, deputy chairman of the AUCCTU.[1] Making no reference to the collapse of Poland's official unions, Prokhorov said that Soviet unions enjoyed "full freedom of action"; they were, he claimed, "entirely independent in deciding their internal affairs." While recognising that the Communist Party exercised a leading role where the unions were concerned, Prokhorov denied that it interfered in the unions' affairs or that it practised "petty tutelage" over them. Instead, he asserted, Soviet trade unions possessed the "widest possible powers to demand and obtain the adoption of whatever measures they deem necessary for the interests of the workers."

Prokhorov's was the first of a number of interviews in which AUCCTU officials lavished praise on the achievements of the Soviet unions.[2] It was followed, too, by a series of weighty journal articles in which the case was closely argued that independent trade unions were irrelevant in a socialist society.[3]

On 25 September, *Pravda* followed up with a long article entitled "V. I. Lenin on the Trade Unions," written by a Professor G. Alekseev. Published under the guise of a book review, this article made no direct reference to the Polish events, but its emphasis on Lenin's doctrine that unions in socialist countries must remain under the "direct leadership" of the Communist Party left little doubt that it had been written with them in mind. Lenin, the article stressed, "sharply criticised those who advocated so-called 'free' trade unions that would stand apart from participation in the solution of general state tasks, 'free' from the ultimate goals of the working-class struggle for socialism and communism, and 'independent' of the overall interests of the working people." Lenin, the article said, denounced such views as being "either a bourgeois provocation of the grossest kind, or extreme stupidity."

The official Soviet media had made no mention of the establishment of independent unions in Poland at the time Alekseev's article was published, but its categorical rejection of the concept of free unions under socialism was widely seen as criticism of the concessions made by the Polish authorities, and was echoed throughout the Soviet press. *Sovetskya Litva*, for example, wrote on 1 October of the Party's leading role as "objectively necessary." "No public organisation," the newspaper of the Lithuanian Party stated, "and this includes the trade unions, can replace the Party of the working class in this respect."

A steady flow of articles followed, all bent on showing what a crucial role the official unions were playing in helping Soviet workers to raise their living standards and resolve shopfloor disputes. On 5 November, the literary weekly *Literaturnaya gazeta* devoted a full page of small print to the activities of the AUCCTU. Not a single measure touching the interests of working people, it was asserted, could be drafted or implemented without reference to the trade unions. As an example of their power, *Literaturnaya gazeta* reported that 6,174 enterprise managers had been brought to book during the previous year, at the demand of trade union committees, for failing to fulfill the terms of collective agreements. Of these managers, the newspaper added, 146 were subsequently dismissed from their posts. A similar article was carried on 5 November by the weekly news magazine *Novoe vremya*.

A spate of reports of such dismissals followed. In November, for example, TASS gave wide publicity to the case of the director of a gas equipment works in the Lithuanian capital of Vilnius who had been removed from his post at the demand of the local union committee because he had left lying idle "large sums of money" earmarked for employee housing.[4] The Lithuanian trade union council, TASS added, had in 1980 investigated more than 20 conflicts between unions and enterprise managements, all of which had been resolved to the benefit of the working people. (Twenty cases does not really seem very many. When it was reported some months later that the director of a mine in the

Ukrainian town of Donetsk had been dismissed for failing to modernise the mine, a local union representative was quoted as saying that the case was exceptional in Soviet practice.[5])

On 26 December 1980, *Pravda* published a long theoretical article entitled "Trade Unions in Socialist Society." Its author was Professor Marat Baglai, pro-rector of the Higher School of the Trade Union Movement in Moscow. In it, Baglai denounced attempts which, he alleged, were being made "even now" by "opponents of socialism" to "impose upon the unions the notion that it is necessary to 'struggle' against the socialist state, as happens under capitalism, where the state represents the interests of the monopolies." Under capitalism, Baglai argued, strikes and trade unions were "a weapon in the struggle against the bourgeois state," but under socialism their nature was fundamentally different. In socialist countries, Baglai went on, no grounds existed for political confrontation between workers and state. Therefore, the unions no longer had any need to resort to strikes to defend the interests of working people. Under socialism, the article stated, the trade unions "always perform their work under the ideological and political guidance of the Communist Party; it is simply impossible that the situation could be otherwise."

"Recent events in Poland," Baglai went on, "show that in socialist countries work stoppages at enterprises--whatever their causes--play into the hands of antisocialist elements seeking to...deflect society from the socialist path of development." The overall thrust of the article conveyed uncompromising repudiation of Poland's new trade unions and of their claim that strikes constituted a legitimate instrument under socialism. This point was rammed home by Radio Moscow, broadcasting in Polish to Poland on 6 January 1981, when a lawyer by the name of Aleksandr Petrov declared:

> In accordance with the principles formulated by Lenin, there is an objective need for the Communist Party to direct the trade unions.

The sixtieth anniversary of the Tenth Congress of the CPSU's predecessor--the Russian Communist Party (Bolsheviks)--fell in March 1981 and provided a further opportunity for the Soviet authorities to discuss the role of unions under socialism. (As detailed in Chapter 2, the Party's Tenth Congress in 1921 was the scene of an earlier, unsuccessful, attempt to establish autonomous trade unions.) *Pravda* marked the anniversary with a stridently doctrinaire article.[6] Its author, an historian by the name of Professor V. Ivanov, stressed Lenin's precept that, under socialism, the Communist Party must retain the leading role in society and that "all other organisations, the trade unions included, must work under its guidance." "Even now," Ivanov stated in an echo of Baglai's thesis, "present-day anticommunists are seeking to undermine the foundations of the new [socialist] system."

It is appropriate to note at this point that publications such as *Literaturnaya gazeta* and *Novoe vremya* are addressed to specific audiences: the first to the Soviet cultural intelligentsia, the second to a largely foreign readership. Even *Pravda* has, in its way, a specific function as the fountainhead of doctrinal orthodoxy. A different picture of the work of the unions was to be found in the pages of *Trud*, the daily paper of the AUCCTU.

INTERNAL DOUBTS AND CRITICISMS

In contrast to the image of confidence and reassurance projected for mass and foreign consumption, media materials intended for specific domestic audiences--such as local Party officials and trade union activists--adopted a critical attitude. Here the aim seemed to be to galvanise grassroots union organisations into greater activity on their members' behalf for, as Georgian Party leader Eduard Shevardnadze was to tell a congress of trade unions in his republic, the emergence of "the so-called free trade union movement 'Solidarity'" was to be blamed on "serious mistakes in the handling of trade union work and in Party leadership of the unions."[7]

Fresh emphasis on the need to improve the work of the unions could be detected as early as August 1980 in Ukraine and the Baltic republics; this accent on the western borderlands will be discussed later in the chapter. Nationwide, the campaign was spearheaded by *Pravda* with the publication on 15 September 1980--two weeks after the signing of the Gdansk Accords--of a front-page editorial calling on industrial and agricultural managers and local Party officials to show greater responsiveness to workers' complaints and suggestions. Without making any reference to the events in Poland, *Pravda* said that public criticism must be encouraged and that workers must feel able to speak out openly about problems on the shopfloor.

Leonid Brezhnev sounded the same note when he addressed a plenum of the CPSU Central Committee on 21 October 1980. "An attentive, concerned approach to people," the Party leader said, "should imbue the whole style of work of Party, soviet and economic organs and, of course, of the trade unions."[8] *Trud* was later to characterise the spirit of the October plenum as "concern for working people and for the fuller satisfaction of their needs and interests."[9]

A shift of emphasis could also be detected in the slogans published in October 1980 to mark the sixty-third anniversary of the 1917 Revolution. (These slogans, which are inscribed on banners and carried through Red Square during the parade that takes place every year on 7 November, are considered by sovietologists a source of clues to current policy, and closely examined from year to year for signs of change.) In 1980, the slogans enjoined the trade unions to work for "the improvement of the working and living conditions of the workers," whereas in 1978 and 1979 the emphasis had been on the need to boost production by increasing workers' participation in socialist competition.[10]

The new focus was much in evidence, too, at a plenary meeting of the AUCCTU held in Moscow on 13 November 1980. Whereas earlier plenums of the AUCCTU--in 1979 and earlier in 1980--had stressed the need to increase productivity while largely ignoring health and safety issues,[11] on this occasion "serious attention was devoted to the question of increasing the activity of the unions in improving the workers' living and working conditions."[12] S.N. Zaichenko, a member of the presidium of the AUCCTU, reported that there had been "strong criticism" of the fact that:

> trade unions do not always check as they should to ensure that labour laws are adhered to. Let's be frank, there are still quite a few instances in which regulations pertaining to work and leisure have been infringed and where there has been unjustified overtime work.[13]

The press was mobilised to give the new campaign full coverage. A conference of journalists working on trade union newspapers and magazines, as well as staff of the AUCCTU's "Profizdat" publishing company, was convened in Moscow on 21 November 1980 and addressed by an official from the CPSU Central Committee's Propaganda Department. AUCCTU secretary Lyudmila Zemlyannikova reminded participants that the November plenum of the AUCCTU called upon the union press to step up its attention to "questions directly related to the improvement of the living and working conditions of the Soviet people, as well as measures to increase consumer goods production and to implement programmes for the construction of housing and social amenities."[14]

Further evidence that Soviet leaders were drawing practical conclusions from the events in Poland was provided in January 1981, when blue-collar workers were elected to the Buros of the Central Committees of the republican Party organisations (that is, to the regional counterparts of the Politburo of the CPSU Central Committee) in the Baltic states of Lithuania and Latvia, and in the three Transcaucasian republics of Armenia, Azerbaidzhan and Georgia. This was the first time in at least 25 years--and possibly longer in some republics--that an ordinary worker had been elected to a republican Central Committee Buro. Radio Liberty's analyst Ann Sheehy commented:

> One aim is presumably to give the ordinary worker the idea or the illusion that one of his colleagues will be taking part in the decision-making at the highest local Party instance. Another aim could be to ensure that those who wield power in the republic are more aware of the feelings of workers at the factory-floor level.[15]

The campaign peaked in February 1981, when Brezhnev discussed the role of the trade unions in a speech on the opening day of the Twenty-sixth Congress of the CPSU. Adopting a strikingly worker-oriented approach, Brezhnev criticised the unions for their failure to defend their members' rights and interests. "At times," he said,

> our trade unions lack initiative in exercising their extensive rights. They

> are not always persistent in questions of fulfilling collective agreements and observing safety regulations, and they still react only feebly to violations of labour legislation and to cases of bureaucracy and red-tape.[16]

And Brezhnev went on to remind his audience that "the events in Poland convince us once again how vital it is for the Party to strengthen its guiding role by lending a sensitive ear to the voice of the masses."

Brezhnev's remarks at the Party Congress of 1981 were in marked contrast to the tone he had adopted at the Party's Twenty-fifth Congress five years before, when he had asserted that the trade unions could play their role as defenders of the interests of the workers only if certain preconditions were met first, namely, "the development of production, the strengthening of labour discipline, and the raising of productivity"; the unions' primary concern, Brezhnev concluded in 1976, must be to boost production.[17]

Reference to Brezhnev's criticism immediately became an essential component of any official Soviet article or speech relating to the unions. Further complaints about "shortcomings and unresolved problems" in the work of the unions came from AUCCTU chairman Aleksei Shibaev at the March 1981 plenum of the AUCCTU. The Politburo and Central Committee of the CPSU, Shibaev said on this occasion, had recently begun to show "new concern" for the unions' activities.[18]

Most devastating of all was the criticism voiced by AUCCTU secretary Kazimeras Matskyavichyus, addressing the AUCCTU plenum that met at the end of July 1981. On the basis of letters received from workers, Matskyavichyus "strongly reproached" local union officials. The central trade union authorities in Moscow, he reported, were receiving "a flood of reports of serious infringements of working people's legitimate rights and of inadequate monitoring of their protection." Many letters, he went on,

> tell of contraventions of the system of housing allocation and of cases where working people's most vital needs are dealt with in an insensitive and bureaucratic manner.... Letters and verbal appeals on matters of social insurance and pensions, citing numerous instances of infringements and indifference on the part of various officials, are a cause for alarm and concern.... There has been no reduction in the number of complaints and applications concerning other questions in whose solution the unions have a dominant role to play. In 1980 there was an increase in the number of letters received by the AUCCTU concerning incorrect bonuses and miscalculations in the payment of wages.... It can only be a cause of concern, too, that the number of letters complaining about working conditions is not only not diminishing, but actually increasing.... Working people's written and verbal appeals show that trade union committees and councils are not combatting labour law violations sufficiently actively and consistently.... The number of illegal dismissals is still high.... Why are many working people forced to go to court? The answer is that, in many instances, they are not receiving the support they need from their trade union organisation. This is a serious indictment of our local trade union bodies.

"Our society's strength," Matskyavichyus concluded:

> lies in the fact that the masses are, in Lenin's words, able to judge everything and approach everything with a high level of awareness. Nonetheless we are receiving many letters from working people who say, "we were not consulted," "we were not informed," "it was not explained to us." And this reluctance to consult with working people is causing justified resentment and dissatisfaction.[19]

The plenum underlined its concern by adopting a resolution requiring all union organisations to devote closer attention to workers' letters and complaints.[20] (This topic is discussed in detail in Chapters 5 and 6.) Official concern over working conditions could also be seen in the creation, at the end of July 1981, of a new body responsible for work safety: the State Committee for Working Practices in Industry and for Mine Supervision, which was established by upgrading a previously existing committee under the USSR Council of Ministers.[21] New regulations barring women workers from 460 occupations involving hard physical labour were, moreover, introduced on 1 January 1981.[22]

EXPOSES OF UNION MISCONDUCT

Efforts to prod the unions into greater activity were backed up by the publication in *Trud* of a series of often horrifying accounts of the violation of workers' rights by enterprise managers. Trade union officials were portrayed as conniving with management in these abuses, turning a blind eye to violations of industrial safety regulations, and doing nothing to prevent unfair dismissals. To be sure, such articles were not an innovation inasmuch as *Trud* had often, over the years, drawn attention to such abuses.[23] Critical articles on this theme nonetheless seemed, in the period under review, to appear more frequently than before.

In November 1980, for example, *Trud* described the situation in the Central Asian republic of Tadzhikistan as one where there were frequent cases of "flagrant infringement of the labour law, including illegal dismissal and transfer of workers to other jobs, the witholding of pay for work already done, and compulsory overtime on weekends and holidays." Such evils would not occur, *Trud* wrote, if local unions were not, through their passivity, lending tacit approval to managerial abuses.[24]

This article was followed by another highly critical piece in which *Trud* detailed the failure of trade union officials in the Ukrainian city of Voroshilovgrad to ensure that safety regulations were observed at local plants. The officials were depicted as drowning under a rising tide of paperwork and red-tape, incapable of checking whether the countless instructions they issued were being followed or not. "We have to go to so many meetings," they wailed, "that we haven't the time or the energy to get on with the really important things!"[25]

Next, *Trud* printed a letter from a group of women workers at a shoe factory in the city of Orenburg. The women complained that, because the factory was behind on its production schedule, they were being forced to work overtime almost every Saturday. The more compulsory overtime was declared, the more staff left in search of jobs elsewhere, and production slipped further and further behind. The management responded by ordering yet more working Saturdays; sometimes they asked the trade union's permission for this, but as often as not they did not.

The women hated having to work on Saturdays

because many of them had young children and, as the kindergarten was shut on Saturdays, they had to take their children to the factory with them. Toddlers ran round the workshop and risked injuring themselves on the machinery. One of the supervisors had fixed up a makeshift creche in a tiny office, but there was nothing there for the children to play with and before long they became bored and tearful. At no point in the article was the factory trade union committee shown as protecting the interests of the employees.[26] And when, shortly before the appearance of this particular report, *Trud* discussed the plight of miners from the Ukrainian city of Donetsk who were also being required to put in long hours of overtime, the newspaper added the comment: "No-one ever asks the permission of the trade union when days-off are cancelled or double-shifts are ordered."[27]

A number of articles published by *Trud* at this time focussed on bribery and corruption among managers and trade union officials, particularly where the allocation of housing and vacations was concerned. Trade union officials were portrayed at best as apathetic toward managerial abuses, at worst as actively involved in corrupt practices. *Trud* described the situation at a paper-manufacturing combine in Karelia where the personnel director had for years been engaging in corrupt deals, moving workers' families out of desirable apartments and putting his own cronies in instead. Since these friends had no right to new housing, minutes were forged to make it look as if the allocations had been sanctioned at meetings of the trade union. In this way, the director's son and his wife obtained a luxurious three-roomed apartment, while workers' families were left in cramped communal flats where they had to share cooking and washing facilities with other families.[28] It was, *Pravda* editorialised on 6 May 1981, in the realm of living and working conditions that the trade unions were showing least persistence.

Another case of union passivity was exposed by *Trud* with an article examining the allocation of housing at a cement factory in the Tadzhik capital of Dushanbe. There, too, the trade union committee was portrayed as playing a purely formal role. Its members raised no objection when asked to allocate a desirable new flat not to a needy worker--who was living, with his family of five, in a single room with no cooking facilities--but to a close friend of the enterprise director, the republican minister of industrial construction. The union officials kept silent, *Trud* explained, because "they were well aware that their opinion was not of the slightest interest to anyone, and that the matter had already been decided, at a much higher level...."[29]

Perhaps the most revealing expose concerned a much decorated coalminer from the Central Asian republic of Kirgizia who was elected chairman of his local trade union committee. It did not take him long to get accustomed to the comforts and privileges of his new position, and to forget his erstwhile workmates toiling underground. Turning a blind eye to violations of safety regulations, he stopped visiting the mine altogether "because when he did he had to find answers to the miners' questions." In an effort to curry favour with the bosses, he began instead to engage in the corrupt distribution of holiday vouchers. As *Trud* told the story, the moral degradation of this miner turned union official took less than two years; the paper did not inquire how it was that so outstanding a worker could sink so low in so short a time.[30]

ACCENT ON THE WESTERN BORDERLANDS

This propaganda campaign was accompanied by efforts to strengthen Party influence within the trade unions and in the workplace. As already mentioned, such efforts were particularly noticeable in Ukraine and the Baltic republics--that is, in those of the USSR's border regions that are closest to Poland both geographically and culturally.

As early as August 1980, Lithuanian and Ukrainian officials began to call for greater activity from their republican trade union organisations. At a plenary meeting of the trade union council of Ukraine's Crimean oblast that met in the middle of that month, the work of the local unions came in for extremely heavy criticism, and Party members were exhorted to play a more active role in local union activities. Unusually, this plenum was attended by a brace of high-level functionaries from the republican capital of Kiev, including the chairman of the Ukrainian Council of Trade Unions himself, Vitalii Sologub.[31]

A few days later the Central Committee of the Communist Party of Lithuania devoted a plenary meeting to discussing ways of increasing the numbers of workers in the Party's ranks and of generating prompter responses to workers' concerns on the part of officials. The republican Party second secretary, Nikolai Dybenko, castigated the trade unions for failing to protect workers from illegal dismissal and demanded that officials be "penalised much more severely for disdainful attitudes" toward working people's opinions.[32] (By contrast, a plenary meeting of the Central Committee of the Communist Party of Latvia which met at the end of July--two weeks before the outbreak of strikes in Gdansk--was devoted to a discussion of ways of strengthening labour discipline.[33])

In his study of the impact of the Polish events in the Soviet Baltic republics, Stanley Vardys notes that in the autumn of 1980 "all Baltic newspapers featured stories about workers abused by managers of factories or other state enterprises." But, the American scholar adds, expressions of concern of this kind "slackened after the introduction of martial law in Poland in December 1981."[34]

At the end of October 1980, Ukrainian Party first secretary Vladimir Shcherbitsky told a plenum of the Central Committee of the Communist Party of Ukraine that the republican Party Buro had worked out concrete measures aimed at "strengthening the influence of primary Party organisations in the work collectives."[35] These measures were followed in June 1981 by the convening of an unusual meeting between Shcherbitsky--accompanied by other members of the Ukrainian Party Buro--and officials of the republican Council of Trade Unions and of local trade union organisations. This meeting called for "further improvement" of union activity and, in particular, for the exercise of tighter control over the construction and allocation of housing and the operation of consumer services such as shops, canteens and kindergartens.[36]

"LENDING A SENSITIVE EAR TO THE VOICE OF THE MASSES"

The policy of trying to improve the public image of the official trade unions, which characterised the first phase of the Soviet leaders' response to the Polish crisis, was most closely identified with Party leader Brezhnev and his long-time associate, Politburo member and Central Committee secretary Konstantin Chernenko. The need for officials to pay careful attention to public opinion--as expressed through sociological surveys and in letters sent to the authorities by members of the general public --had long been a theme of Chernenko's writings.[37] Underlying his recommendations was concern that, unless the CPSU could project itself in the public eye as a worthy leader, then Party and people--rulers and ruled--might drift irrevocably apart.

The strikes in Poland and the rise of Solidarity lent fresh urgency to Chernenko's calls for wider popular participation in the management of society. In the opinion of the historian Richard Pipes--who was serving during that time on the White House National Security staff--Chernenko seemed, of all the Politburo members, "to have understood best that what happened in Poland could not be handled by mere repression." Chernenko was, in Pipes' view, particularly concerned about the collapse of the PUWP and about "the loss of contact between the Party and the people at large."[38]

This concern could be clearly discerned in Chernenko's writings. In an article published in *Kommunist* in November 1980, for example--three months after the emergence of Solidarity--Chernenko urged a switch of emphasis in official trade union policy. The unions' "most important duty," he stated, was "the defence of working people's rights and interests, and an attentive attitude toward their needs and demands and their working and living conditions."[39]

In April 1981 Chernenko delivered the keynote address at the annual Kremlin ceremony marking the anniversary of Lenin's birth. There again he stressed the Party's need to stay in touch with public opinion so as to avoid "inaccurate and mistaken steps," and to "react sensitively" to new problems arising in society. "The Soviet communists know only too well," he added, "from their own and others' experience, that a high price has to be paid for any departure from Leninist norms."[40] Again, writing in *Kommunist* in September 1981, Chernenko called on the unions to show themselves more responsive to workers' concerns, and he issued an explicit warning that in socialist countries "disregard for the interests of any class or group" is "fraught with the danger of social tension and of political and socioeconomic crisis." The failure of the Polish leaders to appreciate the mood of the public, Chernenko seemed to be saying, was an important cause of Poland's labour unrest and, unless Soviet leaders took heed of the wishes of their own population, the USSR might risk a similar outbreak of popular discontent. "We have seen," Chernenko wrote, "from our own experience and from that of the other socialist countries, that firm ties with the masses...cannot be established once and for all.... The people judge the Party's wisdom and maturity not by its words and promises, but by its ability to work out and implement a policy that yields tangible results."[41]

Chernenko repeated this point in an article published in February 1982, in which he wrote that the Polish events showed the "vital significance" of heeding popular opinion. The most serious danger for the Party, he reiterated, was that of becoming divorced from the masses, while the "harsh lessons of recent years" showed that "unless the Party daily reaffirms its right to lead society...the political situation can take on a crisis character."[42]

The views of Chernenko and of others who thought like him enjoyed particular influence during this first phase of the Soviet response to the Polish events, when efforts were made to improve the image of the official unions, more attention was paid to public opinion, and concern was expressed over the quality and quantity of consumer goods. But while the Polish events clearly served the Soviet leaders as an object lesson, different leaders drew different conclusions from them. Proposals made by leaders such as Mikhail Suslov and Yurii Andropov also, as will be shown, had an impact on Kremlin policy-making.

FOOTNOTES TO CHAPTER 4

1. *TASS*, 18 September 1980.
2. See, for example, interview with AUCCTU

Secretary Aleksei Viktorov, *TASS*, 23 October 1980; press conference by AUCCTU Secretary Aleksandra Biryukova, *TASS*, 4 February 1981; and interview with AUCCTU Secretary Lyudmila Zemlyannikova, *TASS*, 10 June 1981.

3. These included V. Prokhorov, "Partiya i profsoyuzy," *Politicheskoe samoobrazovanie*, No 2, 1981, pp. 25-32; A. Shibaev, "Samaya massovaya organizatsiya trudyashchikhsya," *Kommunist*, No 4, 1981, pp. 72-83; Yu. N. Korshunov, "Sovetskie profsoyuzy: zashchita interesov trudyashchikhsya," *Sovetskoe gosudarstvo i pravo*, No 4, 1981, pp. 123-31; L. Petrov, "Profsoyuzy--shkola kommunizma," *Partiinaya zhizn'*, No 12, 1981, pp. 30-35; G. V. Sharapov, "Leninskie printsipy partiinogo rukovodstva profsoyuzami," *Voprosy istorii KPSS*, No 11, 1981, pp. 3-18.

4. *TASS*, 20 November 1980.

5. *Radio Budapest*, 4 May 1981.

6. *Pravda*, 8 March 1981.

7. *Zarya vostoka*, 2 February 1982.

8. *Pravda*, 22 October 1980.

9. *Trud*, 25 November 1980.

10. In 1979, the slogan read: "Soviet trade unions! More widely encourage socialist competition and the movement for a communist attitude to work!" (*Pravda*, 14 October 1978). In 1979 the slogan read: "Soviet trade unions! Play an active role in the management of state and public affairs, in the resolution of political, economic, social and cultural questions! Improve socialist competition and the movement for a communist attitude to work!" (*Pravda*, 14 October 1979). In 1980, the wording changed to: "Soviet trade unions! Play an active role in the management of state and public affairs, in the solution of political and economic affairs, *and in the improvement of the working and living conditions of the workers!*" (*Pravda*, 12 October 1980, emphasis added).

11. Foreign Broadcast Information Service (FBIS) Trends, "Soviet Trade Union Officials Outline Expanded Role," 1 April 1981.

12. *Radio Moscow*, 13 November 1980.

13. *Ibid.*

14. *Trud*, 22 November 1980.

15. RL 57/81, "Blue-Collar Workers Elected to Central Committee Buros in Five Union Republics," by Ann Sheehy, 5 February 1981.

16. *Pravda*, 24 February 1981.

17. *Ibid.*, 25 February 1976.

18. *Trud*, 21 and 22 March 1981.

19. *Ibid.*, 29 and 30 July 1981.

20. *Ibid.*, 31 July 1981.

21. *Izvestia*, 28 July 1981.

22. RL 110/82, "Easing the Workload of Soviet Women--in Theory and in Practice," by Sergei Voronitsyn, 8 March 1982.

23. Details of a number of such instances are to be found in Betsy Gidwitz, "Labor Unrest in the Soviet Union," *Problems of Communism*, November-December 1982, pp. 25-42 at p. 27.

24. *Trud*, 2 November 1980.

25. *Ibid.*, 21 November 1980.

26. *Ibid.*, 20 January 1981.

27. Reported in the *Daily Telegraph*, 20 November 1980.

28. *Trud*, 5 May 1981.

29. *Ibid.*, 2 July 1981.

30. *Ibid.*, 18 November 1980.

31. *Robotnycha hazeta*, 21 August 1980, cited in RL 303/80, "Criticism of Local Trade-Union Organs in the Ukraine: Impact of Polish Developments?" by Roman Solchanyk, 27 August 1980.

32. *Sovetskaya Litva*, 27 August 1980, cited by V. Stanley Vardys in "Polish Echoes in the Baltic," *Problems of Communism*, July-August 1983, pp. 21-34 at p. 33.

33. *Sovetskaya Latviya*, 1 August 1980, cited

by Vardys, *op. cit.*

34. Vardys, *op. cit.*

35. *Radyans'ka Ukraina*, 30 October 1980, quoted in Roman Solchanyk, "Poland and the Soviet West," in S. Enders Wimbush (ed), *Soviet Nationalities in Strategic Perspective*, Beckenham, 1984, pp. 158-80 at p. 164. See also RL 303/81, "Ukrainian Party Shows Concern for Trade Unions and Workers," by Roman Solchanyk, 4 August 1981.

36. *Radyans'ka Ukraina*, 3 June 1981, and *Trud*, 4 June 1981, cited in RL 303/81.

37. For analyses of Chernenko's views, see RL 331/79, "The Views of Konstantin U. Chernenko," by Terry McNeill, 6 November 1979; RL 356/81, "Kirilenko at 75, Chernenko at 70: What Chance Does Either Have of Succeeding Brezhnev?" by Elizabeth Teague, 9 September 1981; Heinz Brahm, "Leitmotive in K. Tschernenkos Schriften," Berichte des Bundesinstituts fuer ostwissenschaftliche und internationale Studien, Koeln, 1982; Marc D. Zlotnik, "Chernenko's Platform," *Problems of Communism*, November-December 1982, pp. 70-75.

38. Interviewed on American television (ABC's "Nightline") on 14 February 1984.

39. K. Chernenko, "Velikoe edinstvo partii i naroda," *Kommunist*, No 17, 1980, pp. 10-24.

40. *Pravda*, 23 April 1981.

41. K. Chernenko, "Leninskaya strategiya rukovodstva," *Kommunist*, No 13, 1981, pp. 6-22.

42. K.U. Chernenko, "Vopros, vazhnyi dlya vsei partii," *Voprosy istorii KPSS*, No 2, 1982, pp. 3-19.

Chapter 5

INCREASED ATTENTION TO PUBLIC OPINION

The initial reaction of the Soviet leaders to Poland's upheaval was to call for greater responsiveness on the part of officials to the needs and concerns of the population. Stressing the need for attention to public opinion, this approach emphasised the study of working people's letters as an indicator of the popular mood.

To keep abreast of developments in all corners of their vast empire, the Soviet leaders have a number of sources of information at their disposal. These include, first of all, Communist Party and KGB channels. There exists, too, a large number of institutions which provide the leadership with access to the general public mood, such as the trade unions, youth organisations, the constituency meetings supposed to be held regularly by delegates to the local soviets, and so on. Increasing use has been made in recent years of sociological methods, including public opinion surveys, questionnaires, and statistical analyses.[1]

Aside from some studies conducted in the 1920s, the study of public opinion and its parent discipline, sociology, fell into disfavour during Stalin's time. In the late 1950s, interest in sociology was revived, and public opinion polling was encouraged throughout the 1960s. Before long, however, the fledgling science came into fresh conflict with conservative Party officials, who saw empirical research as a threat to established doctrines and insisted, as had Stalin before them, that historical materialism was the only appropriate instrument for the explanation of social phenomena. As a result of Party intervention, sociological research came in the early 1970s under a cloud for which it began to emerge only toward the end of that decade.[2]

Since then there has been a further revival of interest in sociological research and in the study of public opinion in the Soviet Union. In contrast to the "chief ideologist" of the CPSU, Mikhail Suslov, who warned sociologists to beware of slipping into "pragmatism" and "empiricism,"[3] Konstantin Chernenko was a consistent advocate of sociological research, arguing that public opinion surveys were essential to provide the Party with "knowledge of the mood among the masses."[4]

It would be difficult, and perhaps impossible, to prove conclusively that the Polish events of 1980 increased the leadership's concern about the monitoring of public opinion, though this conclusion seems probable. But it can be shown that in public discussion about the study of public opinion, statements concerning the need for such monitoring were linked explicitly to the Polish example. Writing in *Pravda* on 25 September 1981, for instance, a senior researcher at the Institute of State and Law of the USSR Academy of Sciences, Rafael Safarov, described public opinion as "a sensitive barometer whose readings can, if carefully analysed, tell us a great deal about the hidden processes of social life, often scarcely perceptible or still only incipient." The events in Poland, Safarov stated, showed the necessity of utilising this barometer to give advance warning of "contradictions and conflict situations in socialist society."

Soviet leaders have traditionally made use of letters and verbal complaints addressed by citizens to state and Party bodies, the mass media, and so on. Indeed, Alex Pravda describes the writing of critical letters (for critical is what many of them are) as the only form of spontaneous activity on the part of the ordinary citizen to receive official approval and even encouragement in the USSR.[5]

Letterwriting was a tradition even in pre-revolutionary Russia. According to Michael Binyon:

> For generations, any Russian with a grievance has traditionally picked up a pen and written to his country's leaders. In early Tsarist days a basket used to be lowered from a window of the Old Kremlin Palace, in which petitioners could place their missives.[6]

This kind of letterwriting received strong support from Lenin, persisted through the Stalin period,[7] and was encouraged under Khrushchev. It received further endorsement under Brezhnev, and was granted comprehensive legal provision in 1968, with the adoption by the Presidium of the USSR Supreme Soviet of a decree (amended in 1980) laying down the procedures to be followed in the examination of citizens' letters, appeals and complaints.[8]

That decree guaranteed the right of Soviet citizens to make written or verbal representations to all state and social organisations. It required that citizens be assured ready access to local officials, and called for the establishment of regular consulting hours, during the evening as well in the daytime, both in residential areas and at people's places of work. Time limits were specified within which appropriate action must be taken on each letter and the person lodging the request was to be kept informed of its outcome.

To be sure, these provisions are not always met. One reader wrote to the newspaper *Sovetskaya Rossiya*:

> It's impossible to see the chairman of our local soviet. "A delegation has arrived," we were told, "and he's completely tied

> up." But when we poked out heads round the door, there he was, all alone.[9]

Officials who treat citizens' letters in a bureaucratic manner can, the law specifies, be held legally accountable. Nonetheless there are constant complaints of "formalism," "disdain" and "paper-shuffling," summed up by the descriptive Russian term *otfutbolivanie*, or "passing the buck."

Citizens are required to address their "suggestions and appeals" to the organisation directly responsible for resolving the matter in question; "complaints," on the other hand, are to be lodged with the official body immediately superior to the official or organisation whose behaviour is at issue. The accusation is constantly heard, however, that "complaints are often referred to those about whom they are written," even though the decree expressly forbids such a procedure.[10]

Following the Twenty-fifth and Twenty-sixth Congresses of the CPSU in 1976 and 1981, Central Committee resolutions were adopted that called on Party bodies to improve their handling of letters and appeals from the public.[11] Particular emphasis was laid on the importance of such work by Chernenko who at that time headed the General Department of the CPSU Central Committee. Chernenko had a vested interest in such work because the functions of the General Department include "registering, examining and initiating action on complaints made [to the central Party bodies] in writing or in person by members of the public."[12] Even when a new Letters Department was set up within the Central Committee in 1979,[13] it remained under the supervision of the General Department and was headed by Boris Yakovlev, one of Chernenko's former deputies.

During the Polish crisis, Chernenko charged more than once that the Polish leaders' lack of understanding of the population played a role in the disturbances and that, unless leaders paid close attention to public opinion, they could not gauge and direct the public mood. In a speech in April 1981, Chernenko called on Party officials to study letters as a means of "increasing and deepening links with the masses," "reacting sensitively to changes and new phenomena in society," and avoiding "inaccurate and mistaken steps."[14]

Chapter 6 describes how, following the Polish crisis, the Soviet leadership began to encourage a new form of work, the "Open Letter Days." This was not the only development. Radio programmes devoted to workers' letters also made an appearance at this time, while a television series entitled "Daily Attention to the Needs of the People" was screened for the first time in October 1981.[15] This was succeeded in 1982 by a television series, launched on the initiative of the Central Committee's Letters Department and entitled "Solutions are Found on the Spot."[16]

Attention to working people's letters was maintained following Brezhnev's death. One of the first acts of the Andropov leadership was to start publishing brief reports of the weekly meetings of the Politburo and it was recorded that, at its first regular meeting since Brezhnev's death, the Politburo "discussed the issue of working people's letters."[17] This was shortly followed by a *Pravda* editorial which stressed that the Central Committee was devoting "constant attention" to citizens' verbal and written appeals, "regarding them as an effective means of expression of public opinion."[18]

The number of letters, complaints and requests made by Soviet citizens to local officials and to the central authorities is huge. (Failure to obtain the desired response or, indeed, any response at all at the local level often, of course, requires a complaint to be resubmitted at a higher level.) The numbers involved are sometimes so large as to rule out any possibility that the officials responsible will be able to give them all adequate attention. (In 1959, for example, the chairman of the executive committee of an oblast soviet was reported to have received, in one year, 7,815 written requests and 1,561 personal visits in his office![19]) Moreover, all sources agree that the numbers of letters and visits are constantly increasing.[20]

Chernenko revealed that in 1978 the CPSU Central Committee received 560,000 letters,[21] while some 20,000 people were at that time being received annually for interviews in the Central Committee's Reception Office in Moscow.[22] In 1978 the Central Committees of the Communist Parties of the Union republics examined a total of 683,000 letters, and granted personal interviews to 215,000 people.[23]

Of the leading Soviet newspapers, *Pravda* in the early 1980s was said to receive half a million letters a year (slightly fewer than the Central Committee).[24] The trade union newspaper *Trud* (which in the early 1980s was printing 15 million copies a day, as compared with *Pravda*'s 10 million) was receiving nearly 2,000 letters daily, more than either *Pravda* or the Central Committee. *Trud* maintained a staff of about 100 people to deal with this postbag; each letter was reportedly turned round within seven days (either answered directly or forwarded to the appropriate authority) and, where appropriate, *Trud* monitored the outcome.[25]

Reports claim that older people write the most letters, amd that young people write comparatively rarely. Men are usually said to write more letters than women, and city dwellers more than country people. Pensioners make up the largest single group among those who write to the press, followed in descending order by blue-collar workers, office workers, farm workers and technicians.[26]

The sheer quantity of letters involved and the complexity of many of the problems raised--to say nothing of the characteristic unwillingness of Soviet bureaucrats to take decisions--mean that many letters go unanswered. Others are propelled into a kind of vicious circle:

> Someone thinks he's been discriminated against in the vital matter of housing. So he writes to the authority next up the ladder. From there his complaint is referred back to the body that made the original decision. The people "on top" seem to think that those "down below" will immediately see the error of their ways and put matters straight. But those "underneath" are interested only in saving their skins, and they defend their original decision at any cost. So the complainant writes to the authorities *two* steps up the ladder. They send his letter down to their subordinates, who refer it back down again to those who made the original decision. This goes on indefinitely.[27]

The central authorities complain constantly about "formalistic and disdainful attitudes toward citizens' legitimate rights, unjustified refusals of requests and tardy answers to their letters" on the part of local officials.[28] Addressing the Twenty-sixth Party Congress in February 1981, and evidently with the Polish events in mind, Brezhnev criticised Party officials more sharply than on any previous occasion for their failure to deal sympathetically with letters from the public. Of the 1,500 letters received every day by the Central Committee in Moscow, he charged, "many unfortunately testify to serious failings at the local level. Many of the questions raised by working people could and should have been settled by the managers of enterprises and by district and city organisations."[29]

Why Soviet citizens write so many letters is something of a mystery. The fact that many letters are written, and that their numbers are constantly growing, suggests that Soviet citizens look on letterwriting as a useful activity, offering at least some chance of achieving the desired end. Writing a letter is, after all, a solitary activity requiring a fair amount of individual motivation. Unlike attendance at a May Day parade or at a *subbotnik* (a day's unpaid work), it is not something that people can easily be pressured into doing just for a quiet life.[30] At the same time, the press speaks of countless letters unanswered or rejected out of hand. Cases of victimisation are by no means unknown.[31] *Pravda* took up the case of a young woman, an exemplary worker from Krasnodar krai (region) named Nadezhda Turovskaya, whose application for Party membership had been inexplicably rejected by the local Party committee (*raikom*). It transpired that two years earlier Turovskaya had been assigned an apartment in a new block. The building was poorly finished; there was no heating, even in winter, and no running water. Failing to obtain satisfaction locally, Turovskaya and her neighbours bombarded the local press and the krai authorities with letters of complaint. The water was eventually turned on and everybody forgot all about the incident. Everybody, said *Pravda* pointedly, except the *raikom*....[32]

Fear of victimisation leads many letterwriters not to sign their names:

> We're afraid! Yes, we're afraid that reprisals will be taken against us. We all have families and children, and we've all seen with our own eyes how the bosses get even with anyone who makes their criticism openly....[33]

Anonymous letters--with their echoes of Stalinist denunciations--are a constant topic of debate in the Soviet press. The point is often made that, if only the authorities ignored *anonimki*, people would stop writing them. To that the ministry of internal affairs replies that it investigates all the letters it receives, that 25 percent of the anonymous accusations turn out to be founded in fact, and that it cannot afford to ignore so valuable a source of information in the struggle against crime.[34]

Research conducted among recent Soviet emigres in Israel and the United States of America suggests, however, that letterwriting ranks low in Soviet citizens' perceptions of "the best way to influence a Soviet government decision," with only 4.5 percent of those interviewed recommending this option. The largest group (35.5 percent) preferred the option of "using personal or family connexions" as promising the best chance of success.[35]

There are several possible explanations why Soviet citizens persist in writing letters--though none seems wholly satisfactory. Of course, letter-writers may simply be without the influential "personal or family connexions" the emigres referred to. However, the practice has deep roots in pre-revolutionary Russia. While Western societies tend to regard informing, or "sneaking," on neighbours and workmates as a despicable act, it was the tradition for princes in mediaeval Muscovy to conclude treaties whereby each swore to inform the other of any matter concerning him. In the course of time, these reciprocal princely arrangements took on the character of one-sided obligations, whereby a vassal was obliged to report whatever information he heard to the sovereign and his boyars.[36]

Another explanation may be found in the relative weakness in pre- and post-revolutionary Russia of the concept of the rule of law as it is generally understood in the West. Neal Ascherson's desciption of the phenomenon in its modern Polish setting will be recognised by anyone who has lived in the Soviet Union:

> Except at the very summit, no official decision is final in Poland. A visit to a [district] headquarters usually reveals a queue of supplicants waiting with petitions or grievances, and many of them will be petitioning against a decision taken at the lower ... level of local government. In practice, there is almost no real devolution of power, no area in which a subordinate state or Party body has complete authority. Any decision at any level can be overturned by the next tier if the petitioner has a good case, good connections, or--on occasion--the resources for a convincing bribe.[37]

The motives of those who write petitions and complaints in the USSR are, then, unclear. It may be that, as the emigre evidence suggests, letter-writers do not as a rule have very high expectations that their letters will achieve their objects. At the same time, there seems little reason to doubt official Soviet reports about the volume of letterwriting. The phenomenon is not one that shows Soviet society in a particularly good light or about which there is an unequivocal official view. Reports about it do not, therefore, fall into the category of official boasting and the phenomenon appears, in short, to be real enough.

And, while the motives of letterwriters remain obscure, those of the central authorities are clear. Letterwriting is repeatedly lauded as an important activity because it provides the leadership with "a sensitive barometer of public opinion." Summaries of working people's letters are regularly circulated among members of the Politburo and Secretariat.[38] Such letters supply the leaders with feedback about the mood of the population and their reaction to policies; they also enable local officials to identify potential trouble spots. Guram Enukidze, secretary for ideology of the Central Committee of the Communist Party of Georgia, has stated that such research is valuable "because it enables us to discern the first symptoms and trends of this or that deviation, and to elaborate recommendations for its elimination."[39] T.M. Dzhafarli, deputy head of the Centre for the Study, Moulding and Prognosis of Public Opinion of the Central Committee of the Georgian Party, has been equally frank:

> The Central Committee of the Georgian Party is interested above all in detecting opinion that for one reason or another does not conform with the official point of view, because in such cases it is possible to review the official position critically--from the "sidelines," so to speak--and to ascertain why a particular social group holds a different point of view, and to determine whether they had sufficient and reliable information about those facts concerning which their opinion was formed.[40]

Letters also enable the central authorities to monitor the performance of local officials. Brezhnev himself recognised the risk that:

> When information is "ferried" from one level to another it may be distorted, while the edge of vital issues tends to be dulled.[41]

This tendency is exacerbated by the Soviet Union's administrative structure. Despite the high centralisation of some areas of state activity, provincial Party leaders exercise wide powers of their own, much in the manner of a prefect or satrap, and frequently have it within their ability to make or break initiatives from Moscow. They are, moreover, extremely likely to supply the central authorities with information that redounds to their own credit, and to suppress any that does not. In the words of a leading Central Committee official:

> Some Party committees willingly inform higher organs about positive features and good results, but prefer not to direct attention to errors and shortcomings.[42]

In order to maintain control over the activities of local leaders, therefore, the central authorities must find alternative sources of information about what is going on at the grassroots. Workers' letters are valued by the leaders as just such a source of independent information.

As to the topics about which people write, all sources agree that more letters concern housing than any other single subject; 15 percent of all letters to newspapers are reported to relate to this question.[43] Also frequently raised are problems concerning working conditions. As the last chapter noted, the Soviet media devoted considerable attention to this subject at the time of the Polish events, with the trade unions coming in for a good deal of criticism. Speaking at the July 1981 plenum of the AUCCTU, trade union official Kazimeras Matskyavichyus complained specifically that a very large number of workers' letters related to "contraventions of the system of housing allocation."[44]

This point was picked up some months later by *Trud*, which stressed that it was not housing itself that most people wrote about, but corrupt practices relating to it. The newspaper said it was receiving "many letters complaining about unfair distribution of housing."[45] Boris Yakovlev, head of the CPSU's Letters Department, told Radio Moscow on 5 February 1983 that:

> Letters about housing stand out for their quantity among the great variety of letters arriving at the Central Committee.... The most alarming letters on this theme relate to...infringements of the law in...the distribution of housing.

In light of Yakovlev's remarks, an unconfirmed report takes on especial interest. The Associated Press reported from Moscow on 26 March 1982 that, according to "Soviet Communist Party sources," the initiative for the crackdown on corruption then under way came from the Letters Department. The department head was reportedly so overwhelmed by the number of complaints about corrupt practices that he approached his boss to see what could be done. His boss, of course, was Chernenko. Chernenko was said to have raised the matter in his turn at a meeting of the Politburo and, as a result, a campaign against corruption was launched in November 1981.

Now it has generally been assumed that the campaign against corruption was masterminded by Yurii Andropov, then head of the KGB, in an attempt to discredit Chernenko in the struggle for the Brezhnev succession. Following his election as Party leader in November 1982, Andropov certainly seemed to use the issue of corruption as a weapon to shake up the Party apparatus and replace leaders of the Brezhnev era with appointees loyal to himself (see Chapter 13). Andropov's role in the campaign against corruption is, therefore, hardly open to doubt. But it would not have been beyond a politician of Andropov's skill and intelligence to exploit for his own purposes a campaign set in motion by another. The campaign against corruption takes on a new irony if it is speculated that it originated with Chernenko's concern about popular resentment of widespread corruption. The Polish example would certainly have given the Kremlin leaders food for thought; in the words of one of Solidarity's representatives in the West, Aleksander Smolar:

> Of all the unsavory and unpopular features of the Communist system in Poland, perhaps none aroused more hostility and outrage, or contributed more to the outburst of discontent in the summer of 1980, than the existence of widespread social inequalities, blatant disparities of income, social privileges, and material well-being between the bulk of the population on the one hand and the small ruling elite on the other.[46]

Plentiful evidence is provided by the letters published in the Soviet press in the period 1980-82, and by reports of the "Open Letter Days" that began to be held throughout the country at that time, to indicate that social injustice and inequality were indeed giving rise to strong feelings of resentment among ordinary Soviet citizens. The interesting phenomenon of "Open Letter Days" will be discussed in the next chapter.

FOOTNOTES TO CHAPTER 5

1. See RL 142/78, "Growing Interest in the Study of Public Opinion," by Sergei Voronitsyn, 27 June 1978; and RL 109/83, "Revival of Public Opinion

Polls in the USSR," by Elizabeth Teague, 9 March 1983.

2. See Mervyn Matthews' introduction to *Soviet Sociology, 1964-75, A Bibliography*, by Mervyn Matthews in collaboration with T. Anthony Jones, New York, 1975, pp. 1-24; and Walter D. Connor, "Public Opinion in the Soviet Union," in *Public Opinion in European Socialist Systems*, by Walter D. Connor and Zvi Y. Gitelman, with Adaline Huszczo and Robert Blumstock, New York, 1977, pp. 104-31.

3. M. Suslov, "Istoricheskaya pravota idei i dela Lenina," *Kommunist*, No 4, 1980, pp. 11-29 at p. 26.

4. K. Chernenko, "The CPSU's Leninist Tradition: Working For and With the People," *Problems of Peace and Socialism*, No 5, 1979, pp. 3-11 at p. 9.

5. Alex Pravda, "Spontaneous Workers' Activity in the Soviet Union," mimeo, undated.

6. *The Times*, 12 July 1982.

7. The use made during the Stalin era of *donosy*, or anonymous denunciations, is notorious. It is interesting to learn that Leonid Nikolaev, the man whose assassination of Sergei Kirov served as Stalin's pretext for the purges of the late 1930s, was an inveterate letter writer who "had written denunciatory letters to every official who had ever made him miserable, and if he received no satisfaction he would write to their superiors." It is said to have been this habit that brought Nikolaev to the attention of the secret police. See Robert Payne, *The Rise and Fall of Stalin*, London, 1968, p. 445.

8. "On the Procedure for the Consideration of Citizens' Proposals, Appeals and Complaints," *Pravda*, 26 April 1968; for amendments see *Spravochnik partiinogo rabotnika*, Moscow, 1981, pp. 355-60.

9. *Sovetskaya Rossiya*, 14 October 1984.

10. *Literaturnaya gazeta*, 22 August 1984.

11. *Pravda*, 4 May 1976 and 4 April 1981.

12. Leonard Schapiro, "The General Department of the CC of the CPSU," *Survey*, No 3, 1975, pp. 53-65 at p. 63.

13. *Pravda*, 26 April 1979.

14. *Pravda*, 22 April 1981.

15. *Zhurnalist*, No 7, 1982, pp. 11-12.

16. *Trud*, 8 March 1983; *Sovetskaya Litva*, 16 April 1983.

17. *Pravda*, 11 December 1982.

18. *Ibid.*, 28 December 1982.

19. Theodore H. Friedgut, *Political Participation in the USSR*, Princeton, NJ, 1979, p. 225.

20. For example, K.U. Chernenko, "Leninsky stil' raboty i kommunisticheskoe vospitanie trudyashchikhsya," *Voprosy istorii KPSS*, No 9, 1979, pp. 3-18.

21. *Ibid.*

22. *Pravda*, 24 February 1981.

23. Chernenko, *op. cit.*

24. *Pravda*, 24 August 1983.

25. *Trud*, 10 October 1982.

26. *Guardian*, 29 July 1980; *Sovetskaya Rossiya*, 6 March 1983.

27. *Literaturnaya gazeta*, 22 August 1984.

28. *Pravda*, 24 February 1981 (report of the Central Auditing Commission of the CPSU to the Party's Twenty-sixth Congress).

29. *Pravda*, 24 February 1981.

30. This point is elaborated in Michael B. Bowker, "Why People Participate in the Soviet Union," MA dissertation, University of Essex, 1980.

31. See Nicholas Lampert, *Whistle-blowing in the Soviet Union: Complaints and Abuses under State Socialism*, London, 1985, for a discussion of this subject.

32. *Pravda*, 19 August 1984.

33. *Literaturnaya gazeta*, 22 August 1984.

34. *Ibid.*

35. Wayne Di Franceisco and Zvi Gitelman, "Soviet Political Culture and 'Covert Participation' in Policy Implementation," *American Political Science Review*, No 3, 1984, p. 610.

36. A.M. Kleimola, "The Duty to Denounce in Muscovite Russia," *Slavic Review*, December 1972, pp. 759-79.

37. Neal Ascherson, *The Polish August: The Self-Limiting Revolution*, Harmondsworth, 1981, pp. 11-12.

38. K. Chernenko, "Resheniya XXVI s"ezda KPSS -- leninizm v deistvii," *Politicheskoe samoobrazovanie*, No 5, 1981, pp. 3-20.

39. *Pravda*, 13 January 1982.

40. *Radyanks'ka Ukraina*, 7 December 1982, quoted in RL 460/84, "Sociology and Politics: Top-Level Meeting in Kiev," by Roman Solchanyk, 30 November 1984.

41. Brezhnev as paraphrased by Chernenko, *Problems of Peace and Socialism*, *op. cit.*, p. 7.

42. P. Smolsky (deputy head of the Central Committee's Organisational-Party Work Department) in *Partiinaya zhizn'*, No 20, 1983, pp. 26-34.

43. *Izvestia*, 4 June and 12 July 1981, 18 January 1982; *Radio Moscow*, 5 February 1983.

44. *Trud*, 30 July 1981.

45. *Ibid.*, 20 January 1982.

46. Aleksander Smolar, "The Rich and the Powerful," in Abraham Brumberg (ed), *Poland: Genesis of a Revolution*, New York, 1983, p. 42.

CHAPTER 6

OPEN DISCUSSION OF WORKER'S COMPLAINTS

The Polish events prodded the Soviet leaders into paying increased attention to public opinion in general, and to workers' letters in particular. A decree issued by the CPSU Central Committee in April 1981 showed that the central authorities were dissatisfied with the work being done at lower levels:

> The CPSU Central Committee notes that in certain central state, economic and social bodies and in some local Party, soviet, and other organisations, serious shortcomings occur in the examination of citizens' letters and verbal submissions. There are cases of callous and bureaucratic handling of legitimate requests and justified appeals, and of promises made that are subsequently broken. This obliges citizens to apply to higher organisations and institutions, and to make long journeys to get their requests satisfied. Certain Party and soviet bodies fail to show a due sense of principle and exactingness in appraising the work of officials who procrastinate and who deal with workers' letters in a bureaucratic manner; these bodies sometimes fail to react as quickly as they should to letters reporting cases of "eyewash," victimisation for criticism, or signals about shortcomings in the workplace.

The decree of the Central Committee went on to

recommend "more active use of the experience, which has proved its worth, of holding Open Letter Days."[1]

In July 1981 the AUCCTU also issued a decree calling for an improvement in the way the trade unions handled letters, for closer involvement by the unions in this form of work, and for more active implementation of the practice of holding Open Letter Days.[2]

Shortly thereafter reports of Open Letter Days (*den' otkrytogo pis'ma*) began to appear in the press. The newspapers *Sovetskaya Rossiya* and *Trud*, in particular, began to promote the holding of Open Letter Days under their own auspices; they then reported the proceedings and monitored the results.

It has to be remembered that the Soviet media are subject to rigorous central control and have a strong campaigning function. It would be wrong to imagine that the press reflects an undistorted image of Soviet reality, or to assume that the wide publicity given in 1981 to reports of Open Letter Days automatically implied that more such events were being held. Nonetheless, Open Letter Days do seem to have been a new phenomenon in 1981. Exactly when they were first held is not known, but they were enough of a novelty in the summer of 1981 for TASS to describe them as "a new form of work" for Party organisations.[3]

The earliest known reports of Open Letter Days date from 1979--a full year, that is, before the outbreak of worker unrest in Poland. *Sovetskaya Rossiya* noted in an editorial dated 12 February 1982 that it was "almost three years" since the newspaper had, "together with local Party committees," begun to organise such Days. The earliest known Open Letter Day was held in June 1979 in the town of Aleksandrov in Vladimir oblast, not far from Moscow.[4] The next, reported in *Sovetskaya Rossiya* on 9 March 1980, was held on an unspecified date at the Yaroslavl' motor factory, the USSR's largest supplier of diesel engines for lorries and tractors.

At Aleksandrov, people were chiefly concerned about the town's lack of leisure facilities and about the unavailability of certain consumer goods in the shops. So many inhabitants had written to *Sovetskaya Rossiya* to complain, the newspaper explained, that the paper hit on the idea of organising a public meeting, or Open Letter Day, as a means of investigating all the complaints at once. In nearby Yaroslavl', on the other hand, it was working conditions that dominated the proceedings. Workers complained bitterly about the amount of overtime work they were obliged to put in to make up for time lost when, because of shortages of spare parts, machinery stood idle during normal weekday working hours. The management, the workers said, were "indifferent" to their grievances; they had written "dozens" of letters to *Sovetskaya Rossiya*, which responded by organising this Open Letter Day.

The experiment was judged a success and, with the outbreak of Poland's worker discontent in 1980, the authorities evidently decided that both the practice of Open Letter Days, and the publicity given to them, should be extended. In the summer of 1981 the newspaper *Trud*, in conjunction with local trade union committees, also began to organise Open Letter Days.[5] *Trud*'s chief editor, Leonid Kravchenko, said in a subsequent interview that:

> The Polish crisis was greeted with acute attention here. Each of us certainly searched ourselves for ways of eliminating the possibility of such actions here.[6]

One solution, Kravchenko revealed, was the provision of a safety valve for workers' complaints through the holding of Open Letter Days. Similar events, he confirmed, had been held before, but on a smaller scale, and the experiment was extended following the rise of Solidarity. The hope, Soviet officials were quoted as saying, was to put new teeth into the existing trade union organisations.[7]

Throughout the summer and autumn of 1981, reports of Open Letter Days were published in the Soviet media, mainly in *Trud* and *Sovetskaya Rossiya* but also in *Pravda* and *Izvestia*, and often in the republican press. TASS reported from Alma-Ata:

> Every month in the capital of Kazakhstan an Open Letter Day is held.... Now, not only the city authorities but also a number of industrial enterprises have decided to hold such Days every month.[8]

Open Letter Days may be held in factories, on farms, or in specific towns. They are organised as follows. Some two or three weeks before the event is scheduled to take place, boxes are hung up in places where people can easily reach them--in shops and post offices, in social clubs, and so on. Local people are encouraged to place written questions relating to their living and working conditions in these boxes.[9] The forthcoming event receives wide publicity; newspaper and radio announcements may be made; sometimes special telephone lines are opened so that people can call in with their questions.[10] The letters are examined by a special commission which divides them up by subject[11] and, on the appointed day, an open meeting is convened. Local officials such as the heads of city, district, or oblast Party committees, representatives of the local soviet, and those in charge of catering, transport, and so on, are invited to attend and are given prior warning of the topics the workers have raised for discussion. Additional queries may be put from the floor during the course of the meeting.

Open Letter Days seem popular with the general

public. They are normally held in the evenings, after work; one in a village in Omsk oblast in Siberia went on until midnight.[12] They are lively occasions with high audience participation. The questions come thick and fast, and pull no punches. "It was clear," *Trud* commented about the first Open Letter Day the newspaper organised, "that the factory management had not anticipated such a stormy beginning."[13]

Some of the replies are as frank as the questions. A worker in Irkutsk complained that he'd been trying to get a new pair of calipers for three years: "In the meantime, I have to borrow someone else's. The whole situation with tools is chaotic. What are we supposed to work with?" A representative of the management replied, "The factory has to buy some of its tools on the black market; they're of low quality and they wear out sooner than they should."[14]

Other answers were described as "slick,"[15] "superficial," and "obviously just excuses,"[16] and for these audiences showed little patience. "No-one was convinced." "The hall began to buzz." "Everyone could see that all this talk about 'rationalisation' was just a smokescreen hiding an inability to get things organised."[17] When a local transport official claimed that no one had to wait "hours" for a bus because it ran every 22 minutes, his words met "incredulous laughter" from the hall.[18] Workers at another meeting complained to the head of the transport department of the local soviet about the inconvenience caused by the elimination of a certain bus route. Not rising from his seat, the official announced, "We're not going to reinstate the route!" At that, the audience began to shout that transport was supposed to run for the convenience of the public, not vice versa.[19]

Another official, *Trud* reported, "glibly read out a prepared statement about successes in solving social problems. But it was a different matter when he had to answer specific questions."[20] Embarrassed, some officials tried to shift the blame onto their colleagues. In reply to a query why there was no facility for busy workers to buy groceries at the factory, the director of the regional food trade authority blamed the factory managers: "They say there's no room." A worker jumped up from the audience shouting: "Don't blame the factory! The only reason is that you want to avoid extra work for yourself!"[21]

Some officials thought it safer not to show up at all. *Trud* commented caustically: "The deputy director for consumer services did not consider it necessary to attend; he seemed to have made some mistake about the time."[22] Again: "Unfortunately, no-one from the management thought it necessary to meet the factory collective."[23] And again: "People were hoping to hear answers from the chairman of the local soviet. He had been invited to attend in plenty of time, but found it impossible to spare even half an hour to meet the workers."[24]

The topics discussed ranged from questions such as "Why is there so little meat in the shops?"[25] to a complaint that the decision to spend money raised by a *subbotnik* on New Year presents for local children discriminated against workers who had no children.[26] The main areas of concern were, of course, living and working conditions.

Following an Open Letter Day held in the Turkmen capital of Ashkhabad, for example, it was reported that the problem of food supplies aroused the greatest concern among participants.[27] The chief engineer of one of the local bakeries was booed when he rose to answer complaints about the local bread, which was described as "shapeless, dry, hard and undercooked." He protested that his bakery was overfulfilling its plan. Came a voice from the hall: "It's not the plan we're complaining about, it's the quality!"

Another typical complaint was heard when an Open Letter Day was held in the Ukrainian town of Zhdanov. "The water comes on in our house at six o'clock in the morning," local residents reported, "but by that time many of us are already starting our day's work." At first, officials from the town soviet said the problem was insoluble. And yet, *Trud* reported, "within two days water began to flow in Zhdanov at five o'clock in the morning...."[28]

Others were not so lucky. Young people employed at a metallurgical plant in the Tatar autonomous republic made a collective complaint that the only cafe for young people in their area shut at nine o'clock in the evening and that no musical instruments, sports, or games equipment were available. The chairman of the town soviet replied that that was how it was; the situation could not be changed because the cafe was in a residential building. Nor, said he, were funds available to buy equipment, and that was that. One of the youngsters commented after the meeting that the questions had been "concrete," but the answers--"not very."[29]

Sovetskaya Rossiya organised an Open Letter Day in Labinsk, an agricultural centre in Krasnodar krai. The event was held in the regional hospital and focussed on the quality of medical services available to the population.[30] The problems that came to light were so disturbing that a special commission was set up by the local Party committee to examine them. Complaints included the lack of specialists in the area (for example, there was no-one to advise on children's skin diseases). Why, it was asked, was the hospital so short of bed linen that patients had to supply their own? Answer: "Gosplan [the State Planning Committee] and Gossnab [the State Committee for Material and Technical Supply] cut back all the requisitions we make."

Western scholars are sometimes accused of

plucking from the Soviet media examples of particularly flagrant abuses and generalising from them to create a distorted image which they then claim typifies conditions throughout the USSR. In this case, however, *Sovetskaya Rossiya* itself stated that "the problems of the Labinsk medical staff are also typical of many other places," and that the article it was publishing discussed "by no means all" the problems of the area health service. Similarly, *Trud*'s account of poor working conditions in a metallurgical plant in Donetsk oblast in Ukraine explicitly stated that the case was no exception and that the conditions described ("the buildings haven't been repaired since 1948 and the roof's falling in around our ears") were to be found "all too often."[31]

As to working conditions, a bleak picture also emerged at an Open Letter Day held in an electrical equipment factory in the Siberian city of Kemerovo. Workers there had not been paid their wages for an unspecified period of time and were, as a result, suffering real hardship. They also complained about the sparks and fragments of metal which they said flew around the workshop, and about the fierce heat, which meant that doors had to be kept open even in winter, with the result that people caught cold and got sick. "They demand 'production culture' from us," the workers said, "but what kind of culture can you have when you're working in conditions like ours?"[32]

Trud's reports laid the blame for the things the workers complained about on poor management and, specifically, on officials who "put off till tomorrow solving the problems that people are concerned about today."[33] *Sovetskaya Rossiya* came to the same conclusion:

> Officials tried to defend themselves against the barrage of questions by plead-

> ing "objective causes" for shortcomings, but if you dig deeper you see that poor organisation and irresponsible behaviour are wholly subjective things.[34]

In other words, the majority of the press reports laid the blame on the failings of individual officials. Only a few reports came anywhere near hinting that faults in the Soviet economic or political system might be in any way to blame. One such suggestion occurred in *Sovetskaya Rossiya*'s reports on a follow-up visit to the Siberian mining town of Leninsk-Kuznetsky one year after an Open Letter Day had been held there.[35] The newspaper stated that, though some of the workers' suggestions had been implemented, no one could say the situation had really improved. The water supply was still sporadic; the heating was inadequate; people still had to wait up to an hour for a bus. The reason for this state of affairs, the newspaper concluded, was that many different ministries, departments and enterprises controlled different sections of the town, including housing, heating, and the water supply. It is supposed to be up to the local soviet to impose order on this web of urban organisations, local enterprises, all-Union and republican ministries, each of which had what *Sovetskaya Rossiya* did not balk at describing as its own interests at stake. Only 4.0 percent of the town's housing was under the control of the local soviet, while more than 70 percent belonged to enterprises administered by the ministry of coal production, 10 percent to construction enterprises, and 10 percent to textile enterprises. Nonetheless, it was the local soviet that *Sovetskaya Rossiya* blamed for the fact that complaints made the previous year had not been acted upon. In doing so, the newspaper skirted round the lack of systematic accountability on the part of middle-level officials that underlay the inefficiency which the Open Letter Days exposed.

Trud identified another cause of popular discontent, pointing to poor communications and lack of effective information channels between ordinary people and the authorities. Workers in a textile factory in Dushanbe complained at an Open Letter Day that no places were available on tourist excursions during the holiday period. The answer came that there were plenty of places, but that they had been so little advertised that nobody knew of their existence.[36] Another complaint held that bonuses were not paid to workers for products destined for export. Again, the answer revealed that workers did in fact qualify for such bonuses but, asked *Trud*, "what's the use of an incentive if workers don't know their efforts will be rewarded?"[37]

Trud claimed the reason why Open Letter Days were so lively was that "people won't accept generalised answers and vague promises," and that this demonstrated "the worker's acute sense of his position as master of his life."[38] Looked at from another angle, however, the reports of Open Letter Days betray a sense of frustrated helplessness on the part of many Soviet workers not only because of poor management and lack of information but, more fundamentally, because of anonymous and irresponsible bureaucracy. People were well informed, *Trud* found, about global issues, but not about what was going on in their own street. One query read: "There's a rumour our house is to be pulled down. Is it true? There's no one you can ask about it."[39]

Of course, the nation-wide campaign launched by Yurii Andropov in November 1982 to tighten discipline in the workplace (described in Chapter 12) did not fail to be reflected in the Open Letter Days. Both *Sovetskaya Rossiya* and *Trud* devoted full-page reports to Open Letter Days dealing solely with the subject of labour discipline,[40] and *Sovetskaya Rossiya* followed up with a long report on an

Open Letter Day that focussed entirely on problems of alcohol consumption in the workplace.[41] It may be noted, however, that the topic of labour discipline had from the beginning found a ready audience at Open Letter Days. The tone of some speakers was blatantly censorious:

> On our farm there are unfortunately some people who care a lot about how much money they earn, but not much about how hard they work. Labour discipline must be strengthened.[42]

This remark, made at an Open Letter Day held on a state farm in Uzbekistan in early 1982, was reportedly "unscheduled on the agenda" but met with "spontaneous applause" from the audience. This and the many other questions relating to labour discipline raised at Open Letter Days suggest that the general public was concerned about the problem well before Andropov launched his campaign. At the same time, reports indicated an awareness on the part of many workers that the problem would not be easy to solve. In autumn 1981, for example, an Open Letter Day was organised in Kuibyshev, an industrial city on the Volga, in response to letters from local inhabitants complaining about the poor selection of consumer goods, especially shoes, in the shops. Workers from the local footwear factory admitted that often they themselves did not like the models they were producing. However, they pointed out, the factory was meeting its production targets, and more was therefore required than just a tightening of discipline among the workers at the factory. Instead, the workers pointed to a number of other considerations. These included irregular deliveries of raw materials, such as leather, from outside suppliers, and frequent breakdowns of antiquated machinery. In particular, they complained about overcentralisation. For example, the workers said, style- and colour-selection was made in Moscow, not locally. Prices for new lines were also fixed in Moscow. It took time for all these decisions to be passed down so that, even though the workers rushed to meet their targets, the new shoes were no longer fashionable by the time they reached the shops.[43]

Hand in hand with complaints about labour discipline went concern among the population at the amount of corruption they saw around them. An Open Letter Day was called in a Tula yarn-spinning mill specifically to discuss the problem of petty pilfering there. Workers expressed the opinion that the punishments for theft were tough, but inappropriate. Depriving a thief of his thirteenth month salary, they said, was a senseless punishment; all the miscreant had to do was steal another bale of cloth to make up the loss. Demoting a wrongdoer to the bottom of the waiting list for new housing was also an ineffective punishment when housing was in such short supply that there was none to be had in the first place.[44]

Complaints about corruption were heard from many sources. Workers in a Dushanbe textile machinery plant asked at their Open Letter Day, for instance, why it was impossible to find cotton fabrics in the shops. The answer that demand was so high that deliveries were being made "only to specialised shops and direct to enterprises" failed to satisfy the audience. One woman retorted that cotton was not to be found in those places either, "but go down to the flea market and you'll find anything you want. Only you'll have to pay through the nose for it!"[45] A worker at the Donetsk metallurgical plant had a related complaint:

> I don't earn a bad wage--300 rubles a month. But I can't afford to furnish my flat the way a shop assistant earning 80

> rubles can. What are the police and the courts thinking about?[46]

There was no discernible change in the range of topics discussed at Open Letter Days following the declaration of martial law in Poland in December 1981, though reporting of such Days in the central press has gradually declined over the years. Although the conspicuous use made of Open Letter Days in 1981 seems to have been a response to worker unrest in Poland and, in particular, to Brezhnev's call for "a sensitive ear to the voice of the masses," the method seems to have proved its worth to the authorities, and its popularity with the general public has ensured its continuation. It has been claimed, for example, that fewer letters of complaint are written by people in a place after an Open Letter Day is held there, and that anonymous letters sometimes cease to be written altogether.[47] And when, early in 1983, the Party committee in the Crimean resort of Sochi decided to organise the town's first Open Letter Day, 6000 questions and suggestions were received.[48]

How, indeed, could the content of the questions raised by Soviet workers at such events change in so short a time? The problems faced by ordinary citizens showed no sign of improvement as the 1980s progressed. On 10 April 1983, for example, the television series "Solutions are Found on the Spot" reported on an Open Letter Day held in Saratov oblast, south-east of Moscow. A woman construction worker was asked about the food supply in her town and replied:

> "There's absolutely nothing to buy there. All we get is what's available at the construction site, while the shops are left bare. I have two children, and they have to be fed."

The local Party secretary assured the audience that a shop would be provided. A brigade leader spoke from the audience:

> "There'll be a crush when you open that shop. People will spend all day standing in the queue, they won't do any work. I shan't be able to hold my workers back. They'll all run there--and so shall I!"

FOOTNOTES TO CHAPTER 6

1. *Pravda*, 4 April 1981.
2. *Trud*, 31 July 1981.
3. *TASS*, 31 August 1981.
4. *Sovetskaya Rossiya* published a follow-up report on 29 June 1980.
5. The first Open Letter Day organised by *Trud* was held in the Irkutsk heavy machine building plant and reported in the newspaper on 28 July 1981.
6. *Christian Science Monitor*, 15 March 1982.
7. *Ibid.*
8. *TASS*, 1 October 1981.
9. *Trud*, 23 August 1981.
10. *Sovetskaya Estoniya*, 13 October 1981.
11. *Izvestia*, 13 September 1981.
12. *Sovetskaya Rossiya*, 2 October 1981.
13. *Trud*, 28 July 1981.
14. *Ibid.*
15. *Ibid.*, 23 August 1981.
16. *Sovetskaya Rossiya*, 11 August 1981.
17. *Trud*, 5 August 1981.
18. *Sovetskaya Rossiya*, 11 August 1981.
19. *Trud*, 23 August 1981.
20. *Ibid.*, 5 August 1981.
21. *Ibid.*
22. *Trud*, 23 August 1981.
23. *Sovetskaya Rossiya*, 11 August 1981.

24. *Trud*, 23 August 1981.
25. *Ibid.*, 28 July 1981.
26. *Turkmenskaya iskra*, 9 December 1981.
27. *Ibid.*
28. *Trud*, 23 August 1981.
29. *Sovetskaya Rossiya*, 11 August 1981.
30. *Ibid.*, 20 September 1981.
31. *Trud*, 23 August 1981.
32. *Ibid.*, 11 August 1981.
33. *Ibid.*, 28 July 1981.
34. *Sovetskaya Rossiya*, 11 August 1981.
35. *Ibid.*, 11 December 1981.
36. *Trud*, 5 August 1981.
37. *Ibid.*, 28 July 1981.
38. *Ibid.*, 23 August 1981.
39. *Ibid.*, 11 August 1981.
40. *Sovetskaya Rossiya*, 25 December 1982; *Trud*, 15 March 1983.
41. *Sovetskaya Rossiya*, 10 June 1984.
42. *Pravda Vostoka*, 11 February 1982.
43. *Sovetskaya Rossiya*, 20 October 1981.
44. *Ibid.*, 17 January 1982.
45. *Trud*, 5 August 1981.
46. *Ibid.*, 23 August 1981.
47. *Literaturnaya gazeta*, 22 August 1984.
48. *Sovetskaya Rossiya*, 15 May 1983.

Chapter 7

"CONSUMERISM" IN OFFICIAL SOVIET PRIORITIES*

In the "Final Testament" which he wrote in his retirement, deposed Soviet leader Nikita Khrushchev spoke of his concern lest food shortages and consumer goods price increases should lead to manifestations of discontent among the Soviet population. The Polish events of 1970, Khrushchev stated, "were a lesson for us."[1]

Such fears seem to have revived in the summer of 1980 when, following a decision of the Polish government to raise meat prices, strikes broke out throughout Poland. The Polish crisis of 1980 coincided, moreover, with a period of marked economic slowdown in the USSR. As Poland's labour unrest continued into 1981, the Soviet government found itself facing its third failed harvest in as many years. As a result, the food situation in provincial areas of the USSR was reported in 1981-82 to be worse than at any period in the previous twenty years. Meat was regularly on sale in state shops in only about half a dozen of the big cities, while other staple foods such as butter, eggs and fish were said to be virtually unobtainable in many parts of the country.[2]

Estimates made by the US Central Intelligence Agency (CIA) show annual real increases in Soviet gross national product (GNP) at between 1.7 and 3.0 percent during the period 1980-83.[3] Meanwhile the Soviet population was growing at about 0.9 percent a year,[4] so that per capita GNP growth was averaging slightly less than 2.0 percent a year. In circumstances of slow and slowing economic growth, Soviet leaders found their scope for trade-offs between the main end-uses of expenditure--consumption, investment and defence--severely restricted.

Total per capita consumption, for example, is estimated to have increased in 1981 by about 1.0 percent, but is then believed to have declined in 1982 by, again, almost 1.0 percent.[5] It seems likely, therefore, that decisions made by the Soviet leaders in this period were taken with a particularly keen awareness of the danger that consumer discontent might erupt in the Soviet Union in the same way as it had in Poland.

Some analysts maintain that Soviet priorities are not affected by worries about the popular mood, that Soviet citizens are submissive and can be forced to tighten their belts whenever their leaders wish it, and that (even more to the point) Soviet leaders are well aware of this.

That view is not, however, consistent with the available evidence. In fact, there is evidence to suggest that increased priority was given to consumption during the 1970s. Soviet spending on food imports, for example, rose from less than 20 percent at the beginning of the decade to about 40 percent (in 1980-81) of all hard-currency imports, while a smaller share was allotted to machinery and pipe imports (see Table 7.1 on the following page). The balance shifted back somewhat in 1982, when large machinery and pipe imports were recorded in connexion with the Urengoi pipeline project, but the share devoted to food remained high.

The extent of policymakers' anxiety over food supplies was also suggested by the rising share of agriculture (widely defined) in total Soviet investment, as the following percentage figures show.[6]

1966-70	1971-75	1976-80	1981-85 (Plan)
23	26	27	27+

Such figures point to serious concern on the part of the leaders about the maintenance and, if possible, the raising of average consumption levels.

Table 7.1 USSR: Reported Hard Currency Merchandise Imports ($mn, current prices)[7]

	Total imports	Food	Machinery and pipe	Food as % total	Machinery and pipe as % total
1970	2701	280	1095	10.4	40.4
1971	2943	405	1179	13.8	40.1
1972	4157	981	1533	23.6	36.9
1973	6547	1841	2167	28.1	33.1
1974	8448	1001	2989	11.8	35.4
1975	14257	3319	6102	23.3	42.8
1976	15316	3401	6239	22.2	40.7
1977	14664	2412	5915	16.5	40.4
1978	16951	3175	7238	18.7	42.7
1979	21593	6568	7656	30.4	35.5
1980	25428	9792	7507	38.5	29.5
1981	27945	10525	6290	37.7	22.5
1982	25588	8210	8583	32.1	33.5

Method: Derived from Soviet foreign trade returns. 1970-78 from P.G. Ericson and R.S. Miller, "Soviet Foreign Economic Behavior: A Balance of Payments Perspective," in US Congress Joint Economic Committee, *Soviet Economy in a Time of Change*, Washington DC, Vol. 2, 1979, pp. 208-44. 1979-82 calculations made by Philip Hanson.

Note: Coverage of food, machinery and pipe is incomplete because Soviet trade returns do not provide figures for all trade partners, and exclude some items among those country-by-commodity data that are published. "Food" is defined here as food, fodder, beverages and tobacco, i.e., ETN (Soviet foreign trade classification) sections 7 and 8 excluding small imports of live animals for breeding. "Machinery and pipe" is defined as ETN section 1 and group 266. Conversion rates are the averages of Gosbank fortnightly rates in each year.

And this at a time of economic stringency, when resources committed directly or indirectly to consumption entailed high opportunity cost in investment and defence spending forgone.

Against this background, can variations in policymakers' "consumerism" be detected during the early 1980s? And do such variations correspond to other changes in domestic policy that can be linked with the demonstration effect of the Polish events, and with the evolution of Soviet leaders' attitudes toward those events? To answer these questions it is desirable first to look in a little more detail at what was happening in the late 1970s, in order to place the developments of the 1980s in a slightly longer-term perspective. (The economic data used here will be chiefly Soviet data, the justification for this being that Soviet policymakers are likely to pay attention to those, rather than to CIA or other Western recalculations.)

PRIORITIES IN THE LATE 1970S

A period of especially low economic growth--superimposed on a longer period of more gradual growth retardation--began in the mid-1970s. Net material product utilised (which is akin to total final domestic expenditure, but without depreciation and without most of the services sector) grew at 5.1 percent a year in 1971-75 and at 3.9 percent a year in 1976-80.[8] In the Tenth Five-Year Plan (1976-80), national income utilised had been targetted to grow by 4.7 percent a year.[9] The growth rate planned for all investment was exactly the same--4.7 percent--but that was growth between the 1971-75 total and the 1976-80 total. Investment funded by the state alone was to rise by only 2.8 percent a year between 1975 and 1980. The planned growth rate for all investment between the base-year and end-year of the plan was not published, but it would seem from the targets mentioned above that it must have been equal to or (more likely) less than the planned growth of net material product utilised. This was a striking decision, given past Soviet history. High rates of investment growth had hitherto been sacrosanct. Actual investment growth in the previous five years (1971-75) had been at 7.0 percent a year--well above the national income growth rate.[10]

The outcome of the Tenth Five-Year Plan (henceforth 10 FYP) was a 3.9 percent annual growth rate of national income utilised, as has already been mentioned, and a 3.4 percent annual growth (between base-year and end-year) in total investment.[11] Thus investment growth actually lagged behind national income growth. Some Western analysts were inclined to see this development as the result of Soviet policymakers' opting for more growth in defence spending at the expense of investment. That interpretation now looks less plausible in the light of CIA assessments that the real growth of Soviet defence spending in 1976-81 slowed from an earlier rate of 4.0 - 5.0 percent a year to about 2.0 percent. A report produced jointly by the CIA and the DIA (Defense Intelligence Agency) in 1986 repeated the assessment of a mid-1970s slowdown. It contained an appendix showing CIA recalculations of Soviet GNP and defence growth in real terms, using 1982 ruble prices. Here the CIA estimated a 3.0 percent annual inflation rate in total Soviet defence expenditure, and implied that growth of the military effort in real terms was even less than 2.0 percent a year.[12] The interpretation of the slowdown in defence expenditure is contentious--as, indeed, is the actual measurement of it--but there is evidence that it entailed some deliberate slowing-down of the growth of inputs allocated to the military, and not just increasing difficulty in converting inputs into outputs.[13] If this is correct, it would appear that the maintenance of some significant growth in per capita consumption at a time of stringency was being consciously aimed at from at least the mid-1970s.

Brief mention has already been made of the fact that there was in this period (1976-80) a clear policy emphasis on agricultural development. At the plenary meeting of the CPSU Central Committee that took place in July 1978, Brezhnev set out agricultural targets for the 1980s.[14] The enunciation by Soviet leaders of major economic targets substantially ahead of the publication of draft five-year plan guidelines[15] had been a rare event since the days of Khrushchev, yet Brezhnev listed several specific targets for 1981-85 and, indeed, for 1986-90: an average grain harvest of 238-243 million (mn) metric tons in 1981-85 and a harvest equivalent to 1 metric ton per head of population by 1990 (about 290 mn tons); meat output of 19.5 mn tons by 1990; and the maintenance or increase in 1981-85 of agriculture's 1976-80 share in total investment. This setting of agricultural targets before other targets had been set--or at least before other targets had been published--may possibly have been a preemptive strike against other members of the leadership who wanted to restrict the farm sector's claim on resources; this, however, is only speculation. The July 1978 speech was certainly a forerunner of the "Food Programme" publicly launched by Brezhnev in 1982, in which again agricultural targets for 1986-90 were enunciated in a preemptive way.[16] In his 1978 speech, Brezhnev asserted that it was desirable to assist, rather than restrict, the private agricultural sector--another "consumerist" policy that would be emphasised later on. The July 1978 plenum approved a dozen resolutions on specific agricultural issues: farm machinery, veterinary services, seed selection, feed additives, and so on.[17]

One aspect of agricultural policy has particularly strong political overtones, and therefore merits separate consideration. This is policy toward private plots. Relaxation of restrictions on them, to say nothing of policies of positive encouragement for their cultivation, has always been politically sensitive. Steps in the direction of relaxation are therefore not taken lightly, and must be presumed to be prompted by serious concern over food supplies. Encouragement of private plots will appeal to those able and willing to pay above state retail prices for better food supplies from private producers as well, of course, as to the cultivators themselves. In the late 1970s there were around 43 mn private plots, if urban family allotments are included,[18] and this must have meant that not far short of half the population had a direct stake in private agricultural production.

In September 1977 a decree was issued that widened the rights of non-collective farm households in the utilisation of private plots. It was not published at the time, and appears to have been referred to in the Soviet press for the first time only in May 1979, when it cropped up in an interview with a senior planning official in *Literaturnaya gazeta*; this reference was followed by numerous (published or cited) letters of enquiry.[19]

To sum up: evidence of slow planned and actual investment growth, a high priority for agriculture, and policies favouring private plots show that there was already a consumer-oriented element in Soviet policymaking in the late 1970s. The direction and timing of subsequent changes will now be examined.

POLICY DECISIONS IN THE EARLY 1980S

The 1981-85 plan would necessarily incorporate public statements and targets indicating the weight attached by the Soviet leaders to consumer concerns. Recent practice had been to publish the draft guidelines for the first time in the December of the last year of the old plan, and this was the practice followed in 1980.[20]

In October 1980, not long after the outbreak of labour unrest in Poland, Brezhnev used the opportunity of a CPSU Central Committee plenum to make some general remarks about the forthcoming plan and to emphasise its consumer-oriented features.[21] Admitting that the USSR was still experiencing difficulties in supplying its cities and industrial centres with foodstuffs such as meat and milk, Brezhnev declared it to be the Party's top priority to produce enough food to guarantee the population an adequate diet. He stressed--as he had at the July 1978 plenum--that agriculture must continue to receive a large share of investment, and that industry Group B would receive special attention.[22] It was on this occasion that Brezhnev first made mention of the Food Programme, then still in the planning stage, and that the Party's agriculture secretary, Mikhail Gorbachev, was promoted to full Politburo membership. Gorbachev had spent an unusually short probationary period of one year as a candidate member of the Politburo and, at the age of 49, was by far its youngest member.

At the end of 1980 Brezhnev made an unusual personal appearance on Soviet television (his first New Year television address since 1973). He stressed, among other things, that the authorities were paying particular attention to the question of food supplies.[23]

The draft guidelines published in December 1980 did indeed show a strong consumer orientation. Total investment, which competes for resources with defence and consumption (private and public consumption combined), was to increase by only 12-15 percent between 1976-80 and 1980-85. This was an unprecedentedly low rate (2.3 - 2.8 percent per annum), compared with past investment growth or with the planned growth of net material product utilised (18-20 percent between 1980 and 1985). Within that slowly-growing investment total, investment in rural social infrastructure was targetted to increase much faster: 25-30 percent. Moreover, industry Group B was targetted to grow slightly faster than industry Group A: 27-29 percent, as against 26-28 percent.

In January 1981, a remarkable joint decree on the private sector of agriculture was adopted by the CPSU Central Committee and the USSR Council of Ministers. Calling on cultivators of private plots to step up their output of a whole range of foodstuffs--in particular, meat and other animal products--the decree recommended collective farms (*kolkhozes*), and ordered state farms (*sovkhozes*), to enter into contractual agreements with individual farmers whereby the farms would provide the farmers with young breeding stock and poultry for raising, together with winter feed and pasturing facilities. In return, the farmers would contract to sell meat and animal products to the *sovkhozes* and *kolkhozes*, to be counted toward the farms' annual production and procurement plans.[24] The key provision of the decree--"representing a veritable ideological break-through"[25]--was that, where a farmer entered into such a contractual agreement, the previously pre-scribed upper limits for private livestock holdings by individual farmers would cease to apply.

The fact that produce from the private plots was to be marketable to the socialised sector at a negotiable rate was described as "a major pragmatic concession."[26] The emphasis which the decree placed on the importance of increasing production of meat and animal products suggested how concerned Soviet leaders were about the possibility of consumer discontent in the USSR. The official Soviet figure of 58 kilograms (kg) annual per capita meat consump-tion was, according to Keith Bush of Radio Liberty:

> widely considered to embrace not only unmentionable subproducts and slaughter

> fats but also to include a generous measure of pure statistical inflation. The actual per capita consumption figure in 1980, in measurements comparable with those employed in East European and Western calculations, would be closer to 40 kilograms, i.e., about half of the amount that makes Poles protest.[27]

The decree certainly seems to have been controversial. It was suggested at the time that the fact that it was published only in the newspaper *Sel'skaya zhizn'*, which is intended for the rural population, and that no details found their way into either *Pravda* or *Izvestia*, indicated that opposition was being put up to its provisions by dogmatic members of the Party hierarchy.[28] *Literaturnaya gazeta*, for example, was reminding readers at about this time that:

> Poland is the only country among the socialist states within which private agriculture and enterprises exist.... These factors...are now subject to intense efforts of exploitation by world reactionary forces.[29]

It was rumoured in Moscow that the decree was Gorbachev's brainchild but that, as a result of opposition from political diehards, its publication in the central press had been blocked and that the decree itself was "quietly buried, leaving only a diluted version of the liberalisation to be actually implemented."[30] At their best, Moscow rumours are unverifiable; at worst, they may be disinformation deliberately intended to mislead. They cannot be ignored, however, because sometimes they turn out to contain a valuable grain of truth. All that can be said in this instance is that Gorbachev is on record as asserting, in April 1981, that the contribution of private plots to Soviet agricultural production "could be a great deal larger than it is at present."[31] And subsequent evidence suggests that, for whatever reason, the decree failed to boost private plot production. All it seemed to achieve was a halting--not a reversal--of the overall trend toward declining production.[32]

The draft guidelines for the Eleventh Five-Year Plan were again discussed at the Twenty-sixth Congress of the CPSU in February 1981. In his address to the Congress, Brezhnev dwelt at length on the subject of agriculture,[33] but no substantial new or amended plan data were provided.

Over the next few months, a spate of decrees on agriculture appeared. State procurement prices for certain crops were raised substantially; new provisions for agricultural chemicals and equipment were set out; major development programmes were outlined for the Non-Black-Earth and Central Black-Earth Regions of the RSFSR (the Russian republic, largest of the USSR's fifteen constituent republics);[34] and a decree on the production of horsemeat was adopted--described by a Western observer as "one indication of the government's desperation over meat supplies."[35]

The summer of 1981 saw the publication of two further decrees of the CPSU Central Committee and the USSR Council of Ministers whose titles are eloquent expressions of the desire of the Soviet leaders at least to appear to be doing something for the consumer: "On Measures for Improving the Production of Goods of Prime Necessity in 1981-85 and for the Fuller Satisfaction of the Population's Demand for These Goods," and "On Raising the Output of Goods in Mass Demand, [and] Improving Their Quality and Assortment in 1981-85."[36] The first dealt with production and supplies of textiles, clothing, footwear, soap, detergents and dyestuffs.

The second dealt with consumer durables and targetted increases of 130 percent in the output of colour television sets, 120 percent in the output of cassette recorders, 60 percent in the output of washing-machines, and so on. The wording of both decrees implied that some new resource-allocation decisions had been taken that shifted additional resources toward consumption and were covered by special new programmes. Whether this was true is impossible to say. Plan figures published earlier had been less detailed: for example, a 40 percent increase in the total of all *kul'tbyt* goods (roughly, consumer durables) taken together. Whether the implicit claims made in the decrees were true or not is, in any case, perhaps not a crucial question. Either there were new resource allocations toward the consumer, or the Soviet leadership wanted to give the impression that there were.

Meanwhile, the food situation was becoming acute. Since food accounts for the largest share of the average Soviet family budget and must be bought on a daily basis, fluctuations in food supplies are commonly viewed by Soviet citizens as the main barometer of their standard of living. By all accounts, the shortages that occurred at this particular time gave rise to widespread resentment among the general public. They were reported to have sparked scattered demonstrations and the circulation of leaflets in 1980 and 1981 in Kiev, Sverdlovsk, Odessa, Tobol'sk, Donetsk and Krasnodar. Food shortages were said to have triggered work stoppages at the Tol'yatti and Gor'ky car and truck plants in May 1980 (see Chapter 3).

Visiting the Soviet Union in 1980 after an absence of ten years, the American author George Feifer reported "increasing popular discontent." The reason, he wrote, was "the resentment of huge numbers of white- and blue-collar workers" whose "chief grievance is nothing more elevated, or less significant, than the system's failure to provide them with what they regard, with Russians' traditionally low expectations, as a tolerable standard of living." Feifer gained the impression, too, that public rancour was increasing. Despite the fact that "the Soviet consumer has never had it better," he reported, people's perceptions were that life was getting *worse*.[37]

Western journalists reported extensively on food supply problems at this time. In February 1981, for example, the *New York Times* described severe meat shortages:

> Westerners who returned last week from Novosibirsk in Siberia said that shops there had simply closed their meat departments for the duration. They had received no supplies in months and had no prospect of getting any.[38]

Following a visit in October 1981 to the old Russian city of Vologda--traditionally a dairy-producing area--David Satter of the *Financial Times* reported that

> meat, butter, cheese and fresh vegetables are all unavailable in the state stores and long queues form for milk, which runs out by mid-morning.

And, Satter went on,

> At four o'clock in the afternoon in Cherepovets, a grimy steel-producing town two hours away from Vologda, there was no milk on sale anywhere in the city, except at special "milk kitchens" where parents of small children were able to receive a liter of milk a day by prescription for a

> child under the age of one, and half a liter of milk for a child between the ages of one and two.

In conclusion, Satter reported that

> housewives in queues, cab drivers and sales girls agreed that the food supply situation was getting worse.[39]

Another Western journalist reported that the population was making its discontent known by the traditional means of writing letters of complaint to the authorities:

> According to reliable Soviet sources, the Central Committee is deluged with letters, many in blunt terms, about half of them signed, complaining of the discrepancy between promises of a better diet and reality. The letters are said to reflect a feeling widely felt among ordinary Russians that the food situation is steadily deteriorating.[40]

In response, the Soviet media began to lay heavy emphasis on the importance of satisfying the population's daily needs. *Pravda* wrote on 20 July 1981 that "today this task is, very likely, one of the most important; to a large extent it will determine both the mood of the people and their working activity." The spring and summer of 1981 saw, too, the introduction of a nationwide campaign aimed at encouraging people to conserve bread and bread products. Recipes for tasty puddings that could be made with stale bread were widely distributed; *Pravda* announced the adoption of a new Party and government decree on bread conservation; and posters bearing the slogan "Bread is the Wealth of Our People" were put on show in bakeries.[41]

Part of the problem was that subsidised bread prices were so low that farmers were buying bread to feed to their pigs since it was cheaper than orthodox animal feedstuffs. In general, Soviet food prices were being maintained at artificially low levels. The result was that, as money incomes rose, popular demand for quality foodstuffs also increased, and supply was unable to keep pace. The authorities seemed not to dare to take the obvious step of reducing food subsidies and controlling demand by regulating prices. Were they influenced by an awareness that attempts to raise food prices had led in Poland in 1970 and 1976 to food riots, and in 1980 to the strikes that resulted in the foundation of Solidarity?

Further evidence of high-level concern at the worsening food situation was provided when, in the summer of 1981, the CPSU Central Committee sent a letter to all local Party organisations. According to a *samizdat* source the letter, dated 13 August, was read out at closed Party meetings. Warning of the possibility of further food shortages during the winter months, it stressed that public panic must be averted and promised that the authorities would not allow that year's poor harvest results to be "the deciding factor in the national food situation." That is, the state would import the necessary food supplies or use its reserve stocks to prevent any drastic deterioration in the situation. A system of internal food distribution had, the letter stated, been worked out to keep major industrial enterprises supplied with food, and contingency plans for the rationing of certain products had been drawn up. The letter was also reported to have said that the authorities were considering holding a series of show trials of shop assistants caught speculating in scarce foodstuffs and that "criminal sanctions, including imprisonment," would be applied to people found hoarding food in their homes.[42] (The Criminal Code of the RSFSR was indeed toughened in September 1981 by the extension of laws against black-marketeering in the retail trade and consumer services sector; for details, see Chapter 14.)

In the autumn of 1981, an informal system of food rationing (which had been reported from scattered areas of the USSR since 1977) was introduced in many areas of the country.[43] Under this system, food purchases by individual customers were limited to set amounts; these quantities were not, however, everywhere identical.[44]

According to the *New York Times,* for example, a customer in Moscow was in early 1982 entitled to purchase no more than one kilogram of meat at any one time. In addition, a schedule was in operation whereby people were allowed to make their purchases only at predetermined hours; local residents were organised into shifts, block by block. In many cities outside Moscow, on the other hand, a coupon system was said to have been introduced at the beginning of 1982 for certain foodstuffs. Customers were reported to have reacted with anger to find that often their coupons were useless because the stores had none of the rationed commodities, such as meat, to sell.[45]

A system of special distribution of foodstuffs through the workplace, which originated in the late 1970s, was substantially expanded at this time. In the Lithuanian city of Klaipeda, for example, a system of placing advance orders for scarce foodstuffs was devised with the declared aim of achieving a fair distribution among the population:

> In Klaipeda, 260 enterprises and establishments are regular customers of the store that fills such orders. This means that 100,000 people have the opportunity of using the store's services in a city

> with a population of 185,000.... Like other cities, Klaipeda receives its allotment of foodstuffs according to the number of its inhabitants. Ten tons of meat a day: the amount is not large, but it is enough to ensure that every family has one and a half to two kilograms of pork or beef a week.[46]

A striking development occurred at the plenary meeting of the CPSU Central Committee held in November 1981. On this occasion Brezhnev spoke in sombre tones of the "food problem" as "the central problem of the Five-Year Plan, on the political as well as on the economic plane"[47]--words that were, according to one commentator, "about as close as the Soviet leadership comes to admitting that there is public disaffection with the Party's continued failure in this area."[48]

The Soviet grain harvest that year had been bad--the USSR's third failed harvest in as many years. No figure was officially revealed but a later, semi-official leak put it at 149 mn tons, which is equivalent to 554 kg per head of the population.[49] This was far below Brezhnev's long-run target, already cited, of a metric ton per head of population. Nor was it much better than the equivalent figure for Russia in the late tsarist period--an annual average of 450 kg per head of population in 1909-13. The Soviet leaders therefore had every reason to feel apprehensive about food production. Indeed, the output per head of population of every major food item except eggs fell in the USSR between 1978 and 1982.[50] Seen against this background, the Polish example must have seemed all the more worrying.

These circumstances appear to have led the Soviet leadership to make a very significant revision to the 1981-85 Plan. In his speech to the

November 1981 plenum, Brezhnev stressed that a cut was being made in the resource allocation to investment, which was now to grow by only 10 percent. Presumably this increase was measured between the 1976-80 total and the planned total for 1981-85, as in previous announcements. If so, then it was a reduction from the range of 12-15 percent previously cited. Brezhnev was clearly stressing a shift in favour of consumption, and referred to a cut in planned investment amounting to 30 billion (bn) rubles. According to the Economist Intelligence Unit (EIU), this way of presenting the cut made it look as large as possible, for the reduction was calculated from the top end of the range originally projected for investment. The EIU also noted that the new planned investment growth rate was only 1.9 percent a year, and commented: "The original figures were unprecedentedly low; the revised investment targets are so low as to look totally un-Soviet."[51] Once again, the impression was of a leadership making strenuous efforts to convey a public image of favouring the consumer, and of favouring the consumer to an increasing extent. In the case of total planned investment, there was clearly, moreover, a change in plans between late 1980 to early 1981, on the one hand, and November 1981, on the other.

This may have been a repetition of the revisions that were reportedly made, in very similar circumstances, to the Ninth Five-Year Plan. According to Roy Medvedev, the plan for the years 1971-75 that was presented to the Twenty-fourth Congress of the CPSU in 1971 differed markedly from an earlier draft which he had seen. In Medvedev's opinion, the changes were attributable at least partly to the shock of the Polish riots of December 1970.[52]

The final version of the 1981-85 plan emerged in the speech delivered by the chairman of USSR

Gosplan, Nikolai Baibakov, to a session of the USSR Supreme Soviet that took place immediately after the November 1981 plenum,[53] and in the plan law passed by the Supreme Soviet.[54] Most of the final targets were set at the bottom end of the ranges given earlier in the guidelines. The volume of retail sales, however, was targetted to grow by 23 percent, against a guidelines target range of 20-25 percent. As has already been noted, investment was meanwhile set to grow at a rate below even the bottom of the range given in the guidelines. Agriculture's share in total investment was to remain approximately unchanged. The "Food Programme" was still not spelt out, but the Party leaders were committed at this stage to elaborating such a programme and presenting it to the world at large.

The Food Programme was finally unveiled at the Central Committee plenum of May 1982,[55] that is, after martial law had been imposed in Poland and after Soviet domestic propaganda about the Polish events had adopted--as will be detailed in Chapter 12--a harder, more self-assured tone. Targets for the years 1986-90 were mentioned for certain items. The grain target was not given in a form directly comparable to that set out by Brezhnev in July 1978, but it was in effect scaled down somewhat; the target for meat production seemed, on the other hand, to have been pushed up a little. Targets for per capita food consumption around 1990 were given which were quite ambitious. In kg per head of the population per annum they were:[56]

meat	70	dairy products	330-340
fish	19	eggs (numbers)	260-266
potatoes	110	bakery products	135
sugar	45.5	vegetables and melons	126-135
		fruit and berries	66- 70

To what extent this programme reflected

continuing anxiety on the part of the leadership about popular discontent, and to what extent it was a delayed expression of earlier worries that had abated by the time it appeared, is impossible to say. It can however be noted that the farm production targets were not markedly different from targets that had been mentioned earlier. It can also be noted that the share of agriculture and of the "agroindustrial complex" (whose organisational structure was being redesigned) in total investment continued to be set at the same levels as in 1976-80 and in the earlier versions of the 1981-85 plan. More precisely, the former was set in the range 27-28 percent (against 27 percent in earlier statements) and the latter in the range 30-35 percent (against 33 percent in the earlier statements).[57] If anything, however, these shares tended in practice to decline slightly in the years that followed (see below), suggesting that day-to-day operating priorities began to shift slightly away from agriculture and in favour of other branches.

The Central Committee's decree on the Food Programme referred to the desirability of encouraging private-plot production. There were occasional approving references to private plots in later statements of an authoritative nature,[58] but decrees in their favour appear to have been concentrated in the earlier (1981) phase. The Soviet press had evidently been instructed to feature cautiously approving discussion of private plots in early- to mid-1981,[59] but this press emphasis did not, by and large, continue in 1982.

Western journalists who travelled outside the Soviet capital in the autumn of 1981 reported considerable concern over food shortages but "little evidence of serious discontent":

In comparison with Moscow, the Soviet

> provinces ... demonstrate a difference in the level of consciousness which is just as striking as the difference in the level of food supplies. For the residents of areas such as the Vologda oblast, Soviet propaganda is the definitive substitute for reality and the elements of xenophobia, spymania and aggressive nationalism in the Soviet world outlook are constantly stressed.[60]
>
> "We don't have enough food here because America is attacking us," one woman told me [in Vologda]. "Where is all the food going?" I asked. "To the army," she replied.[61]

Reports like these suggest that the danger of an outburst of popular discontent such as that evidently feared by the Soviet leaders in 1980 and 1981 had (if it ever really existed) been averted by the end of 1981. Consumer-oriented decrees and statements did not, of course, disappear from the Soviet media overnight, and assertions of top-level concern about living standards continued even after the Polish crisis had abated. However, substantive policy changes in this direction became less frequent, and the evidence suggests that resource reallocations in favour of consumption continued if anything to be outweighed by shifts in favour of other final uses. Some statistical evidence on this is provided in Table 7.2 (see overleaf).

CHANGING PRIORITIES, 1980-84

Table 7.2 is a compilation of Soviet data all of which, it may be argued, shed light on fluctuations in Soviet priorities as between consumption and other final expenditure categories (defence and investment).[62] These indicators relate to private

Table 7.2: USSR: selected economic indicators relating to consumer policies, 1975–84, Soviet official data

	Percentage change over preceding year in "volume"[1] of:					
	National income utilised	Total invest-ment	Investment in agri-culture[2]	State and cooperative retail sales[3]	State and cooperative retail sales per head of population[4]	New housing floorspace constructed
1976	5.0	4.5	4.2	4.6	3.7	−3.4
1977	5.7	3.6	3.7	4.5	3.6	1.5
1978	4.6	6.1	3.9	3.9	3.0	0.9
1979	1.8	0.7	1.4	3.8	2.9	−5.1
1980	4.3	2.4	2.3	5.5	4.7	3.6
1981	3.2	3.8	3.6	4.7	3.9	1.3
1982	3.5	3.6	3.0	−0.6	−2.4	1.4
1983	3.5	5.7	6.0	3.4	2.5	4.2
1984	2.6			4.2	3.2	0.5 (approx)

Official retail price index for state and co-operative trade (% change over previous year)	Average money wage of state employees (% change over previous year)	Average real wage of state employees (% change over previous year)	Output of industry Group B as % all industrial output[5]	Annual-plan % growth in output of industry Group B *minus* annual-plan % growth in output of industry A
0	3.8	3.8	26.0	−2.2
0.3	2.5	2.2	26.1	−1.0
0.7	3.0	2.3	26.0	−1.0
1.3	2.1	0.8	26.0	−0.4
1	3.4	2	26.2	0
1	2.1	1	26.3	0.1
4	2.8	−1	24.9[6]	−0.2
0	2.7	3	25.1	0.4
	1.6			0.3

Table 7.2 continued

Sources:

Derived from *Narkhoz 79*, pp. 7, 49, 136, 363, 370, 394, 413, 453, 467; *Narkhoz 83*, pp. 5, 39, 41, 121, 355, 362, 393, 417, 458, 471; *Pravda*, 3 December 1975, 30 October 1976, 12 December 1977, 30 November 1978, 29 October 1980, 20 November 1981, 23 November 1982, 29 December 1983, 24 January 1985; *Ekonomicheskaya gazeta*, No 50, 1979.

Notes:

(1) In so-called "constant prices," usually not allowing fully for inflation and therefore tending to exaggerate volume growth.

(2) Agriculture in the broad sense, including agricultural research and land improvement, but not the whole "agroindustrial complex."

(3) *Narkhoz*-reported sales figures deflated by official retail price index.

(4) Previous column deflated by population growth (year-end to year-end).

(5) In current enterprise wholesale prices and therefore (a) excluding turnover tax and (b) not necessarily reflecting reported growth in industry A and industry B output volumes.

(6) The fall in 1982 in part results from the wholesale price revision of that year, which raised many fuel and raw material (Group A) prices.

rather than to public consumption, since it is reasonable to assume that categories such as state expenditure on health and education are seen by both leaders and population as less immediately relevant to levels of discontent or satisfaction in the population. (The indicators in Table 7.2 all have to do with year-to-year changes, it should be noted, so the timing of policy changes is suggested in only an approximate fashion.)

The reasons for choosing these particular indicators are as follows. The growth in national income utilised (column 1) is the official measure of year-to-year changes in the available supply of goods for final consumption, investment or defence purposes. When total investment (column 2) grows more slowly than national income utilised, the prima facie conclusion is that consumption is being favoured, and vice versa. It is difficult to be sure about this, however, in the absence of reliable measures of the third of the main claimants on resources, i.e., defence. The CIA's estimates (in both 1970 and 1982 ruble prices) of "real" defence spending growth at or slightly below 2.0 percent a year after 1975 are subject to a large margin of error; they are not reliable so far as changes from one year to the next are concerned, but the 1986 CIA assessment seems to suggest that slow growth in defence spending continued at least through 1984. But there is some disagreement between the CIA and the DIA over what happened in 1982-84, with the former maintaining that there continued to be no growth in Soviet military hardware procurement and the latter detecting an increase.[63]

The third column shows growth in agricultural investment. This seems to be less subject to year-to-year fluctuations than total investment spending. In the period 1980-83, as a whole, it tended to grow very slightly more slowly than total investment. This means that, despite Brezhnev's pronouncements and the introduction of the Food Programme, the priority accorded to agriculture in the investment programme tended, very slightly, to decline. There is otherwise no clear sign of a shift in this particular priority--within the period 1980-84, that is.

Changes in the volume of retail sales (column 4) and retail sales per head of population (column 5) show sharp fluctuations. There is in particular an abrupt change in 1982 from the 3.0 - 5.0 percent annual growth of per capita retail sales in previous years to an absolute decline of 1.5 percent. Reductions in food supplies resulting from the especially bad harvest of the previous year--a development outside the control of the policymakers--might have contributed to this. In fact the official series for the column of total retail food sales shows an increase in 1982, albeit a very small increase, while the fall in volume occurs in non-food sales.[64]

One factor was the increase in official retail prices in 1982 (column 7), which was concentrated on alcoholic drinks (+ 11.4 percent, officially) and non-food items (+ 3.0 percent, officially).[65] That was clearly a discretionary action by policymakers. It was not offset by any special increase in average money wages (column 8) or in pensions and other social benefits. The result was a fall in average real wages (column 9): an unprecedented development in the postwar USSR--at least insofar as such developments are reflected in the official Soviet statistics. This supports the hypothesis that at some time toward the end of 1981 or the beginning of 1982 the Soviet leadership became less anxious about consumer grumbles and more inclined to adopt tough measures vis-a-vis the population.

The development of housing construction (column 6) does not show any major change in 1982. It is possible that a decision to commit more resources to housing construction shows up in the floorspace of new housing completed only after a couple of years. In that case, the figures in column 6 would support the notion of a change in priorities--toward the consumer in 1981, and against in 1982--but that is speculative.

The last two columns relate to the priority for consumer goods as against producer goods in industrial production. Group A output is not the same as industrial output of investment goods, but the relative growth of Group A and Group B is often stressed by Soviet leaders and official commentators as a measure of the degree of priority being given to heavy industry as against consumption.[66] The Group A and Group B growth rates appear to have at least a symbolic importance as signals to the Soviet population and to the outside world about current official priorities.

The figures in the last column but one of the table show that Group B held its share of total industrial output in the late 1970s, and that this share edged slightly upward in 1980 and 1981, before falling sharply in 1982. The fall in 1982 is attributable in part to major changes in wholesale prices introduced in that year.[67] This means that it is not a good indicator of "real" changes in output. Indeed, the change in volume was reported to be slightly larger for B than for A (2.9 as against 2.8 percent).[68] On the other hand, the 1982 annual plan for real output changes in Group A and Group B favoured the former--the first time this had been the case since 1979 (see the final column of the table). If, therefore, the A and B targets are seen as signalling devices, the 1982 annual plan (published in November 1981) was "anti-consumption," whereas the 1981 annual plan (published in October 1980) was "pro-consumption."

CONCLUSIONS

The sequence of major economic policy decisions in

the early 1980s suggests that 1980-81 was a period of heightened concern about consumer dissatisfaction. That is indicated above all by the amendments made in the course of 1981 to the consumption-investment balance of the draft 1981-85 plan, and by the prominence given by Brezhnev to consumer affairs in his public pronouncements. The encouragement given to the private sector of agriculture at this time is also striking. How far the changes that Soviet policymakers were claiming to make at this time corresponded to real resource shifts in favour of consumption, it is hard to say. There is no doubt, however, that Soviet leaders felt it advisable to make "consumerist" noises. Such noises subsequently became less audible. This sequence of events supports the idea of a switch at least of public stance in late 1981 or early 1982 toward a less "consumerist" position.

Available indicators from official Soviet statistics do not show a clear and unmistakable shift in resource-allocation priorities around this time. They are not, however, inconsistent with it. Changes in retail prices and money wages--both amenable to strong central control and capable of responding swiftly to it--were sharply unfavourable to Soviet consumers in 1982, but not in 1980-81. The "signalling" of annual-plan targets for industry Group A and Group B shows a similar shift. This shift occurred before Soviet industry and the Soviet grain harvest showed any clear sign of recovery from the doldrums of 1979-82, so it cannot be simply ascribed to an "objective" easing of conditions at that time.

Resource allocation decisions which would take effect more slowly, and which therefore promised smaller immediate domestic political returns of a "consumerist" nature, do not show any clear pattern of change. The statistical evidence, in fact, is that actual investment spending grew faster than planned in the 11 FYP, right from the start of the plan period, accelerating in 1983 and decelerating in 1984. Agriculture's share of investment scarcely changed, but was if anything shaded slightly downward. And the marked improvement in housing construction comes through in completions only in 1983. Altogether, however, the official statistics do not contradict the impression given by public policy pronouncements, and could tentatively be said to give it some support.

FOOTNOTES TO CHAPTER 7

* Particular thanks are due to Philip Hanson for help in the preparation of this chapter.

1. *Khrushchev Remembers: The Last Testament*, Volume 2, London, 1974, p. 145, quoted by Archie Brown in Archie Brown and Michael Kaser (eds), *The Soviet Union Since the Fall of Khrushchev*, second edition, London, 1978, p. 223.

2. *Financial Times*, 11 November 1981.

3. CIA, *Handbook of Economic Statistics 1984*, Washington DC, 1984, p. 37.

4. *Narodnoe khozaistvo SSSR v 1983 g.* (hereafter *Narkhoz 83*), Moscow, 1984, p. 5.

5. US Congress Joint Economic Committee, "USSR: Economic Trends and Policy Developments," Washington DC, September 1983, p. 6.

6. *Narodnoe khozaistvo SSSR: 1922-1982*, Moscow, 1982, p. 372.

7. Reproduced by kind permission from Philip Hanson, "Western Policies on East-West Trade with Particular Reference to the Pipeline Issue," paper presented at the annual conference of the British National Association for Soviet and East European Studies, Cambridge, March 1983.

8. *Narkhoz 83*, p. 39.

9. This and other Tenth Five-Year Plan infor-

mation come from the final version of the plan as published in *Pravda* on 27 October 1976.

10. *Narkhoz 83*, p. 355.

11. *Ibid.*

12. CIA/DIA, "The Soviet Economy Under a New Leader," report presented to the Subcommittee on Economic Resources, Competitiveness, and Security Economics of the US Congress Joint Economic Committee, Washington DC, March 1986, p. 35.

13. See Richard F. Kaufman, "Soviet Defense Trends," study prepared for the Subcommittee on International Trade, Finance and Security Economics of the US Congress Joint Economic Committee, Washington DC, September 1983.

14. *Ekonomicheskaya gazeta*, No 28, 1978.

15. The 11 FYP guidelines were first published in the central Soviet press on 2 December 1980, along with some rather vague remarks about developments in 1986-90.

16. *Pravda*, 25 May 1982.

17. *Ekonomicheskaya gazeta*, No 30, 1978.

18. RL 233/78, "Soviet City Dwellers Encouraged to Grow More Food," by Andreas Tenson, 24 October 1978.

19. Marie Lavigne, "Nouvelle Reforme Economique en Union Sovietique," *Le Monde Diplomatique*, September 1979, pp. 2-3.

20. *Pravda*, 2 December 1980.

21. *Ibid.*, 22 October 1980.

22. Industry Group B refers to industrial production of objects of consumption, as opposed to industrial production of the means of production (intermediate goods and investment goods), which is referred to as industry Group A.

23. *Daily Telegraph*, 2 January 1981.

24. "On Additional Measures for Increasing the Output of Agricultural Produce on Citizens' Private Plots and Livestock Holdings," *Sel'skaya zhizn'*, 18 January 1981.

25. RL 38/81, "Major Decree on Private Plots and Livestock Holdings," by Keith Bush, 26 January 1981.

26. *Ibid.*

27. *Ibid.*

28. *Ibid.*

29. Feliks Kuznetsov, "Front bez krovi," *Literaturnaya gazeta*, 6 May 1981, p. 14.

30. A. Beichman and M.S. Bernstam, *Andropov: New Challenge to the West*, New York, 1983, Chapter 17.

31. *Za vysokoe kachestvo i deistvennost' ideologicheskoi raboty*, Moscow, 1981, p. 117.

32. RL 402/81, "Has Official Support for the Private Farm Sector Come Too Late?" by Allan Kroncher, 8 October 1981; and RL 224/83, "The Impact of Official Policy on the Number of Livestock in the Soviet Private Farming Sector," by Karl-Eugen Waedekin, 9 June 1983.

33. *Pravda*, 24 February 1981.

34. Economist Intelligence Unit (EIU), *Quarterly Economic Review of the USSR*, No 2, 1981, pp. 8-9; *Pravda*, 15 April and 7 May 1981.

35. EIU, *Quarterly Economic Review of the USSR*, No 3, 1981, p. 9.

36. *Pravda*, 12 August 1981.

37. George Feifer, "Russian Disorders: The Sick Man of Europe," *Harper's Magazine*, February 1981, pp. 41-55.

38. *New York Times*, 8 February 1981.

39. *Financial Times*, 11 November 1981.

40. Robert Gillette in *The Guardian*, 21 January 1982.

41. *Financial Times*, 13 August 1981.

42. AS 4496.

43. RL 321/82, "Food Rationing in the Soviet Union," by Andreas Tenson, 11 August 1982.

44. *Reuters*, 12 October 1981; *Frankfurter Allgemeine Zeitung*, 15 February 1982.

45. *New York Times*, 15 January 1982.

46. *Trud*, 8 January 1982; see also "Kak torgovuyut v Klaipede," *Partiinaya zhizn'*, No 20, 1982, pp. 70-72.

47. *Pravda*, 17 November 1981.

48. *Baltimore Sun*, 17 November 1981.

49. RL 157/83, "Recent Developments in Soviet Agriculture," by Philip Hanson, 18 April 1983.

50. *Ibid.*

51. EIU, *Quarterly Economic Review of the USSR*, No 4, 1981, pp. 6-7.

52. Roy Medvedev, *On Socialist Democracy*, London, 1975, p. 404, quoted by Archie Brown in Brown and Kaser, *op. cit.*, p. 329.

53. *Pravda*, 18 November 1981.

54. *Ibid.*, 20 November 1981.

55. Brezhnev's report and the Central Committee's decree are to be found in *Pravda* of 25 May 1982. Further details were given by *Pravda* on 27 May 1982, and in a *Pravda* editorial of 31 May 1982.

56. *Pravda*, 27 May 1982.

57. For the figures, see *Pravda*, 31 May 1982.

58. See, for example, Yurii Andropov at a meeting of regional Party first secretaries, *Pravda*, 19 April 1983. This was, however, only a passing reference.

59. *Pravda*, 18 February 1981; 15 May 1981; 10 June 1981.

60. David Satter in *Financial Times*, 11 November 1981.

61. Andrew Nagorski in *Newsweek*, 3 November 1981.

62. Thanks are due to Philip Hanson for permission to reproduce this working table.

63. CIA/DIA, "The Soviet Economy Under a New Leader," report presented to the Subcommittee on Economic Resources, Competitiveness, and Security Economics of the US Congress Joint Economic Committee, Washington DC, March 1986, p. 8.

64. *Narkhoz 83*, p. 437.

65. *Ibid.*, p. 471.

66. For example, Brezhnev's speech at the Central Committee plenum of October 1980; *Pravda*, 22 October 1980.

67. See *Vestnik statistiki*, No 9, 1984, p. 79, for details.

68. *Pravda*, 23 January 1983.

Chapter 8

THE EVOLUTION OF PUBLIC OPINION

The Polish events aroused keen interest at many levels of Soviet society. In July 1981, a well-known Soviet journalist, Spartak Beglov, commented:

> Today, regardless of what kind of Soviet audience one addresses with a lecture or discussion on a topic of international affairs, the first question asked of the speaker invariably touches on Poland.[1]

This interest notwithstanding, the efforts of the Soviet authorities to prevent the spread of rebellion from Poland's striking workers to the population of the Soviet Union bore the desired fruit. Solidarity's example failed, in the final analysis, to evoke an echo among the general Soviet population. By the time martial law was declared in Poland in December 1981, the majority of Soviet citizens had come, it seems, to hold opinions hostile to the aspirations of their Polish neighbours --or, at least, to those aspirations as portrayed in the official Soviet media.

Western newsmen based in Moscow during the Solidarity period noted how hostile the reactions of many ordinary Soviet citizens were. Robert Gillette reported in December 1980 that while discreet and guarded expressions of sympathy and even admiration for the Poles could "occasionally" be heard, such sentiments were "largely confined ... to the better-educated elite in Moscow and a few other larger cities" and that among ordinary people, particularly those in provincial areas, the Polish events tended "more often to arouse resentment toward the upstart

Poles than sympathy for their complaints." Such resentment, Gillette went on, "is deeply rooted in centuries of mutual ethnic antagonism and is reinforced by fears that Soviet aid to Poland will worsen food shortages that are already serious across much of the Soviet Union." Westerners travelling in Ukraine and Belorussia, he added, were reporting a rising incidence of ethnic slurs about "shiftless, lazy Poles."[2]

Although the opposite is in fact the case, the view is commonly held among Soviet citizens that Poland and the other nations of Eastern Europe are net importers of food from the USSR. Another American correspondent who was in Moscow during the Solidarity period, Andrew Nagorski, reports that a Moscow taxi-driver complained to him, "We spill our blood for them and now we'll have to feed them. The Poles have more to eat than us anyway."[3]

On the other hand, Nagorski recalls finding widespread sympathy for the Poles among Moscow intellectuals who, he writes, "were fascinated by the revolution taking place in Polish society and dreamed that it might succeed." "Among intellectuals here," an economist told him, "Afghanistan is in tenth place as a topic of conversation. Poland is in first place." A prominent intellectual explained, "I don't know anything about the situation [in Afghanistan]. In Poland, I know the situation well." These intellectuals, Nagorski states, "knew their views were not held by the majority of Russians," yet he warns against assuming that the opinions of the handful of Soviet citizens interviewed by Western correspondents were typical of those of the entire population, or that people's opinions were determined by their social class or educational level. He recalls discovering negative reactions among intellectuals as well as "pockets of sympathy" among workers. "I had no illusions," Nagorski explains, "that Solidarity was a popular cause among

Russians as a whole, but I was increasingly wary of making sweeping generalizations about their attitudes...."[4]

Of particular interest was the variation that Nagorski observed in the attitudes of citizens in different parts of the USSR. His trip to Lithuania in July 1981 provided "a picture of near-universal opposition, both active and passive, to the Soviet government and everything it represented," while a visit three months later to the old Russian town of Vologda furnished a total contrast: "an image of complete support."[5]

Despite the ethnic slurs reported by Gillette, there is evidence to suggest that considerable interest was aroused among some sections of the population in the USSR's western borderlands, that is, in the non-Russian republics closest to Poland: Ukraine and Belorussia (where there are significant Polish-speaking minorities), and the three Baltic republics of Lithuania (where there is also a large Polish-speaking minority), Latvia, and Estonia.

Some of these areas are, of course, close enough to the Polish border to receive Polish television and radio broadcasts. In the Ukrainian city of L'vov, for example, Polish broadcasts are easily picked up, and toward the end of 1980 Western newsmen reported that people there were showing great interest in the Polish events.[6] In Estonia, Finnish television is obtainable, and the Estonian language is close enough to Finnish to be easily understood. What is more, the Baltic states, Western Ukraine and Western Belorussia are areas that were incorporated into the USSR relatively recently, and deeply-rooted nationalism and strong anti-Soviet sentiments are still to be found there.

National feelings run particularly high in Ukraine. At 45 million, Ukrainians make up by far the largest non-Russian nationality in the USSR. In addition, a Ukrainian minority of some 250,000 people living in Poland is viewed with mistrust by the Soviet authorities as providing a potential opening to the West for their co-nationals in the Ukrainian Soviet Socialist Republic.[7] The Ukrainian Catholic Church--a major symbol of national identity in Western Ukraine--was outlawed in 1946 when Moscow regained control of the region but, complete with clandestine hierarchy, clergy and religious schools, it survives today in the underground as the USSR's largest unauthorised religious denomination. Subjected to unrelenting persecution by the authorities, the Church appears nonetheless to have undergone a resurgence in the past few years that some observers believe is due at least partly to the example set by Solidarity.[8]

Lithuania also borders on Poland. Many Poles trace their family roots back to the region, and Lithuania has the highest percentage Roman Catholic population of any Soviet republic. The Estonians, while they number only one million people and are the smallest of the nationalities of Union-republican status, have been among the most stubborn of the nations of the USSR in defending their culture and language. There have in recent years been a number of demonstrations in Estonia by crowds of young people protesting against what they see as the Russification of their republic. Access to Finnish television, moreover, makes the Estonians the most open to Western influence of all the nationalities of the USSR.

By all accounts, the populations of these areas took a lively interest in the Polish events. The American journalist David Willis visited the Latvian capital of Riga in September 1980, and reported that the inhabitants were snapping up copies of Polish newspapers and tuning in to shortwave radios to find out what was going on in Poland. The daily newspaper of the Polish Communist Party, *Trybuna Ludu*, normally on regular sale, was selling out so fast that Riga residents were having to hunt "from kiosk to kiosk" to find copies. They were also turning for information to the daily newspaper of the British Communist Party, the *Morning Star*, which was broadly sympathetic to Solidarity. Willis reported a number of conversations with Riga inhabitants who showed great enthusiasm for the Polish events. "Events in Afghanistan are remote from us here," he quoted one woman as saying:

> "But Poland--well, we have a long history of close ties with Polish culture--unlike the Lithuanians who have fought the Poles for centuries. We know the Poles have more freedom to travel than we do. Frankly, we are envious that the Polish workers have been able to strike and to win concessions from their government."[9]

Willis quoted the words of a Riga factory worker: "Just look at what the Poles are achieving. But Moscow won't allow it here." And of a Latvian intellectual: "It just can't happen here. But we hope that local Party and government bosses will take account of what happened in Poland, and fight against corruption here in Latvia, or replace older trade union leaders with younger men."

Nagorski describes very similar impressions from a trip he made to Vilnius in July 1981, when Solidarity's activity was at its height. There too, he found the inhabitants tuning in to foreign radio broadcasts; they could also pick up Polish radio and television. "It seemed clear," Nagorski recalls, "that the Polish events were having a considerable effect on many Lithuanians":

> ...no one we talked to--and we talked to dozens during our stay in Vilnius--expressed anything but sympathy for the

> Poles. "Everyone talks about Poland all the time," said one woman of mixed Polish-Lithuanian background. "Some of the Russians here ask what those Poles want and say we should just partition them out of existence again. But the Lithuanians say that the Poles are smart and know what they are doing. If only it could be like that here."
>
> ...Throughout our conversations, Poland kept intruding. What was happening there seemed an impossible dream, a renewal that Lithuanians could only pray for but not realistically expect to emulate. So long as Solidarity survived, it provided hope that someday they could win a small measure of what the Poles had already achieved. But people voiced fears of a Soviet invasion of Poland. They knew that the anxious men in the Kremlin worried that the Polish "disease" might infect Lithuania....[10]

From the start, the Soviet authorities went to considerable lengths to ensure that the general public received only a "sanitised" version of the events. Details of the real nature of Solidarity's demands were not published in the Soviet press at any time. Instead, the media issued a stream of denunciations both of Solidarity and of the very idea of independent trade unionism under socialism.

Jamming of Western radio broadcasts to the USSR, lifted in 1973 as a gesture toward East-West detente, was reimposed by the Soviet authorities in August 1980,[11] just ten days after the outbreak of strikes in Gdansk and four days after TASS carried its first commentary on Poland's labour unrest.[12] Polish publications--even, apparently, the official newspaper, *Trybuna Ludu*--were removed from newsstands and public libraries in Moscow and other Soviet cities.[13]

Travel between Poland and the USSR, as well as the normal flow of routine and officially sponsored exchanges between the two countries, was cut back. In an effort to isolate Poland from its neighbours, border restrictions were imposed not only by the USSR but also by Czechoslovakia and the GDR.[14] At least one Latvian tourist trip to Poland was cancelled in August 1980,[15] and Poles studying at the Institute of Civil Aviation in Riga said they returned that autumn from holiday to find themselves forbidden to share living quarters with Soviet students.[16] In November 1980, two Western newspaper correspondents planning to visit Vilnius were told the city was "temporarily closed"; no explanation was given.[17]

Nagorski reported from Vilnius the following summer on the restriction of contacts between Lithuania and Poland:

> ...once-routine visas for family visits are now granted rarely and grudgingly. Lithuania's Polish minority complains that letters from Poland arrive weeks late, if at all. "I don't know what is happening with my family," said one elderly woman who had not received a single note since the Polish strikes began a year ago.[18]

The Soviet authorities appeared particularly conscious of the danger of worker unrest spreading to areas of the USSR where such conflict might spark against existing national tensions. Sporadic strikes and labour disputes were indeed reported during the period 1980-81 from the Ukrainian capital of Kiev, from the Latvian capital of Riga, and from Tartu in Estonia, while in September and October of

1980 demonstrations provoked by social and economic discontent were staged in the Estonian cities of Tallinn, Tartu and Parnu.[19] It is surely significant that Pyatras Grishkyavichus, Party first secretary in Lithuania, was the first Party leader of a Soviet republic to refer openly to the Polish events. Speaking at the Twenty-sixth Congress of the CPSU in Moscow in February 1981, Grishkyavichus admitted that "Soviet communists and the workers of our country [the USSR] are following the development of the situation in Poland with anxiety."[20] Only a few weeks earlier, at the congress of the Communist Party of Ukraine, the chairman of the Ukrainian Trade Union Council, Vitalii Sologub, had denounced those who sought to "shatter the socialist system from within" by "speculating on demagogic slogans about the independence of trade unions."[21]

Studies by Western scholars have found that the Soviet authorities took particularly strict measures to prevent the flow of what they considered harmful ideas from Poland to the USSR's western regions.[22] The KGB's crackdown against nationalist dissent and religious observance was especially harsh in those regions,[23] and was accompanied by a propaganda barrage designed both to discredit Solidarity in the eyes of the population and to counteract the influence of ideas and contacts from outside.[24]

Western journalists have recorded their impression that Soviet public opinion underwent a process of evolution during the period 1980-81. In the early period, the USSR's virtual news blackout meant that many Soviet citizens were confused and bewildered by--though not necessarily hostile to--the rise of Solidarity. As Poland's crisis deepened, and as the Soviet propaganda campaign gathered momentum, the opinions of the Soviet public seemed gradually to harden.[25] Such impressions cannot, of course, be confirmed, but they do tally with the findings of a series of opinion surveys conducted under the auspices of Radio Liberty during the period in question.

In an effort to track listening habits among its target-population, Radio Liberty has for many years carried out audience surveys among Soviet travellers in Western Europe. Interviews are conducted not by Radio employees, but by public-opinion institutes in several countries, so as to obtain a sufficiently large and diverse sample to estimate audiences reliably within stated margins of error. The demographic composition of the survey group is not representative of the parent population, since it is weighted in favour of middle-aged, educated, urban males, who are members of the CPSU and resident in the European areas of the USSR. Raw polling results are therefore adjusted by computer simulation techniques. The results are generally accepted by other Western broadcasters as the most satisfactory audience research available.[26]

Starting in the autumn of 1980, Radio Liberty's Soviet Area Audience and Opinion Research unit (SAAOR) made a systematic effort to monitor the attitudes of Soviet visitors to Western Europe to the events in Poland.[27] The results, which are detailed below, suggest that during the period dating from the outbreak of strikes in Poland in the summer of 1980 and ending with the declaration of martial law in December 1981, there was a perceptible hardening of public opinion among Soviet citizens concerning the Polish events. From the very beginning of the period, in fact, the majority of Soviet citizens interviewed for Radio Liberty expressed a hostile attitude not only toward Solidarity but also to the very idea of strikes and independent trade unions under socialism.

When evaluating these data, it is of course necessary to add the caveat that Soviet citizens granted the privilege of travelling abroad are by definition atypical of the mass of the Soviet population; they are also likely to have been warned to be careful about what they say and to whom they say it. In defence of the findings, it may however be said that they provide one of the very few alternatives to the other sources of information available to Western scholars, that is, the official Soviet media, *samizdat* documents, and the reports of Western correspondents based in Moscow. Moreover, the SAAOR findings show remarkable internal consistency both over time and between sampling points, while exhibiting a range of responses of which many run counter to the official line. For all their limitations, these surveys of tourists' views do not merely elicit "safe" replies consistent with official Soviet statements. This will be seen from the responses cited here. It is evident, too, in the striking correspondence between the SAAOR findings and the results, also summarised here, of an unofficial opinion poll conducted inside the USSR.

The findings of a preliminary survey commissioned by SAAOR and conducted among 125 Soviet citizens interviewed while travelling to the West between 1 October and 15 November 1980, showed that even at that early stage the majority of respondents viewed recent events in Poland in an unfavourable light: 60 percent of them expressed negative opinions; 20 percent, positive ones; and 20 percent had no opinion. Statements of disapproval thus outnumbered those of approval by a margin of three to one and, although a sizable majority expressed some sympathy for the Polish workers, the very notion of strikes in a socialist society seemed ridiculous to others. Some expressed resentment at the fact that the Poles lived--in their opinion--better than Soviet citizens. This, they felt, deprived the Poles of the right to complain.

Further interviews were conducted in an attempt to chart the evolution of Soviet public opinion, and earlier material was also incorporated into the findings. For the period of September 1980 to February 1981, the data suggest that, despite certain percentage shifts, the attitudes of Soviet citizens remained largely consistent. Respondents expressing strong disapproval of the independent Polish trade unions continued to outnumber those voicing any degree of support for the movement. Although there was no significant growth in negative attitudes, denunciations of the strikes were nonetheless found to be increasingly vehement in that the proportion of strongly hostile comments was judged to have risen from 32 percent in the early survey period to 37 percent in the later period. The proportion of only mildly hostile comments was, on the other hand, found to have declined (Table 8.1).

Table 8.1
Soviet Attitudes toward the Polish Strike Movement
September 1980 to February 1981
(Percentages of Survey Group)

	Sept-Nov N = 52	Dec-Feb N = 214	Overall Period N = 366
Strongly supportive	7	7	7
Mildly supportive	20	18	19
Strongly opposed	32	37	35
Mildly opposed	15	10	12
No opinion	26	29	27
	100	100	100

Further data were compiled on the basis of interviews conducted during the period March to August 1981, and combined with the earlier findings (relating to the period September 1980 to February 1981). These data suggest that, as time progressed, the views of Soviet citizens moved toward more negative assessments of the situation in Poland. One reason for this increase in hostility--which appears to have begun in the spring of 1981 and to have accelerated during the summer months--is likely to have been the fact that the official Soviet media campaign against Solidarity intensified during that period.

The principal direction of change in the two later time periods charted in Table 8.2 (March to May and June to August 1981) was from "no opinion" to "mildly negative," which suggests that those who had only lately formed an opinion of the events in Poland had tended to adopt a critical viewpoint. The tone of the negative responses was judged, moreover, to have undergone an evolution in the second six-month period (March to August 1981), taking on increasingly anti-Polish overtones (Table 8.2).

Table 8.2
Soviet Attitudes toward the Polish Strike Movement
September 1980 to August 1981
(Percentages of Survey Group)

	Sept-Feb N = 398	March-May N = 188	June-Aug N = 260
Strongly positive	7	9	10
Mildly positive	17	16	12
No opinion	32	24	14
Mildly negative	11	17	25
Strongly negative	33	34	39
	100	100	100

These findings closely resemble those of an unofficial poll of attitudes toward Solidarity that was carried out by Soviet sociologists during conversations with 618 residents of Moscow and nearby towns in the period between mid-September 1980 and late December 1981.[28] Again, it must be noted that the sample was skewed toward urban, educated males. For a comparison of the overall results of the Soviet internal poll and the SAAOR survey described above, see Table 8.3.

Table 8.3
Attitudes of Soviet Citizens to Solidarity
(Percentages of Survey Group)

	Internal Poll N = 618	SAAOR Survey N = 846
Favourable	32	26
Unfavourable	55	47
No opinion	13	27
	100	100

As can be seen, the two sets of results are broadly similar. The unofficial Soviet researchers noted that, "weighting the response categories so as to coincide with the various social and national groups of the Moscow population, we can conclude that 20 to 25 percent of Moscow's inhabitants are to some degree sympathetic to Solidarity." Nonetheless, the results of both surveys suggested that the majority of all age, sex and occupational groups gave negative evaluations of Solidarity, as did both Party members and non-Party members alike, though, as might be expected, both studies found that Solidarity enjoyed more support among non-members of the CPSU than among members. Educational attainment seemed to be the most important predictor of attitude, since a positive correlation was discovered between educational levels and sympathy for Solidarity, but negative opinions predominated even among university graduates.

Finally, the data from a survey conducted among Soviet citizens travelling in Western Europe in the period between 13 December 1981 (when martial law was declared in Poland) and May 1982, are included in Table 8.4, which also reviews the overall pattern.

Table 8.4
Evolution of Soviet Attitudes toward the Crisis in Poland
September 1980 to May 1982
(Percentage of Survey Group)

	Sept 1980- Feb 1981 N=398	Mar- May 1981 N=188	June- Aug 1981 N=260	Sept- Nov 1981 N=366	Dec 1981- May 1982 N=505
Support liberalisation	24	25	22	23	15
No opinion	32	24	14	14	13
Oppose liberalisation	44	51	64	63	71
	100	100	100	100	100

These data suggest that, after the imposition of martial law in Poland, attitudes among Soviet respondents grew increasingly hostile. Only 15 percent of those interviewed between December 1981 and May 1982 held favourable opinions, against 71 percent with negative views. The imposition of martial law seems to have been welcomed by many respondents.

Lack of data precluded a thorough attitudinal breakdown by nationality. However, the data were adequate to suggest an attitudinal dichotomy between Slavs and non-Slavs. Thus, Slavic respondents tended to view the Polish developments more negatively than did their non-Slavic compatriots, particularly those of Baltic or Transcaucasian origin.

Russians registered the highest ratio of negative to positive views, with negative opinions outnumbering positive ones by more than two to one. Among Poland's Slavic neighbours--the Ukrainians and the Belorussians--attitudes toward the Polish events were also found to be decidedly negative; as with the Russians, their negative assessments ran at least two to one.

Data for non-Slavic respondents, on the other hand, showed that among the Balts positive and negative attitudes were about equal. Among those of Transcaucasian origin, however, positive views on the Polish developments were found to outnumber negative ones. (The Baltic and Transcaucasian areas have consistently distinguished themselves from other areas of the USSR in surveys conducted by SAAOR. For example, the highest rates of listening to Radio Liberty broadcasts are found in these republics.[29])

To sum up, reactions gathered between September 1980 and February 1981 indicated that a large number of respondents held negative attitudes to the Polish events from the outset, even though many others were undecided. From March 1981 onward, there was a shift away from "no opinion" attitudes and a corresponding increase in the number of negative attitudes toward Solidarity. It appears that, as the Soviet propaganda campaign intensified, Soviet public opinion swung behind the official interpretation of events. The data suggest that the campaign began to bear fruit in the spring of 1981, when that proportion of the respondents who had until then held no opinion began to move into the negative camp. Following the declaration of martial law, the ranks of those expressing favourable attitudes toward the free trade union movement further declined. The final data show opponents outnumbering supporters by a margin of almost five to one.

The opinion samples cited here suggest that the attempts made by the Soviet authorities to discredit Poland's free trade union movement were successful in playing on Soviet citizens' inherent distrust of disorder, anarchy and chaos; on their deep, if latent, anti-Polish sentiments; and on their simple human envy of Poles who, even though materially better off than Soviet citizens, could still demand more. Apprehension comes across strongly in the replies of a number of Soviet travellers interviewed in Western Europe on behalf of Radio Liberty. The following quotations are typical:

> "It is impossible to introduce the right to strike without bringing about the overthrow of the regime."

> "We have managed to achieve a minimum of organisation. If the right to strike existed, it would all be lost overnight. It would lead to the failure of our system and the ruin of our country."

> "Our economic system would not be able to withstand this kind of freakish notion."

Hand in hand with such attitudes went a generally negative to the right to strike:

> "May God preserve us from strikes. They would only lead to famine."

> "I don't understand how ideas can be more important than food for children."

> "I do not understand how a strike could have got under way in a socialist country, or why the authorities can not put a stop to it."

An influential factor in Soviet citizens' negative reaction to the events in Poland appeared to be envy and dislike of the Poles:

> "The Poles are behaving like spoiled children. The more they get, the more they want."

> "The Poles are a dissolute people ready to betray their allies and their principles for a few consumer goods."

> "The Poles are a pain in the neck. They throw their country into disorder because they know the USSR will not let them down, and will intervene when necessary to restore order and give them bread--even if it means taking it out of our own mouths."

> "Their mouths full of butter, they still find something to complain about.... They travel abroad as they wish, and they do not want for many items that are lacking in our country, such as butter, meat and milk."

> "I wonder what they would do if they were in our shoes?"

Last but not least, the Stalin era's legacy of fear still plays a role in shaping the opinions of Soviet citizens. This conclusion can be drawn from a number of the replies received:

> "Soviet workers are totally helpless and defenceless. If they could go on strike without being shot or imprisoned, they could recover a sense of human dignity."

> "Striking is the basic right of the workers, but it is not possible to strike in the USSR. There are KGB agents infiltrated into all the factories to spy on the workers. Acts of opposition are severely prosecuted."

Finally, the opinion of a Russian industrial worker, interviewed while travelling in the West on holiday:

> "The Polish people have awoken to an awareness of their rights; hence the current agitation in Poland. Eventually the same thing will happen in our country. But it will take time, for the consciousness of our people is impregnated with fear born of the tragic fate that has always been Russia's."

FOOTNOTES TO CHAPTER 8

1. *APN*, 7 July 1981.
2. *Los Angeles Times*, 9 December 1980.
3. Andrew Nagorski, *Reluctant Farewell*, New York, 1985; p. 54.
4. *Ibid.* The passages quoted here are from pp. 53, 56, 152 and 241.

5. *Ibid.*, p. 99.

6. *Frankfurter Allgemeine Zeitung*, 27 November 1980.

7. RL 19/84, "Poland and the 'Ukrainian Connection,'" by Roman Solchanyk, 11 January 1984.

8. The Ukrainian Catholic Church was forcibly incorporated into the Russian Orthodox Church in 1946 in an attempt to quell nationalist sentiment in Ukraine. Virtually the entire hierarchy and clergy of the Church was arrested and many subsequently lost their lives. See RL 3/85, "Chronicle of the Catholic Church in the Ukraine," by Ivan Hvat, 7 January 1985; Bohdan Nahaylo, "Moscow's Ukrainian Predicament," *Wall Street Journal*, 31 October 1984; *idem,* "The Church Rumbling beneath the Kremlin," *The Times*, 12 January 1985; Philip Walters, "Cardinal Slipyi: The Man and his Church," *Religion in Communist Lands*, Vol. 13, No 1, 1985, pp. 91-93; George Zaryky, "Soviet Journal on Religious Dissent May Embarrass Kremlin," *Christian Science Monitor*, 6 March 1985.

9. *Christian Science Monitor*, 30 September 1980.

10. Nagorski, *op. cit.*, pp. 61 and 65.

11. *Neue Zuercher Zeitung*, 30 August 1980. The programmes affected by the reintroduction of jamming were those of the BBC, the Voice of America and Deutsche Welle; jamming of Radio Liberty had never been suspended.

12. *TASS*, 19 August 1981; *Pravda*, 20 August 1981.

13. *Christian Science Monitor*, 17 November 1980; *Baltimore Sun*, 27 April 1981; *Newsweek*, 3 August 1981. These reports related not only to Moscow but also to Latvia and Lithuania where, it was said, the sale of all Polish newspapers was discontinued after 12 October 1980. The British Communist Party's *Morning Star* was also said to have been withheld from distribution for a time during

the autumn of 1980 (*Christian Science Monitor*, 30 September 1980), as was the daily newspaper of the Italian Communist Party, *L'Unita*, following the declaration of martial law in December 1981.

14. *AP*, 5 and 6 October 1980.

15. *Christian Science Monitor*, 30 September 1980.

16. *Ibid.*, 17 November 1980.

17. *New York Times*, 24 November 1980.

18. *Newsweek*, 3 August 1981.

19. V. Stanley Vardys, "Polish Echoes in the Baltic," *Problems of Communism*, July-August 1983, pp. 21-43.

20. *Pravda*, 26 February 1981.

21. *Radyans'ka Ukraina*, 12 February 1981.

22. Vardys, *op. cit.*; Alexander R. Alexiev, *Dissent and Nationalism in the Soviet Baltic*, Santa Monica, Calif., 1983; Roman Solchanyk, "Poland and the Soviet West," in Enders Wimbush (ed), *Soviet Nationalities in Strategic Perspective*, Beckenham, 1984.

23. RL 364/83, "The Arrest of Enn Tarto and the Crackdown on Baltic Dissent," by Saulius Girnius, 29 September 1983.

24. RL 70/81, "Ukrainian Party Journal Raises the Specter of Poland," by Roman Solchanyk, 17 February 1981; RL 422/81, "Ukrainian KGB Chief Warns of Ideological Sabotage," by Roman Solchanyk, 22 October 1981. On the activities of the KGB in Lithuania at this time, see Nagorski, *op. cit.*, pp. 60-1.

25. See Anthony Barbieri in the *Baltimore Sun*, 16 December 1981: "At first there was admiration and sympathy for Poles in their struggle to form free trade unions.... But as the Polish crisis ran through its endless cycle of confrontation and as the Soviet government became increasingly harsh in its condemnation of the Polish unions, the opinions of ordinary Russians began to harden"; and John

Darnton in the *International Herald Tribune*, 11 June 1982: "The attitudes of everyday Soviet citizens toward Poles, a blend of suspicion and resentment, appear to have hardened through the two-year-old Polish crisis."

26. For details of the surveys and how they are carried out see R.E. Parta, "Listening to Radio Liberty in the USSR, 1976-77," Analysis Report 3-78, published by Radio Free Europe/Radio Liberty Soviet Area Audience and Opinion Research (RFE/RL SAAOR), 28 June 1978; and Sig Mikelson, *America's Other Voice: The Story of Radio Free Europe and Radio Liberty*, New York, 1983, pp. 210-11.

27. Full details of the opinion surveys summarised here are to be found in the following publications of RFE/RL SAAOR: Analysis Report 1-81, "Attitudes in the USSR toward the Right to Strike," January 1981; Background Report 2-81, "Soviet Citizens Comment on Events in Poland," 13 January 1981; Background Report 3-81, "Attitudes of Soviet Citizens to the Strike Movement in Poland," May 1981; Analysis Report 8-81, "Developing Soviet Citizen Attitudes toward Poland," October 1981; Analysis Report 5-82, "Attitudes of Some Soviet Citizens to the Solidarity Trade Union Movement," May 1982; and Analysis Report 6-82, "Soviet Citizen Attitudes toward Poland since Martial Law," September 1982.

28. These data were published in the Danish newspaper *Berlingske Tidende* on 21 March 1982, and in *L'Alternative* (Paris), No 16-17, 1982, pp. 54-6.

29. SAAOR Analysis Report 3-78, "Listening to Radio Liberty in the USSR, 1976-77," 28 June 1978.

Chapter 9

THE POLISH EVENTS REFLECTED IN *SAMIZDAT*

The last chapter tried to determine what impact the Polish events had on the general Soviet population, but found the evidence to be inconclusive. A certain amount of sympathy seemed to be felt for the Polish workers by people in the USSR's western borderlands, but it could not be assumed that such feelings were uniformly shared by people living in areas of the USSR further removed from Poland's frontiers. On the contrary: the available evidence suggested that the measures adopted by the authorities to insulate the Soviet people from the "Polish disease" were extremely effective, and that a fair proportion of the population came to share their government's antipathy to Poland's independent trade unions.

Among members of the Soviet dissident movement, a different picture emerges. This chapter looks at how the Polish events were reflected in the *samizdat* materials that have reached the West from the Soviet Union. To judge from these materials, interest and sympathy for the Polish workers were felt by many dissidents. Such feelings were expressed not only by intellectuals but also by religious believers and by some people of working-class background.

By *samizdat*, or "self-publishing," is meant material written, produced and circulated by private individuals. Because such documents are not submitted for approval to official censors, their reproduction and distribution are illegal. Almost by definition, therefore, anyone who contributes to the prolific network of Soviet *samizdat* materials is a dissident or *inakomyslyashchii*, that is, someone who "thinks differently" from the orthodox opinions sanctioned and promulgated by the state.

Samizdat materials relating to the Polish events may be divided into a number of (inevitably) overlapping categories. These include: declarations of support for the Polish workers; leaflets in support of Solidarity distributed within the USSR; coverage of the Polish events in journals such as the information bulletin published by SMOT, the USSR's embryonic independent trade union movement; and studies of the significance of the Polish events by members of the Soviet dissident movement.

The present study is, of course, restricted to *samizdat* documents that have reached the West, and it is impossible for an outside observer to determine how representative the sample is of those that circulated in the USSR during the Solidarity period.[1] There seems no reason to doubt that the vast majority of the *samizdat* materials that reach the West are authentic, i.e, they are not KGB disinformation. The question inevitably arises, however, as to how reliable they are. In some cases it is possible for Western researchers to cross-check the information contained in a *samizdat* document, but in many others it is not. Some documents are signed by known individuals, upon whose credibility a value can be placed; others are anonymous or signed with a pseudonym. The researcher is therefore obliged to evaluate *samizdat* documents with the same caution he or she would show to any primary source material: neither more nor less.

DECLARATIONS OF SUPPORT BY SOVIET DISSIDENTS

The first reflexion of the Polish events in Soviet *samizdat* appeared in a letter of support for the Gdansk Interfactory Committee issued in Moscow on 30 August 1980.[2] This letter was signed by ten members of the Soviet human rights and democratic movements, several of them members of the Moscow Helsinki monitoring group set up in 1976 to monitor Soviet compliance with the provisions of the

Helsinki Accords. The signatories were: Andrei Sakharov, Elena Bonner, Raisa Lert, Larisa Bogoraz, Ivan Kovalev, Anatolii Marchenko, Feliks Serebrov, Sonya Sorokina, Viktor Sorokin and Mariya Petrenko-Pod'yapol'skaya.[3] Addressed to "Polish friends," the declaration read in part:

> We are sympathetically following your brave struggle for civil and economic rights.... Your struggle is restoring the honour of the working class and sets an example of unity between workers and intellectuals.

Less than a fortnight later, on 11 September, a group of Baltic dissidents issued a statement in which they congratulated Solidarity leader Lech Walesa "and all Poles" on "laying the foundation of the democratic reforms that are so greatly needed by all the socialist countries." The signatories--ten Estonians and ten Lithuanians--included the Estonian national and civil rights activist, Enn Tarto.[4]

September also saw the appearance in a Russian emigre journal of a letter and two statements in support of the Polish strikers issued by the Council of Representatives of the Free Interprofessional Association of Workers (SMOT), the USSR's only surviving independent trade union in embryo. Addressed to "struggling Polish workers," the documents expressed SMOT's "fraternal solidarity in your heroic struggle" against "our common enemy." They were signed by SMOT's representatives in the West and by L. Volokhonsky, V. Skvirsky, S. Kuvakin and A. Yakoreva, who were all in the USSR at that time. "A free Russia," SMOT stressed, "is unimaginable without an independent Poland."[5]

Another message of support was contained in a document appended to the 13th issue of the SMOT information bulletin, published in 1981.[6] Issued by an unknown group calling itself the "Russian Committee for the Aid of Polish Workers," the declaration was undated, but seemed to have been written sometime before the end of March 1981 since at that time, according to the compilers of the SMOT bulletin, the authorities conducted a number of searches in Moscow in connexion with it. Addressed to "Polish friends," the declaration read in part:

> In the name of the majority of the Russian people--whose voice has been replaced by Party slogans--we salute your just struggle for your rights. ...your movement should give a mighty impulse to the struggle for democracy in the "socialist countries." ... We will make every effort to ensure that your movement receives broad support in the USSR.

In August 1981, on the first anniversary of Solidarity's foundation, a group of 36 human rights activists from the Baltic republics (35 Lithuanians and one Latvian) issued a message of greeting to Lech Walesa, declaring that "this heroic movement of Poland's working people ... is significant for the Baltic nations as well."[7]

Early in 1984, a new *samizdat* journal appeared in Western Ukraine. Entitled *Chronicle of the Catholic Church in Ukraine*, it focussed on the plight of the Ukrainian Catholic Church and its struggle for legalisation. Early issues indicated that the events in Poland had struck a responsive chord among Ukrainian Catholics, and suggested that Solidarity's example had contributed to a resurgence of religious activity in Western Ukraine. In a letter to Lech Walesa published in the *Chronicle*, Iosyp Terelya, a leading Ukrainian national activist who had already spent over 20 years in prison and labour camp for his religious beliefs, told Walesa that "your struggle and that of all the Polish people is the hope that gives us the strength to resist." Dated 12 April 1984, the letter continued:

> The steadfastness and courage of the leaders of the workers' movement and of the Catholic Church in Poland give courage to us here, in Satan's very lair.... Difficult times have begun in Ukraine. Since the Stalinist repressions, our people have not experienced such oppression as they do today. It is a matter of life or death.[8]

The *Chronicle* reported that the authorities adopted especially harsh measures to crush dissent and prevent the spread of Solidarity's example in the USSR's western borderlands. The commandant of a labour camp in L'vov is quoted as warning an imprisoned Catholic priest, 71-year-old Antin Potochnyak, "We have instructions now how to deal with Ukrainian Catholics.... We aren't going to tolerate another Poland here!"[9]

CIRCULATION OF LEAFLETS IN SUPPORT OF SOLIDARITY

Reports were also received of distribution in the USSR of leaflets connected with the Polish events. It was reported, for example, that "leaflets expressing support for the struggle of the Polish workers" were distributed in the middle of March 1981 at the Leningrad Technological Institute.[10] In September 1981 similar leaflets reportedly appeared in Novocherkassk.[11] These called on Soviet workers to demand their government refrain from "interference in the internal affairs of other states."

In February and March 1982 leaflets in support of Solidarity and calling for strikes were reportedly circulated in Western Ukraine. They were said to be typeset and "quite lengthy." The KGB took "very energetic measures" in an attempt to discover the source of the leaflets; the police were said to be particularly concerned by the professional skill with which they were produced.[12] Leaflets were also said to have been distributed during a soccer match held in Tbilisi on 17 March 1982 between a Polish and a local team. The text consisted of the slogans, "Let Poland be Poland," "For our freedom and yours," "Poland is not yet defeated" and "*Solidarnosc*"; the leaflets were handwritten in Georgian, Russian, English and Polish.[13]

DISCUSSION IN SOVIET *SAMIZDAT* JOURNALS

Of course, the Polish events did not fail to be discussed in the information bulletins of SMOT. Not all the bulletins issued by SMOT during the relevant period have reached the West, but the available issues show that SMOT gave the Polish events wide coverage, combining factual accounts of major events with commentaries on their significance.

The 10th issue of SMOT's bulletin (compiled sometime prior to the middle of January 1981), contained an item on the unveiling in Gdansk in December 1980 of a monument to the Poles killed in the disturbances of December 1970.[14] The 15th issue (compiled in April-May 1981) included a Russian translation of the Twenty-one Demands made by the Gdansk Interfactory Strike Committee in August 1980. There followed the text of the self-criticism made by former Polish Party leader Edward Gierek after his fall from power.[15] SMOT's editors added a caustic postscript of their own, asking whether it was not time that "the members of our own beloved Leninist Politburo declared a similar readiness to share their privileges with the ordinary people?" The 19th issue (compiled in August-September 1981) reproduced in Russian translation Solidarity's "Message to the Working People of Eastern Europe and the USSR" of September 1981.[16]

SMOT continued to discuss the Polish events after the declaration of martial law in December 1981. Thus, the whole of the 26th issue of the bulletin (compiled between December 1981 and January 1982) was devoted to "Communist Excesses on Polish Soil" and included a statement of support, issued after the declaration of martial law, reasserting SMOT's belief in the inalienable right of working people to set up independent trade unions.[17]

The 26th issue contained a message of support said to be addressed to Polish workers by "the workers of the Central Black Earth region of Russia," while the 27th issue (compiled at the same time as the 26th) devoted 16 closely typed pages to messages of support and sympathy by anonymous Soviet authors.[18] The 29th and 30th issues (compiled in December 1981-January 1982 and February-March 1982 respectively) provided factual information, drawn largely from Western sources, on the situation in Poland under martial law.[19] Issue No 29 contained a brief essay by a young Russian poetess of Polish ancestry, Irina Ratushinskaya. The essay denounced the servility of the silent majority of Soviet citizens who, "while knowing and understanding what is going on in Poland," refused to stand up to their oppressors. SMOT's editors agreed. "Our craven silence ... is a national disgrace," they added.[20]

In Lithuania and Estonia, too, *samizdat* publications carried information about the Polish events. An underground publication in Lithuania commented, for example, that these events could have "serious consequences not only for Poland, but also for the other socialist countries."[21] In Estonia, the 10th issue of the *samizdat* periodical *Some Additions to the Free Flow of Ideas and News in Estonia*, issued in 1981, contained a translation of the Gdansk Accords reached between the Polish government and the Gdansk Interfactory Strike Committee in August 1980.[22] More than half the 13th issue of this journal (also issued in 1981) was devoted to the Polish events and included factual information regarding the declaration of martial law. Its final item was "A Letter on the Events in Poland," signed by a group of academics at the University of Tartu. The letter blamed "the crisis that has arisen in Poland" on "the powerlessness of the socialist order that has been in power for 36 years."[23]

An assessment of the Polish events from a socialist standpoint appeared in a symposium of *samizdat* articles entitled *Sotsialist-82*.[24] Its appearance was unusual, since writings by dissident Soviet socialists do not often reach the West, even though the existence of several *samizdat* periodicals of a socialist or "Eurocommunist" orientation is known of from a variety of sources. The journals *Varianty* and *Levyi povorot*--later renamed *Sotsializm i budushchee*--are both said to have disseminated information about the situation in Poland by means of translations of articles from Western left-wing publications.[25] This information cannot be confirmed, since no copies of either journal are known to have reached the West.

The bulk of the items in the symposium *Sotsialist-82* discussed the "unsocialist" nature of "real socialism." One article, published under the pseudonym "Ya. Vasin," argued that Solidarity was antisocialist in neither aims nor tactics:

> "Don't burn down the PUWP committee, form your own!" This slogan guided the movement along the best path possible in the circumstances, that is, *the path of mass nonviolent resistance and class organisation*.... this was *a revolution that was socialist in its goals.* The concurrent democratisation of the political system and socialisation of the means of production focussed the attention of the

> whole world on the Polish experiment. (Emphasis in original)

A group of well-connected "young socialists," believed to be involved with the journal *Varianty*, were arrested in the spring of 1982. According to one report, this Moscow group had previously worked quietly and been ignored by the authorities, and "it was only when they crossed the line between subtlety and publicity with a formal condemnation of martial law in Poland that they ran into trouble."[26] During searches in connexion with the case, the authorities were said to have discovered large amounts of *samizdat*, including an "Appeal to Polish Workers" signed "Soviet dissenters."[27]

COMMENTS ON THE POLISH EVENTS BY SOVIET WORKERS

Statements about the Polish events by Soviet workers appeared only rarely in *samizdat* materials reaching the West. Particular interest was therefore presented by an open letter addressed by a Ukrainian worker, Mykola Pohyba, to the Ukrainian Helsinki monitoring group and the United Nations Commission on Human Rights.[28] The letter, expressing Pohyba's enthusiastic approval of the events in Poland and their lessons for the Soviet working class, was dated 4 November 1980. It was written in detention, for its author had been sentenced in 1979 to five years' deprivation of freedom for "hooliganism."

Pohyba was at one point imprisoned in the same labour camp in Kiev oblast as the late Yurii Lytvyn, a leading member of the Ukrainian Helsinki monitoring group.[29] Lytvyn--who took his own life in 1984 while under detention in the notorious special-regime camp No 36 in Perm' oblast--called for an alliance between Ukrainian dissidents and workers. Shortly before Lytvyn's last arrest, in August 1979, the KGB reportedly confiscated an unfinished manuscript entitled "The Soviet State and the Soviet Working Class" during a search of his home.[30] It seems possible, therefore, that Lytvyn's ideas may have had an influence on Pohyba. Pohyba himself states, however, that his social position was the major determinant of his opinions.

As a worker, Pohyba wrote, he found himself "on the lowest rung of the social ladder." He had experienced economic, social, political and national oppression at first hand because "it is the Soviet worker who suffers the full brunt of the state's lawlessness and arbitrariness." He went on:

> I could not help thinking about the real causes of this oppression. I gradually came to see that workers such as I are the objects of exploitation and that, the lower a person's position on the social scale, the greater his exploitation.... The main exploiter in the USSR is the state.... Socialism...is only a smoke-screen disguising a system of production and exchange that is far from socialist. In short, our country is a society of state capitalism with a totalitarian form of political power.

Pohyba called on other workers to reject the existing system and to seek "new forms of class struggle that would lead to the real emancipation of the working class" for, his letter continued, "I am not the only person who believes that in the Soviet Union objective conditions are maturing for the establishment of trade unions independent of both Party and state." He drew inspiration from "the recent events in Poland" which, he wrote,

> have clearly shown that the working class is capable of waging a struggle for its rights and freedoms and for a real

> improvement in its standard of living, and that the success of this struggle depends on the degree of solidarity of the working class and on the level of its self-organisation.

Reference to the Polish example was made by another Soviet worker in an open letter dated, like Pohyba's, November 1980.[31] Mikhail Zotov, a former milling-machine operator obliged as a result of war injuries to take less skilled work at a dairy in Tol'yatti, described how his attempts to obtain redress for his grievances were repeatedly thwarted by the authorities.[32] He concluded:

> The authorities' fear of the truth, their refusal to grant the masses the right of free speech, their determination to rule the people not by means of dialogue but with an iron rod--such "methods" will not bring the authorities any good. In Poland this kind of "rule" has forced the people to strike and led to the establishment of free trade unions. Here in Russia, this kind of "policy" has so far given rise among the people only to infinite moral apathy. And it is perhaps here that one should seek the causes of drunkenness, idling, theft, careless attitudes toward labour discipline, and so on.

The following scene is described in a *samizdat* document written in 1981 by a Moscow worker, Nikolai Alekseev:

> "Have you heard what foolishness the Poles are up to?" one of my workmates asked me as we were going home from the factory. Before I could reply, he burst out, "It's

> time it was put a stop to!" "How can you talk like that!" [I asked]. "They're workers like you and me. They're fighting for their rights. Who taught you all this nonsense?" "Nobody," [he answered]. "It's what I think myself. We aren't any better off than they are, but we don't go on strike; we don't put our country's security at risk. It's all being stirred up from outside."

Alekseev commented:

> My friend was quite convinced that violence and aggression are only to be found abroad. How could I make him see that those who hide from their own people in bullet-proof motor-cars, behind stone walls and surrounded with armed guards, are not at all concerned about our security? And that those who've set themselves up secretly as the distributors of goods, fencing their own luxurious holiday homes, sanatoriums and *dachas* off from the population while the rest of us make do in communal flats and wear ourselves out in endless queues--that such people as those don't care at all about the welfare of the people either of their own country or of their neighbour's?[33]

STUDIES BY DISSIDENT INTELLECTUALS

An expression of support for the Polish strikers and a deeply pessimistic evaluation of the possibility that similar events might occur in the USSR were contained in an essay that appeared in *samizdat* under the pseudonym "Ivan Ivansky."[34] Dated 11 December 1981, the document was written from a town in Voronezh oblast. It drew its title, "The Fourth

Civil War in Russia," from its author's assertion that the relationship between the Soviet leaders and the general population was one of open warfare: "the red aristocrats are fighting their own progeny." In such circumstances, the author went on in an attack on the Soviet human rights movement, "it is senseless to prattle...about laws and the constitution."

The author's disgust at what he saw as the impotence and cowardice of the dissident movement was increased by the example of the Polish strikes:

> It is not surprising that in Poland the foundations show the first crack. Poles are Poles. They are not like us Russians. They have already emerged victorious in what is perhaps the most important area, and have won back religion for themselves. They have not allowed their churches to be destroyed. They will win back their freedom too for, you see, they have faith.

"Ivan Ivansky" held out little hope that Soviet dissidents would be able to inspire the general population to follow in the Poles' footsteps:

> Our hands are not stained with blood. We have not even resorted to such traditional proletarian weapons as paving stones. (Future generations will call us fools or, at best, pacifists.) The only weapons we have are words.

Several attempts were made, under the impact of the Polish events, by dissident Soviet intellectuals to communicate with members of the working class. These do not generally seem to have taken the form of direct personal contacts, but a number of *samizdat* works did appear in which Soviet intellectuals analysed the significance of the Polish events for the USSR in general and for Soviet workers in particular.

Vadim Yankov, a Moscow mathematician, was the author of "A Letter to Russian Workers Concerning the Polish Events."[35] The bulk of this quite lengthy document was composed in November 1981, that is, before the declaration of martial law, and a postscript was added in January 1982. Yankov's stated purpose was to inform Soviet workers what had been happening in Poland, but he was unable to conceal his contempt for the Soviet workers to whom his essay was directed.

Yankov attributed the success of the Polish workers to their "restraint and self-discipline." But, he wrote, "it seems to me that you, Russian workers, are not yet capable of exercising such restraint":

> In such circumstances, the Polish path is closed to you. I admire the Polish workers and hope that their example will be followed by workers in other East European countries, but I believe that if you were to follow in their footsteps along the path of mass strikes and political demands, tremendous bloodshed would be the inevitable result.... In order for what has happened in Poland to become possible in Russia, you will have to learn sobriety (both literal and figurative), restraint and humanity.

Yankov put forward several explanations as to why Soviet workers had not attained the maturity of the Poles. In the first place, he said, the multinational USSR could not be compared with "uninational" Poland. The Poles were united, too, by their strong Roman Catholic faith. Russian workers lacked such a unifying force:

> Your religion has been destroyed and, along with it, something very precious: your intimate links both with each other and with virtue. Perhaps this lack of religion is the cause of your weakness of will, of your submission to the authorities. You no longer have any *independent source of goodness,* and all that remains for you is to search instead for base substitutes in drunken debauchery and in the delusionary belief that you and the state are one. (Emphasis in original)

Particular interest was presented by a *samizdat* document that appeared some time in 1982.[36] "The Polish Revolution" is a long work by an anonymous author, evidently a member of the Moscow liberal intelligentsia with access to both Polish and Western sources.

The author was clearly well informed about Polish history and society. In his opinion, "The events taking place in Poland before our eyes--or, rather, deliberately and systematically concealed from us--are of the greatest historical importance." Accordingly, he set himself the task of informing his friends about them. But he also had another purpose in mind: "The Muse of History is today speaking the Polish language," he wrote. "It is our task to teach her Russian."

The document began with an overview of Polish history. To this day, the author wrote, Poles harbour ill feelings toward Russians because of the role played both by tsarist Russia and by the USSR in the four partitions of Poland and the enforced "Russification" and "Sovietisation" that ensued.

However, the author went on, several internal forces acted to retard Poland's Sovietisation. He cited, in particular, the Roman Catholic Church, whose influence he ascribed to the fact that it retained its own independent organisation. The Roman Catholic Church, the author argued, was stronger than the Russian Orthodox because it "combines elements that Orthodoxy has always lacked: religious depth, culture, and organisation." He claimed that while the Russian Orthodox Church inherited from Byzantium a tradition of "cringing servility" before the civil power, the Catholic Church had always jealously guarded its independence from the state. In Poland, which was long deprived of independent statehood, the Church became the guardian of national tradition. Its influence remained strong among the Polish peasantry, who took their faith with them to the towns during Poland's post-war industrialisation. This, the author argued, was the reason for the continuing strength of Roman Catholicism among the Polish working class.

Poland's intelligentsia, the author went on, was traditionally divided into two wings: the "radicals" (usually atheistic or agnostic) and the "conservatives" (who tended to be Catholic). Polish intellectuals never lost this strand of religious belief. In pre-revolutionary Russia, on the other hand, the intelligentsia was, according to the author of this *samizdat* document, "exclusively radical," while "the conservative party was always extremely non-intellectual." Moreover, the author asserted, the Russian *intelligent* placed no great value on his individuality, "joined any social tendency there was around, blindly swallowed its dogmas and programme, and threw his naive, half-baked personality into collective activity." The Polish intellectual, the author asserted, "was never anything other than an individualist." Through the medium of Polish culture, these traditions of independence and individuality passed to the whole Polish nation, and enabled it to withstand Stalin and his heirs. "The psychological climate in Poland has always been different from ours," the author concluded.

The author recognised that the decisive role in the Polish events of 1980-81 was played by the working class. He therefore devoted considerable attention to ways in which Polish workers differed from Soviet ones. In the first place, he stressed, the Poles had had a shorter experience of "slavery and terror." Between the two world wars Poland experienced a period as a parliamentary republic with a pluralist system: trade unions and political parties--both legal and illegal--flourished, and workers gained experience in the use of "the weapon of last resort to defend themselves against their employers--the strike." By contrast, said the author, the Russian workers who had a taste of freedom in 1917 died long ago. "Their children grew up in silence and fear. Therefore, we cannot hope for success by following the Polish example. Nonetheless, we have much to learn from the Poles."

Of special interest were the lessons the author drew from the Polish events for the Soviet situation and, especially, his comparison between the opposition movement in Poland and the dissident movement in the USSR. The author's judgement of the Soviet dissident movement was harsh. Its members were, in his opinion, incapable of offering any serious opposition to the regime because of their deliberate policy of "no politics":

> ...dissidents in the USSR...argue that only bad people take account of the consequences of their actions, while good people express their feelings openly, paying no heed to what the results may be. Such an ideology suits the authorities very well. If it did not exist, they would have had to invent it....

The author mocked such attitudes:

> The legal side of the question deceives ...only naive people like Soviet dissidents. Wherever laws are not applied--and are not even made with the intention that they should ever be applied--legalistic squabbling is only a substitute for more productive forms of thinking for which the dissidents have no aptitude.

The author offered no assessment of the mood of the Soviet working class. Perhaps, like many of the Soviet intellectuals about whom he complained, he had no contact with workers. He had nothing to say, either, about the attempts made in recent years to form independent trade unions in the USSR, and he appeared to consider Soviet workers insufficiently mature to organise structures of their own along the lines of Solidarity. And, although "The Polish Revolution" stressed the important role played in the rise of Solidarity by Polish national sentiment, the author did not discuss the possibility that nationalist tensions might at some time pose a threat to the stability of the Soviet state.

Instead, he pinned his hopes for the future on a change of strategy by the dissident movement, calling for a combination of both legal and illegal forms of organisation and activity. "Why is such a weak regime still in power in Russia?" he asked. The reason, he concluded, was that it was meeting no effective resistance: "the bloody purges destroyed everyone capable of offering resistance, and the tradition that fosters opposition was crushed. But that tradition could be reborn.... When the regime meets with serious opposition it will collapse like a house of cards."

The lessons the Soviet dissident movement should draw from the Polish events were discussed in another important *samizdat* document. This was a collection of notes written not later than the summer of 1982 by the late Vasyl Stus, a poet and leading figure of both the Ukrainian national and the Soviet human rights movements.[37]

One of a group of young intellectuals active in the revival of Ukrainian national culture in the 1960s, Stus fell a victim of the extensive purge of the early 1970s. Having served a sentence of eight years' imprisonment and internal exile on a charge of "anti-Soviet agitation and propaganda," he returned to Kiev in 1979 where he joined the Ukrainian Helsinki monitoring group. Re-arrested within months, he was tried in October 1980 and sentenced, on the same charge as before, to ten years in a special-regime corrective labour camp followed by five years in internal exile.[38] Stus died before completing this sentence, in September 1985, in the same special-regime camp in Perm' oblast as Yurii Lytvyn.

In his notes, Stus expressed warm sympathy for the aspirations of the Polish workers:

> Long live the volunteers in the cause of freedom! The Poles' defiance of Soviet despotism fills us with joy and their national uprisings amaze us: with the sole exception of the army and police, everyone takes part: workers, intellectuals, students, everyone.... No other nation in the totalitarian world would defend its human and national rights with such self-confidence.

Stus considered what lessons the Soviet population could learn. He concluded that only by following Solidarity's example would Soviet workers be able to wring concessions from their government:

> The trade union means of liberation would be especially effective for the USSR. If

> the initiative of the engineer Klebanov[39] were supported throughout the country, the Soviet government would face perhaps its most up-to-date anatagonist.

"Poland is an example to Ukraine," Stus stated. "But will Poland serve as a model for us?" He was not optimistic. "Ukraine is not yet ready to learn from the Polish teacher," he wrote; "we lack one vital characteristic: the sacred patriotism that unites the Poles." The Polish events made Stus reconsider the philosophy of the Soviet human rights movement. He concluded that this movement, in which he himself had played a leading role, did not command sufficient popular support to realise in the USSR the kind of changes that Solidarity sought in Poland:

> In the light of the Polish events, the weaknesses of the Helsinki movement become even clearer, in particular, its cowardly respectability. Had it been a mass movement of popular initiative with a wide programme of social and political demands, had it aimed at eventually taking power, then it would have had some prospect of success. As it is, the Helsinki movement is like a little child that wants to speak in a deep voice.

THE LESSONS OF POLAND

Vasyl Stus' reflexions on the lessons of the Polish events were cited by one Western specialist on Soviet dissent, Bohdan Nahaylo, as evidence of "a growing sense of disillusionment in some quarters with traditional forms of open and legalistic dissent in the USSR."[40]

"Open and legalistic" dissent appeared late in the Soviet Union.[41] Soviet dissent began to assume organised forms only in the mid-1960s, when human rights activists seized on the idea of exploiting openness and publicity--both inside and outside the USSR--to highlight the regime's legal abuses. They hoped thereby to shame or embarrass the authorities into observing the human rights guaranteed both by Soviet law and by the international agreements the Soviet Union had signed. The activists' most powerful weapons were their own scrupulous observance of legal norms, their insistence that what they were doing was fully permissible under Soviet and international law, and their calculated appeal to world public opinion.

Faced with this innovation, the authorities wavered. For an entire decade, it appears, they remained unsure how to respond to the challenge. The early 1970s saw the Brezhnev leadership pursuing a vigorous policy of East-West detente, and anxious not to antagonise Western nations by heavy-handed repressions at home. The authorities made a few attempts to silence the human rights activists but, by and large, the movement was able to spread and diversify throughout the decade.

As the 1970s drew to a close, detente began to founder. It was then, at the end of 1979, that the Soviet authorities decided to launch a comprehensive crackdown on all forms of dissent within the USSR. The British authority Peter Reddaway has singled out the overall deterioration of East-West relations and the fact that, as a result, the authorities felt no further need to placate Western opinion as the major reason why the Soviet leaders chose that moment to silence the dissident members of their population. What clinched the matter, in Reddaway's opinion, was the Soviet decision, taken sometime toward the end of 1979, to intervene militarily in Afghanistan.[42] That action dealt a death-blow to East-West detente. Thereafter the Soviet leaders appeared to feel that they had nothing left to lose as regards Western public opinion.

Other factors may also have played a role in the decision to crack down on dissent. One seems to have been the proliferation of domestic problems that faced the authorities at the turn of the decade, food shortages included. The Polish strikes may have been an additional factor, leading to further waves of repression in 1980-82.

By the autumn of 1981 General Semen Tsvigun, first deputy chairman of the KGB, could boast that the secret police had "rendered harmless" what he described as "antisocial elements camouflaged as 'defenders of human rights' and 'champions of democracy.'" At the same time, Tsvigun betrayed some nervousness about the state of public opinion in the USSR, and called for "heightened vigilance" against what he alleged were new and even more dangerous trends. The KGB was ready, he said, to move against "subversive" groups complaining about food shortages, the lack of consumer goods, and shortcomings in the medical services.[43]

The crackdown was indeed successful from the point of view of the authorities. The disbanding of the Moscow Helsinki monitoring group in September 1982 ended a decade of human rights activity[44] and, in the opinion of many observers, demonstrated the inability of organised dissent to place limits upon the arbitrary use of power by the authorities. The flow of information on human rights abuses decreased sharply, and activists of every persuasion were driven underground. SMOT, for example, which originally publicised the names of its leaders (though not those of its rank-and-file adherents) was reported in 1982 to have split into some twenty groups that would, in the interests of secrecy, carry out future activities independently of each other.[45] More and more *samizdat* documents were issued anonymously, to protect their authors from identification by the KGB.

As several documents quoted in this chapter attest, some dissidents saw the crushing of Solidarity by the Polish authorities as proof of the hopelessness of the trying to change a Soviet-type system by legal and open means. In the words of the anonymous author of *The Polish Revolution*:

> under conditions of "real socialism," the existence of an independent organisation ...threatens the whole system.... Any attempt at independent activity is not only regarded by the authorities as political activity but *is* objectively political inasmuch as it undermines the foundations of the regime. (Emphasis in original)[46]

Instead, several anonymous appeals appeared in *samizdat*, calling for what Nahaylo has described as "a new strain of clandestine, more militant, and broader-based resistance to the regime." Nahaylo points out that Vasyl Stus was the first but by no means the only person to see that "the restrained, apolitical phase of Soviet dissidence, as exemplified by the Helsinki monitoring groups, has had its day."[47]

Particularly striking was a manifesto issued on 1 July 1981 in Moscow by a clandestine organisation calling itself the "Initiative Group for National Democracy."[48] The Soviet population, the group asserted, had no possibility of curtailing the regime's expansionist foreign policy or its domestic repression; all power lay in the hands of a "Party oligarchy consisting of some 100,000 functionaries," and not even the Party's multi-million membership had any real say in decision-making. As an example of the Soviet Union's "imperialist and expansionist policies," the declaration cited "the threat [posed by the Soviet government] to the gains won by popular democracy in Poland."

The declaration poured scorn on the way Soviet dissidents had focussed their activity around the question of the infringement of individual rights. Soviet citizens, it asserted, had no rights, and rights that did not exist could not be violated. The human rights and democratic movements were wasting their breath seeking to influence the regime in this way. As a result, the declaration asserted, the dissident movement was plunged into a crisis that was both organisational and conceptual.

The manifesto went on to call for the creation of a new form of opposition, "a new phase in the dissident movement." This would involve the secret infiltration of the system of Party, state and economic power. The purpose of this "entryism" was to collect information about the exploitation of the masses and the privileges of the elite and to pass this information on to the general public. To reduce the threat of KGB reprisals, members of the new movement would operate individually and maintain only a minimum of links with other members, and "the figure of the professional revolutionary will appear in our public life once again.".

The new opposition, the declaration went on, should work out alternative programmes of economic and social development. It should organise meetings, demonstrations and strikes. "The struggle for popular democracy in Poland," the group stated, "showed that at a certain, decisive moment this form of activity is of crucial importance."

Another call for the creation of a clandestine organisation appeared in a letter that began to circulate in *samizdat* in October 1981.[49] Clearly influenced by the Polish events, the letter's anonymous author complained that the Soviet dissident movement had paid almost no attention to workers' problems. However, "the Polish situation has shown that all the force for the creation of a pluralistic state is to be found in the workers' movement." The Soviet working class, the author went on, must be helped to free itself from Communist Party control: "it must be taught liberation."

The author called for the establishment of a new, clandestine organisation within the working class. Its work would be carried out by means of leaflets and other printed material that would "lay bare the falsity of communist slogans." Leaflets would be distributed wherever large crowds were gathered--for example, at sports stadiums.

Following the outbreak of strikes in Poland in 1980, scattered reports reached the West--many of them through *samizdat* channels--concerning alleged labour unrest within the USSR. Of these, one is of particular relevance since it involved a strike call made in pursuit of political demands.

The call came from a clandestine group calling itself the "Democratic Front of the Soviet Union," a previously unknown group based in Estonia. Toward the end of 1981, the group began to circulate *samizdat* leaflets in Russian, Ukrainian and the languages of the three Baltic states.[50] The leaflets were distributed in Latvia, Lithuania and Estonia, and also in Moscow, Leningrad and Kiev. They called on Soviet citizens to stop work, refrain from using public transport, and remain completely silent between 10 a.m. and 10.30 a.m. on 1 December 1981, and to repeat this half-hour protest on the first working day of every month "until the Soviet Union becomes more democratic." The group's demands included the withdrawal of Soviet troops from Afghanistan, an end to Soviet interference in Poland's internal affairs, the holding of democratic elections, the release of all political prisoners in the USSR, a reduction in the duration of compulsory military service, and the institution of a more equitable system of food distribution.

Western journalists made contact in Estonia

with spokesmen for the group, and were told of the encouragement that the group had received from the Polish example. One source was quoted as saying that "Previously, everyone assumed that nothing could be changed in the Soviet empire. But they have heard ... what strides have been made [in Poland]. And now it does not seem so impossible."[51]

In an article published over a year later, Karl Vaino, Party first secretary in Estonia, described the leaflets as "a vile provocation, similar to those voiced by Solidarity in Poland."[52] Vaino reported that a good deal of what he called "explanatory work" was carried out by "Party and economic activists," suggesting that the authorities went to some lengths to counter the strike call.

In Estonia, the strike call led to scattered work stoppages on 1 December 1981 and again on 4 January 1982. But the strike never became widespread or general and, as far as is known, the call went unheeded in the other Soviet republics. It was, in short, an almost total failure.

Several of the documents cited in this chapter attempted to explain why, when the living and working conditions of Soviet workers were as bad as--if not worse than--those of workers in Poland, Solidarity's example had so little impact in the USSR. Many commentators suggested that one important factor was the almost total lack of contact in the USSR between members of the intelligentsia (in particular, of course, dissident intellectuals) and members of the working class. The crucial role played in 1980-81 by Poland's dissident organisation "KOR" in helping strikers to formulate their demands for independent trade unions led some Soviet dissidents to reexamine their own aims and methods. In the wake of the Polish events, therefore, calls began to be heard for a fresh orientation toward the needs and concerns of ordinary working people.

This question was highlighted by the editors of the independent *samizdat* almanac *Varianty* in their replies (dated not later than November 1981) to a questionnaire compiled by the Paris journal *L'Alternative*.[53] The *Varianty* editors wrote that there was no denying the existence of a "crisis" of traditional forms of dissent in the USSR:

> The orientation of traditional dissent, which gave priority to the development of legal and semi-legal public organisations, has proved ineffectual.... The emphasis put by many dissidents on the non-political character of their movement has not proved its worth.

The key failure of the Soviet human rights movement, in the opinion of the *Varianty* editorial collective, was that although its members understood that "abuse of power is an inherent characteristic" of the regime, "they disarmed themselves politically by their insistence on legality, publicity and openness."

The *Varianty* collective called for a reorientation of dissident activity, the elaboration of "concrete alternatives," the "formation in the near future of political organisations of different tendencies" (that is, the setting up of oppositional political platforms), and a realignment with "those below." "The lessons of the Polish revolution," they went on, "are many-sided and for the time being, unfortunately, the authorities are better able to profit from them than the opposition. For us, the main lesson is that we must seek the springs of our action in the needs of society, ... make concrete criticisms and put forward practical programmes." It had to be admitted, they asserted, "that until now the secretary of the local Party committee has been incomparably closer to real, everyday life than

Sakharov and the members of the Helsinki monitoring groups. One of the lessons of Poland is, of course, the necessity of combining a mass movement with clandestine social and political organisations whose structure is secret."

The *Varianty* document contained a selection of replies to the questionnaire by Soviet citizens from a variety of social backgrounds. Several related specifically to the lessons of the Polish events for the human rights movement, in particular, the desirability of links between intellectuals and members of the working class. As far as this point was concerned, respondents displayed almost total unanimity. Though disagreeing slightly in their assessments of whether or not the Soviet authorities really anticipated a link-up between dissidents and workers, all agreed that in reality the leaders had nothing to fear from that quarter. Sample responses follow.

> "They'd be fools if they were afraid of that. Which of us workers has ever even set eyes on a dissident?" (Moscow stevedore, male, aged 32)

> "If the authorities are afraid of that, they must be afraid of their own shadows. There's no danger of that. And as for the dissidents, they regard the working class in the same way as the Decembrists viewed the *muzhiki* [peasantry]. In theory, they respect them, but in reality they despise them: 'they're drunkards, stupid and submissive, more interested in watching hockey than in reading books.'" (Moscow craftsman, male, aged 33)

> "The authorities are afraid of everything, but to fear a link-up between dissident

> circles and the working class is as absurd as being afraid of meeting a jaguar in the Moscow forest. Unfortunately, there's no likelihood of it at present. And the authorities know that as well as we do." (Teacher from a higher education institute, female, aged 41)

> "[There can be no linkage between the workers and the intellectuals] because they simply don't meet.... [So] who could learn a lesson from the Polish events? The dissidents--yes. But no-one else, because no-one else knows anything about it." (Woman worker from Moscow, aged 30)

The lesson of the Polish events, according to the Moscow craftsman, was that:

> The intellectuals make fine speeches, but it's the people "underneath" who take the action. Nothing sensible is going to come from speeches about human rights. But if they paid more attention to problems like food supplies, vacations, overtime, excessively high production norms--and if they discussed such topics in pamphlets rather than in journals published in five copies--then perhaps in twenty years' time our workers, too, would be persuaded to found a trade union like Solidarity.

The stevedore urged that the human rights movement should "operate on a new basis" by focussing on the living conditions of ordinary people "and not just on the misfortunes of certain dissidents." The main way to get through to people, he added, "is through their stomachs."

A Moscow journalist, male, aged 35, expressed

doubts as to the efficacy of a human rights movement in "a country where it has for centuries been the norm to live by evading rules and laws." There was, he asserted, no "sense of legality [*pravosoznanie*] in Russia," and there was "something slightly absurd about a movement that calls for the observance of laws in such a country."

A Moscow writer, male, aged 29, appeared to express the feelings of the majority when he answered that, while he would like to see the Polish events act as a lesson for the Soviet Union, "Russia isn't Poland.... We shall have to learn to write before we'll be able to print slogans on banners."

CONCLUSION

The materials examined here show that the activities and aspirations of Solidarity met lively interest and warm sympathy among Soviet dissidents. But although numerous cases were reported of leaflets being distributed and declarations of support being issued, no really significant or coordinated incidents of labour unrest are known to have occurred in the USSR under the impact of the Polish example. Nor was there evidence to suggest that attempts were made to form workers' movements, free of state control, at any time during the Solidarity period. The authorities were clearly nervous and on the defensive, as shown by the preventive measures they took when the circulation of leaflets came to their attention and by the ruthlessness with which the KGB pursued its clampdown on nationalist and religious dissent. However, the authorities proved well able to control such isolated and sporadic incidents of labour and social unrest as did occur. And, with the exception of the western borderlands, Soviet society showed itself largely impervious to liberalising influences from outside.

FOOTNOTES TO CHAPTER 9

1. The majority of the documents examined here were published in Radio Liberty's *Arkhiv samizdata* or Samizdat Archive (hereafter AS).

2. AS 4092.

3. This was not the first time Soviet human rights activists had signed declarations of support for East European colleagues. Sakharov, for example, had already spoken in support of human rights movements in Czechoslovakia and Poland; RL 310/80, "Soviet Human Rights Activists Support Polish Workers," by Elizabeth C. Scheetz, 2 September 1980.

4. AS 4452.

5. *Russkaya mysl'*, 11 and 18 September 1980. S. Kuvakin is probably a misprint for V. Kuvakin.

6. AS 4370.

7. The text appeared in the Lithuanian *samizdat* journal *Ausra*. It is quoted here from V. Stanley Vardys, "Polish Echoes in the Baltic," *Problems of Communism*, July-August 1983, pp. 21-34 at p. 25.

8. AS 5373.

9. AS 5371.

10. AS 4370.

11. AS 5127 and 5128.

12. AS 4905.

13. AS 4679.

14. AS 4293.

15. AS 4760.

16. AS 4622.

17. AS 4728.

18. AS 4729.

19. AS 4752 and 4806.

20. AS 4752. Ratushinskaya was later arrested on charges of "anti-Soviet agitation and propaganda" and sentenced to seven years in a strict-regime labour camp and five years' internal exile. She was allowed to leave the USSR at the end of 1986.

21. *Tautos kelias*, November 1980, quoted by Vardys, *loc. cit.*

22. RL 74/82, "Tenth and Eleventh Issues of Estonian *Samizdat* Periodical," by Jaan Pennar, 16 February 1982.

23. RL 57/83, "Fourth, Seventh and Thirteenth Issues of Estonian *Samizdat* Publication," by Jaan Pennar, 31 January 1983.

24. AS 4769; see also RL 41/83, "*Samizdat* Symposium *Sotsialist-82* Reaches the West," by Julia Wishnevsky, 20 January 1983.

25. RL 341/82, "More Details Emerge About 'Socialists' Arrested in USSR Earlier This Year," by Julia Wishnevsky, 23 August 1982.

26. *Christian Science Monitor*, 15 June 1983.

27. Bohdan Nahaylo, "A New Left in Russia," *The New Statesman*, 10 September 1982.

28. AS 4321.

29. RL 427/83, "Ukrainian Dissident Comments on Events in Poland," by Bohdan Nahaylo, 11 November 1983.

30. RL 408/84, "Yurii Lytvyn's Suicide: The Final Protest of an Indomitable Ukrainian Dissident," by Bohdan Nahaylo, 24 October 1984.

31. AS 4331.

32. Zotov, who was active in the human rights movement and a member of SMOT, was arrested in January 1981 and charged with "disseminating fabrications known to be false which defame the Soviet state and social system." Put on trial in July 1981, he was declared not to be responsible for his actions and confined to a psychiatric hospital, from which he was released in 1983.

33. AS 4413.

34. AS 4205.

35. AS 4615. In January 1983, Yankov was convicted on charges of "anti-Soviet agitation and propaganda" and sentenced to four years in a strict-regime labour camp, to be followed by three

years' internal exile.

36. AS 4904; see also RL 319/83, "A *Samizdat* Work on the Events in Poland," by Mario Corti, 24 August 1983.

37. AS 5062 is a Russian-language translation of the Ukrainian original.

38. RL 472/83, "Ukrainian Dissident Comments on Events in Poland," by Bohdan Nahaylo, 11 November 1983.

39. Toward the end of 1977, Vladimir Klebanov announced the formation of an independent trade union; for details, see Chapter 3.

40. RL 472/83.

41. The following sources have been used in the compilation of this section: RL 297/80, "Soviet Policy Towards Dissent Since Khrushchev," by Peter Reddaway, 21 August 1980; contribution by Peter Reddaway in Archie Brown *et. al.*, (eds), *Cambridge Encyclopedia of Russia and the Soviet Union*, Cambridge, 1982, pp. 322-3; Iain Elliot, "Dissent, Opposition and Instability," in Martin McCauley (ed), *The Soviet Union After Brezhnev*, London, 1983; Peter Reddaway, "Dissent in the Soviet Union," *Problems of Communism*, November-December 1983, pp. 1-15; US Department of State, *Human Rights in the USSR*, Washington DC, December 1983; RL 382/84, "The Fall of Khrushchev and the Birth of the Human Rights Movement in the Soviet Union," by Julia Wishnevsky, 8 October 1984; BBC Current Affairs Research and Information Section (CARIS), "Changing Policies Towards Soviet Dissent and Emigration," a series of five interviews with Peter Reddaway conducted by Malcolm Haslett, 3-7 December 1984; RL 89/85, "Dissent under Three Soviet Leaders: Suppression Continues, the Style Varies," by Julia Wishnevsky, 21 March 1985.

42. Reddaway in *Problems of Communism*, *op. cit.*, p. 9.

43. S. Tsvigun, "O proiskakh imperialistiches-

kikh razvedok," *Kommunist*, No 14, 1981, pp. 88-99.

44. *Reuters*, *UPI*, 8 September 1982.

45. *The Times*, 10 August 1982.

46. AS 4904.

47. RL 427/83.

48. AS 4464.

49. AS 4547.

50. AS 4503.

51. BBC CARIS talk, "The Baltic Appeal and the Polish Example," by Malcolm Haslett, 30 November 1981.

52. K. Vaino, "S tochnym znaniem obstanovki," *Kommunist*, No 4, 1983, pp. 51-60.

53. AS 4619, 4653 and 4859. According to AS 4619, *Variant*y has been published since the end of 1977 by a group of people identifying themselves as "social democrats, socialists and Eurocommunists."

Chapter 10

A CHANGE OF TACTICS ON THE PART OF THE AUTHORITIES

Evidence presented in preceding chapters suggested that the Soviet authorities were seriously alarmed by the outbreak of labour unrest in Poland. By the late summer of 1981, however, they seemed to have regained their confidence. The signs indicated that their stop-gap propaganda campaign against the aims and activities of Poland's free trade union movement had so blackened the image of independent trade unionism in the eyes of Soviet citizens that any immediate threat of spillover had been averted.

As this brief chapter tries to show, such a conclusion is prompted by the behaviour of the Soviet authorities, who reversed the emphasis of their propaganda in the autumn of 1981. Instead of being called upon to show more vigorous support of workers' rights, as they were during the early months of the Polish crisis, Soviet trade unions were encouraged to revert to their traditional role of urging their members to work harder and produce more in order to meet the targets of the Five-Year Plan. Further evidence in support of this conclusion, presented in Chapter 8, indicated that from from the start the demands of the Polish workers met with little sympathy among the broad mass of the Soviet population and that, by the summer of 1981, a significant proportion of the Soviet people had come to share their leaders' negative interpretation of the events in Poland.

Reversion to traditional trade union priorities could be traced to the autumn of 1981. An early sign was provided when the slogans published in October of that year in honour of the anniversary of the 1917 Revolution dropped the call they had made in 1980 for the trade unions to concern themselves with workers' living and and working conditions.[1] The shift in emphasis may accordingly be said to have predated the declaration of martial law in Poland in December 1981 and the banning of independent trade union activity there. As it happens, it coincided with a period of intense activity on the part of the Soviet trade unions. In preparation for their Seventeenth Congress, scheduled to take place in March 1982, the unions spent the autumn and winter of 1981-82 holding report and election conferences at every level, from the lowest primary organisation upward. These were followed by republican trade union congresses and all-Union congresses of the branch unions. Advance notice was given by the newspaper *Trud* on 4 August 1981 in an editorial which emphasised that participants "must focus their main attention on the trade unions' active participation in realising plans for the country's economic and social growth."

This remained the keynote of the report and election campaign. As the fortnightly magazine *Agitator* noted in March 1982, at the campaign's close, "The main theme during the report and election conferences was the further development and improvement of socialist competition."[2] And, writing in *Novoe vremya* in January 1982, AUCCTU secretary Aleksei Viktorov returned to the formula which, though never totally abandoned, had been played down during Solidarity's heyday. (It was used, for example, by Brezhnev at the Twenty-fifth Congress of the CPSU in 1976, but avoided by him at the Twenty-sixth in 1981.) In Viktorov's words:

> The trade unions are aware that improvement of people's living and working conditions is impossible without a steady increase in productivity. One can only distribute and consume that which one has first produced.[3]

The work of the unions came in for a fair amount of routine criticism during the report and election conferences. In its editorial of 18 December 1981, for example, *Trud* reported that a number of union officials failed to win reelection because a "formalistic" and "condescending" approach had placed them out of touch with their members. The chairman of the trade union committee in a factory in Alma-Ata was said, for example, to shun meeting the workers altogether. "Unfortunately," *Trud* declared, "such cases are not isolated incidents."

Other union organisations came under fire for the way the report and election conferences were conducted. For example, *Trud* reported how delegates to one such conference were "elected" in a transport depot in Perm':

> "The boss came into the garage with a list of candidates already typed out," the workers recounted, "and told us to vote for the whole lot all in one go."[4]

In other sections of the same depot, delegates were elected even more simply: "Various people were just called by telephone and instructed to turn up for the conference.[5]

When the time came for the trade union to hold its report and election conference in a Dushanbe jewellery factory, *Trud* reported, the enterprise director informed activists "they could have either the conference or the plan, but not both," and ordered elected delegates to stay at the workbench instead.[6]

Though fairly rare, there was some criticism of unions for failing to protect workers' interests. For instance, *Trud* described how the union committee in a Sochi wood-working combine acquiesced in the victimisation of two conscientious workers. The factory director sacked the two after they informed the police that the combine was running a profitable sideline manufacturing leather shoes for sale on the black market, and the trade union committee sanctioned the dismissals.[7]

Even this example, however, was not a clear-cut case of criticism of trade union failure to protect workers' rights since the publicity given to it also contained a strong anti-corruption element. From the autumn on, charges that the unions were slow in seeking better living and working conditions for their members and in protecting workers' rights against managerial encroachment were taking second billing to exhortations that "high labour productivity and increasing prosperity are interrelated."[8]

An editorial in *Trud* of 6 January 1982, published as the report and election campaign neared its close, exemplifed the return to traditional priorities:

> Striving to fulfill their dual task, the trade unions must concentrate first of all on raising efficiency, intensifying production and improving the quality of work.

The renewal of emphasis on production targets should doubtless be viewed against the background of the continued slowdown in the rate of Soviet economic growth which was leading at this time to stagnation, if not actual reduction, of the living standards of the general population. As has already been mentioned, the USSR was facing its third successive harvest failure and found itself forced, in the winter of 1981-82, to introduce widescale food rationing; food riots were even reported from some areas. The Soviet leaders were unlikely to have forgotten that the Revolution of February 1917 was sparked by bread riots in Petrograd, or that the Polish strikes grew out of protests over food shortages and price rises. Uncomfortably aware that many of the conditions that had led to the outbreak of strikes in Poland existed in an even more acute form among the Soviet workforce, Brezhnev and his colleagues appeared to conclude that any threat to their rule was at least as likely to arise out of domestic discontent over shortages of food and consumer goods as from any spillover from events outside Soviet borders. The scope for countering this risk by allocating more resources to the consumer was limited by the economic slowdown; what was needed was a sharp improvement in productivity.

It appears probable, moreover, that by the autumn of 1981 the Soviet authorities were reasonably confident that their ideological and propaganda campaign against free trade unionism and the right to strike had had the desired effect upon public opinion, and that the threat of spillover from Poland had receded. There seems also at this time to have been some recovery of confidence on the part of the leadership in its ability to increase pressure from above without provoking unrest from below. Accordingly, the authorities began to adopt a series of measures aimed at tightening controls at every level of Soviet society.

This trend toward the adoption of tighter social controls could be discerned from the spring of 1982 onward, that is, it coincided with the election of Yurii Andropov to the Secretariat of the Central Committee of the CPSU in May of that year. The trend became even clearer once Andropov was elected, after Brezhnev's death in November 1982, to the post of general secretary. "Thus," in the words of a leading American analyst, Harry Gelman:

> fourteen months after General Wojciech Jaruzelski had taken control of the Polish party, and eleven months after he had imposed martial law and "discipline" on

> Poland, the man who had headed the KGB longer than anyone else in Soviet history became head of the Soviet party. He enjoyed particular support from the minister of defense [Dmitrii Ustinov], and he held aloft the banner of "discipline" for the Soviet Union. It is by no means impossible that the Polish example had contributed to the Soviet result.[9]

It appears, in other words, that a debate over social policy sparked by the Polish events, together with the deepening of the USSR's own economic difficulties, may have provided Andropov with a platform from which to make his bid for power during Brezhnev's last year of life. Alternatively, the tough domestic policy line that emerged following Andropov's promotion may have been worked out by a collective leadership which then chose Andropov as the right man to tackle the job in hand.

FOOTNOTES TO CHAPTER 10

1. The slogan for 1981 read merely: "Long live the Soviet trade unions--the school of communism, an influential force in our society!" (*Pravda*, 11 October 1981). For the 1980 slogan, see Chapter 4, footnote 10.
2. *Agitator*, No 5, 1982, p. 2.
3. *Novoe vremya*, No 3, 1982, pp. 5-7.
4. *Trud*, 27 November 1981.
5. *Ibid.*
6. *Ibid.*, 10 October 1981.
7. *Ibid.*, 8 December 1981.
8. *Ibid.*, 13 October 1981.
9. Harry Gelman, *The Brezhnev Politburo and the Decline of Detente*, Ithaca, NY, 1984, p. 185.

Chapter 11

FOCUS ON "COUNTERPROPAGANDA"

There were at least two schools of thought within the Soviet leadership as to the lessons to be drawn from the Polish events. One, whose spokesman was Konstantin Chernenko, claimed Poland had got into difficulties because its leaders had lost touch with the masses. To guard against a repetition of the Polish events in the USSR, Chernenko argued, Soviet leaders should make greater efforts to foster public confidence in the Party and its leadership. This could best be achieved not by increasing repression and control, nor by instituting radical changes in the economy, but simply by making ordinary people feel more involved in the process of government. In the early months of the Polish crisis, it was this school of thought that carried the day.

Another school--represented by Mikhail Suslov, the CPSU's "chief ideologist"--argued that Poland's troubles were to be blamed on the Polish Party's failure to exercise strong leadership. This group advocated tighter discipline at all levels of both Polish and Soviet society but, like the first, saw no need for social or economic reforms.[1] This chapter focusses on the "disciplinarians," whose views made themselves increasingly felt as 1981 ran its course. Their calls for stricter ideological controls led, in 1982-83, to the introduction of a major "counterpropaganda" campaign.

This is not to say that the Polish events were the sole reason for the introduction of the campaign. Rather, they played a catalysing role in a process that began in the late 1970s with the souring of East-West detente. Soviet Party leaders became uncomfortably aware at that time of the strong influence exercised by Western ideas over the minds and aspirations of many Soviet people. As Soviet economic growth continued its seemingly inexorable slowdown, the authorities displayed acute anxiety lest stagnating popular living standards should increase the allure of Western values still further. Concern was expressed that old-fashioned political indoctrination was becoming increasingly ineffective among young people.[2] Speaking at a plenary meeting of the CPSU Central Committee in November 1978, Brezhnev criticised the propaganda apparatus in unusually blunt terms.[3] A Central Committee decree devoted to ideological work followed soon after, in April 1979. Complaining that propagandists tended "to smooth over and avoid unresolved problems and acute questions and to hush up shortcomings and difficulties existing in real life," the decree called for

> a systematic, purposeful and uncompromising struggle...using all means of propaganda and education...to eradicate ugly vestiges of the past.... It is necessary to use both verbal persuasion and the harsh force of law in the struggle against these phenomena.[4]

The problem was that the quality of propaganda work was not keeping pace with the rising expectations and educational standards of the population. Public opinion surveys conducted in Chelyabinsk oblast revealed, for example, that whereas 59 percent of those questioned in 1970 had been satisfied with the standard of public lectures, by 1980 the figure had dropped to less than 40 percent. The reason for this decline was not that people disliked lectures--the respondents said they would like more lectures "on every topic without exception"--but that lecturers were unwilling to delve into subjects of interest as deeply as their audiences wanted. Of those questioned, 33 percent called for lecturers "to speak more openly about the objective situation inside the country and abroad," and "not to skirt round the existing shortcomings and contradictions of socialism"; while 42 percent criticised lecturers for avoiding difficult problems, and 44 percent for giving unconvincing replies to questions from the audience.[5]

The most serious consequence of the failure of propaganda work, in the eyes of the authorities, was that Soviet citizens were turning with increasing frequency to outside sources of information, Western broadcasts included. This was especially true of young people. Cynicism about official ideology was accompanied by growing interest in religion and national identity. The Polish unrest was marked by similar sentiments, and Soviet authorities began to search for ways of immunising the population against foreign influences in general and against Poland's turmoil in particular.

Brezhnev touched on this question in his report to the Twenty-sixth Congress of the CPSU in February 1981, when the Polish events were at their height. He called for a restructuring (*perestroika*) to bring ideological work up to date. It was one thing, Brezhnev said, "to address our people when they were not yet trained and had little education, but quite another to address the Soviet man of today."[6]

The spring of 1981 saw a series of conferences devoted to the "restructuring" of ideological work. The first was held in Moscow, under the auspices of the CPSU Central Committee, between 20 and 25 April. It was addressed by a glittering array of top Soviet leaders and attended by officials in the field of ideology from every level of the Party hierarchy.[7]

Suslov set the tone. In his opening speech he declared that, in the "deteriorating international climate, ... our class enemies are acting ever more boldly and craftily." The Soviet population was increasingly subject to foreign propaganda that "maliciously exploits our every shortcoming, failure and difficulty in its attempt to destroy Soviet citizens' class consciousness and their faith in our ideals." Suslov warned against underestimating the effect of this propaganda on "a certain section" of the population.[8]

The keynote address was delivered by the Central Committee secretary with responsibility for propaganda, Mikhail Zimyanin. The events in Poland, Zimyanin asserted, provided the clearest example of the "psychological warfare" being waged against the socialist community, and were caused as much by "imperialist subversion" as by such factors as "mistakes by Poland's former leaders." In the light of the Polish events, he said, it was essential to enhance the "assertive character" of propaganda work, and not to ignore its "counterpropagandistic aspect."[9]

To judge from the (incomplete) collection of documents published after the conference, the overall tone of the speeches was conservative. Many speakers warned of the dangers of Western propaganda and called for a reassertion of traditional Soviet values. According to Imants Andersons, secretary for ideology of the Communist Party of Latvia, the importance of counterpropaganda was "repeatedly stressed" by conference participants. Andersons himself called for increased attention to such work on the grounds that, "though the wiles of imperialism are no secret, ... today's Soviet youngsters, who have never lived under capitalism, have only a vague understanding of its true nature."[10] One Western analysis summed up the conference as follows:

> [T]he unacknowledged subject of the 1981 conference was the impact of the Polish crisis on the Soviet population. While

> most of the speakers did not mention Poland specifically, they were clearly concerned about the attitudes of the Soviet population in the light of the crisis in Poland and about what should be done to ensure satisfactory civic behavior. Their diagnoses and prescriptions contained repeated hints that the events in Poland were being studied as an object lesson for the Soviet party.[11]

There were signs, too, of a clash within the leadership between the "Suslov" and "Chernenko" approaches to the Polish question. Chernenko was not among the conference participants--at least, he gave no speech there--yet the official volume of conference papers published after the event included the speech he made on 22 April (that is, while the ideology conference was going on) at the Kremlin ceremony marking the anniversary of Lenin's birth. Incongruously placed between Suslov's opening remarks and Zimyanin's keynote speech, Chernenko's remarks (which have already been touched on in Chapter 4) struck a very different note. Indeed, they took explicit issue with those who saw the answer to Soviet problems in "more discipline"--which Chernenko pointedly equated with "less democracy."

Chernenko advocated practical, rather than doctrinaire, remedies. He spoke of the need to accelerate housing construction and increase the production of consumer goods, to reduce the share of heavy manual labour in the economy, and to raise workers' overall earnings. He warned against attributing (as the 1979 Central Committee decree had done) all the USSR's problems to "vestiges of the past"; the causes were also to be found, he asserted, in "present-day practice" and "the miscalculations of certain people." Finally,

Chernenko urged Party officials "to pay attention to people, to their conditions of work and their everyday life."[12]

Where ideology and propaganda were concerned, however, it was Suslov's views that prevailed. A series of authoritative editorials in the Soviet press at this time warned of the threat posed by a purported increase in anti-Soviet propaganda from the West. *Pravda*'s editorial of 27 April 1981, for example, reiterated Suslov's charge that it was the West's aim to "erode" the ideals of Soviet citizens. The following day, *Izvestia* called for "heightened vigilance" to counter Western ideas.

The conclusions of the April conference were disseminated throughout the USSR by a series of conferences held during the next two months. Speaking in May at a conference of trade union activists, for example, Aleksei Shibaev warned of an increase in "ideological sabotage" and called for "heightened vigilance" in response.[13] Conferences were also convened by the ministry of internal affairs and by the Party organisations of Leningrad, Latvia, Armenia, Estonia, Azerbaidzhan and Ukraine.[14] Speaking in Riga, Latvian Party leader Avgust Voss claimed the Polish events attested to the effectiveness of "Western subversion," and cautioned against underestimating its "economic, political, and moral" impact on the population.[15]

The holding of a national conference of KGB officials--attended, unusually, by Brezhnev himself --also seemed to be linked to the campaign for increased vigilance toward foreign influences.[16] The concern of the secret police about the impact of Western ideas on Soviet youngsters was shown by the publication in May 1981 in the journal of the Soviet youth organisation, the Komsomol, of an article by the deputy chairman of the KGB, Viktor Chebrikov. Painting a lurid picture of moral malaise among some youngsters, Chebrikov asserted that young people were especially vulnerable to foreign ideas, and that the Soviet Union's enemies were using ever more dangerous and sophisticated weapons--revisionism, bourgeois nationalism, religion and consumerism, as well as subversive political concepts such as pluralism--in their attempts to undermine the trust of Soviet youth in their leaders and their socialist system. Chebrikov laid much of the blame on poor propaganda work. "It must be stressed," he wrote,

> that imperialism's ideological sabotage succeeds only where the dissemination of hostile ideology does not meet the rebuff it deserves, and where young people do not receive clear and precise answers to the questions that trouble them.[17]

As Poland's crisis deepened, the anxiety of the Soviet leaders increased. The Moscow correspondent of the London *Times* wrote in early June 1981:

> There are clear signs of nervousness in the air. Intellectuals have reported renewed pressure on them to conform, and ordinary Russians are increasingly being warned not to have anything to do with foreigners. It is as if the Soviet leadership can see a tough period ahead, and is preparing the population for the inevitable return to a harsher climate.[18]

Writing in *Pravda* in July, Richard Kosolapov, chief editor of *Kommunist*, expressed concern at what he saw as a serious loss of class consciousness among Soviet workers. Kosolapov attributed this trend to the growing influence of Western ideas, and cited the Polish experience as an example of what might happen if the trend were ignored. He blamed the spread of "subversive" ideas in Poland on poor ideological work and on encouragement of unrealistically high material expectations among the Polish people. Only effective Party leadership, Kosolapov wrote, would enable workers to develop "spiritual immunity" to bourgeois ideas.[19]

In an article in *Pravda* on 13 November 1981, Academician Petr Fedoseev, vice-president of the USSR Academy of Sciences and a former director of the CPSU Central Committee's Institute of Marxism-Leninism, stated that the failure of Poland's leaders to exercise firm ideological control was a major reason for that country's upheavals:

> The historical experience of the USSR and the fraternal countries teaches us that without combating private property habits, nationalism, religious fanaticism, and petty-bourgeois thinking it is impossible to build and perfect a new way of life.... It is no accident that the present crisis in Poland was preceded not only by a worsening of the economic situation, but also by a sharp deterioration in the ideological climate, the spread of philistine, consumerist sentiments and nationalist prejudices, and the weakening of class vigilance.

A call for the use of "counterpropaganda" to combat Western influences appeared in *Pravda* on 30 November 1981, that is, shortly before the declaration of martial law in Poland. A two-page unsigned editorial, entitled "Raising the Level of Work with the Masses" and bearing Suslov's imprint, was harshly critical of prevailing standards of Soviet propaganda. The international situation was "sharpening": the United States was "concentrating its subversive activity" against Poland and the other socialist countries "in an attempt to erode the class consciousness of the workers." *Pravda* called for "additional measures" to achieve a radical reorientation of propaganda work: the achievements of socialism must be more assertively publicised and the attempts of the ideological adversary to exploit "real or imaginary difficulties and failures" more actively resisted. Summing up, the editorial called for "far more attention to counterpropaganda, both inside and outside the country." Party organisations were instructed to regard counterpropaganda as "one of their most important activities," to be carried out "with due regard both to the specific situation in different areas of the country as well as to the degree of influence exerted by bourgeois propaganda over various sections of the population."

Writing in March 1982 in the journal for propagandists, *Slovo lektora*, Georgii Smirnov, first deputy head of the Propaganda Department of the CPSU Central Committee (later an adviser on ideological affairs to Mikhail Gorbachev and, later still, director of the Institute of Marxism-Leninism), noted "a whole range of objective factors complicating our economic development." Smirnov warned that "a situation of scarcity" was likely to give rise to "pettybourgeois attitudes" ripe for exploitation by the class enemy. In other words, the Soviet authorities were uncomfortably aware that the failure of the economy to satisfy popular demand for consumer goods and services was threatening to lead to discontent and possibly to political unrest. To avert this danger, Smirnov informed his readers, the Party was calling for "significantly increased attention to counterpropaganda, at home as well as abroad."[20]

Fresh impetus was provided by a conference on ideology held in the Estonian capital of Tallinn on 12-14 October 1982. The conference was acclaimed as "the most representative and widest-ranging forum of theoreticians and practitioners in the field of ideological work" ever held in the Soviet Union.[21]

Suslov had died earlier in the year. The keynote address was delivered by Konstantin Rusakov, Central Committee secretary with responsibility for bloc relations. Rusakov claimed that a "qualitative change" had occurred in imperialist propaganda: the class enemy had passed from "ideological struggle" to "psychological warfare." The West, he asserted, was seeking ways of "directly influencing the populations of the socialist countries so as to undermine their confidence in the communist cause and even ... to create some kind of antisocialist opposition." Stressing the "anxiety" aroused in Soviet people by the Polish events, Rusakov said it was essential "fully to reveal the indisputable advantages of socialism over capitalism."[22]

The advantages of socialism must be stressed but so too, asserted other speakers at the Tallinn conference, must "the correct attitude toward difficulties and shortcomings." The population must be educated to reject imperialist propaganda, "which lives like a parasite on real or imagined difficulties and failures." Estonia's experience was held up as an example of successful counterpropaganda work and the republican Party first secretary, Karl Vaino, spoke of the attempts made late in 1981 to start a strike movement in the Baltic republics. (For details, see Chapter 9.) The strike call went unheeded, Vaino boasted, thanks to extensive "explanatory work" undertaken by the Estonian Party.

Following Andropov's transfer in May 1982 to the Central Committee Secretariat, several measures were adopted that suggested the campaign to insulate the population against dangerous foreign influences was intensifying. The most dramatic was the cutting-off, in mid-1982, of direct-dial telephone links between the USSR on the one hand, and the USA, most West European countries, and Japan, on the other. In June the USSR announced it was "cutting back" these facilities; by the end of September, all direct-dial links had been cut. Observers agreed the most likely explanation was that the Soviet authorities wished to reduce the flow of East-West information and to hamper contacts between Soviet and Western citizens.

Repression of dissent seemed to become harsher during the spring and summer of 1982. Artists, writers, religious believers, Jewish activists, Russian nationalists, unofficial trade unionists, and a number of young members of "socialist discussion groups" were interrogated, searched, detained and, in many cases, arrested. The USSR's fledgling independent peace group, which announced its existence in June 1982, became an immediate target of KGB harassment. And in September the Moscow branch of the Helsinki monitoring group announced it was suspending its activities because of the depletion of its ranks resulting from arrests of members and because of threats of arrest made against its few members surviving at liberty.

The "counterpropaganda" campaign received a further boost after Andropov's election as general secretary. A Central Committee plenum held in June 1983 was devoted entirely to ideological work. It was addressed both by the new leader and by Chernenko who, defeated in the succession struggle, now held the post of ideology secretary. Chernenko seized the opportunity to repeat his warning that setbacks in the Soviet economy and in the pace of social development could have a dangerous impact on popular morale:

> Due consideration must be paid to the fact that the views and sentiments of working people are formed under the influence not only of our achievements, but of shortcomings and difficulties too.[23]

Addressing the Central Committee plenum the following day, Andropov laid particular stress on the subject of counterpropaganda and told his audience they were witnessing

> a confrontation, unprecedented in its intensity and acuteness in the whole postwar period, between two diametrically opposed world views: socialism and imperialism. A struggle is under way for the hearts and minds of billions of people.... What we need is a well worked out, coordinated system of counter-propaganda.[24]

The task, Andropov went on, must be tackled without delay. Party organisations in certain regions--Belorussia, Estonia, Kazakhstan, Moscow, Leningrad and Primorsky krai (situated in the Soviet Far East on the Pacific coast) being most often mentioned--had established counterpropaganda programmes well before the June plenum, and their experience was held up for emulation. At a meeting in the middle of October, the Politburo mapped out

> a number of measures for developing the ideological and political content of informational and counterpropaganda work, for organising counterpropaganda, and for coordinating the activities of the mass media and ideological departments.[25]

How does "counterpropaganda" differ from the traditional Soviet forms of agitation?

The concept has its roots in a speech given by Lenin in December 1920. Defending a proposal under attack from other Bolshevik leaders that would have allowed the creation of foreign concessions on Soviet territory, Lenin proposed the use of "counterpropaganda" to dispel any unfavourable impressions made on poverty-stricken Soviet workers by the higher living standards of their capitalist counterparts. Lenin posed the question:

> Can we really not protect ourselves against such propaganda with our own counterpropaganda? Can we really not prove to the workers that, while capitalism can, of course, create better conditions for a certain group of its workers, the conditions of the remaining mass of workers are not improved as a result?[26]

Despite this Leninist seal of approval, the term fell into disuse. It was not to be found, for example, in the 1979 Central Committee decree on ideological work, and it was novel enough for Latvia's ideology secretary Imants Andersons to include a definition when he used it at the ideology conference of April 1981. "Under conditions of ideological struggle and diversion by the class enemy," Andersons declared, "counterpropaganda helps Soviet people to understand the class content of world events, and to perceive the interests that lie behind them."[27]

The official definition is as follows:

> Counterpropaganda is a specialised form of ideological activity aimed at exposing the goals, methods and arguments of propaganda hostile to socialism, and at neutralising ideological subversion. Counterpropaganda is based on a correct understanding of the processes of reality and their *inherent contradictions, which our ideological enemies delight in exploiting.*[28] (Emphasis added)

Propagandists are recommended to "study the content and methods of enemy propaganda to find out what specific campaigns are aimed at which specific social, demographic and occupational groups of the population." Through the use of public opinion polls, interviews and questionnaires, they are required to "determine the ideological and socio-psychological ability of these groups to withstand enemy propaganda." Propaganda techniques specially tailored to suit different audiences can then be elaborated.[29] This differentiation between specific social groups distinguishes counterpropaganda from more traditional *agitprop*.

In Estonia, for example, sociological work and public opinion polling have been carried out on a regular basis for over a decade, and are said to have led to a great improvement in propaganda work among the population. A study conducted in 1979 revealed that schoolchildren in the republic preferred to watch "foreign" (that is, Finnish) television programmes rather than Soviet ones; these findings provided the basis for measures "to boost the political education of schoolchildren" as well as the creation of new programmes designed to appeal especially to young people.[30]

Vera Tolz of Radio Liberty has noted that, following the Central Committee plenum of June 1983, articles in the Soviet press dealing with the darker side of Western life became more informative and descriptive. Details were for example given about where jobless Americans live, how they dress, and what they eat. In order to give such reports greater authenticity, she has pointed out, media reports about the West gradually began to include criticism of relevant aspects of Soviet life.[31]

As for organisational aspects, the following account--published in 1983--of how counterpropaganda was administered in Latvia was typical of many others:

> The Central Committee of the Communist Party of Latvia has created a counter-propaganda council consisting of eminent scientists and leading cultural and educational figures. Similar councils have been established by city and district Party committees, the Central Committee of the Latvian Komsomol, and local Komsomol committees. Their function is to organise and direct the work of lecturers at work places, houses of culture, and people's places of residence.... A republican group of lecturers specialising in foreign policy propaganda ... has been set up. Similar groups have been established in almost all our cities and districts, and measures have been adopted to bring our ideological cadres up to date on world affairs.[32]

In many areas the authorities decided to put their maximum efforts into work with young people. Complaints were voiced by Party propagandists about young people's "political naivete" and "retarded sense of citizenship."[33] These were blamed on the fact that the younger generation "was not steeled in class struggle...and did not experience the horrors of war."[34] Professor Evgenii Nozhin of the Academy of Social Sciences of the CPSU Central Committee lamented that:

> Bourgeois mass culture is making inroads in our society through a certain type of music.... Rock, pop and disco music is immensely--even excessively--popular.... Fashion in clothes can also exert an alien influence over young people....If American jeans, with their fashionable labels, become a materialised fragment of alien

> reality and even a sign of prestige, fashion becomes the bearer of bourgeois "sociological propaganda." Alien symbols on clothing, such as the American flag, rock music "idols" and "free love" slogans, always have some underlying ideological message. Young people ... do not realise that, in pursuit of the bright and the unusual, defiance of what is generally accepted may turn into blasphemy.[35]

Descriptions abound of counterpropaganda techniques employed in work with young people. An official from Brest oblast, which adjoins the Soviet-Polish border, reported:

> We are striving to draw well-trained specialists into organising discotheques and youth evenings. Programmes such as "Music in the Struggle for Peace," "Never Let It Be Repeated," and "My Blue-Eyed Belorussia" are very popular.[36]

"Skilled commentators" were reported to be running the discos in the Crimean town of Kerch' who, "when introducing the next Western singer or pop group, explain the song's political character."[37] Whenever Western films were shown in the northern seaport of Murmansk, "a skillful presentation is first given by an expert, right there in the cinema."[38]

It will come as no surprise to any reader who has followed the story as far as this to learn that the USSR's western borderlands--the Baltic states, Western Ukraine and Western Belorussia--were considered to be at special risk from foreign propaganda, and that it was in these areas that counterpropaganda work was conducted with the greatest vigour. Of particular interest is the following account of how counterpropaganda was organised in Brest oblast--a region which "embarked upon the path of socialist transformation twenty years later than the eastern areas of Belorussia," and which, as mentioned above, borders on Poland:

> Additional measures to intensify the class orientation of the educational process have been adopted by Party organisations in connexion with the aggravated situation in the PPR [Polish People's Republic]. Not one inhabitant [of the oblast] remained indifferent to these events.... As the situation in the PPR unfolded, a new task arose--that of analysing and explaining to people the objective and subjective causes of the situation there, and exposing the slanderous fabrications of Western radio centres aimed at Poland and at our country. Many inhabitants of Brest oblast have close relations in the PPR. The fact that a considerable part of the oblast's inhabitants are able to watch Polish television programmes cannot be ignored. Before martial law was introduced in Poland, programmes of an anticommunist nature were sometimes broadcast.... Historical facts were frequently distorted, and hostile attacks against our country were permitted. The inhabitants of this oblast could not fail to be disturbed by the political carelessness that issued from the mouths of some Polish leaders. In these circumstances, the oblast Party organisation conducted constant and efficient work to explain the situation.[39]

The populations of the Western borderlands were

not the only Soviet citizens for whom special counterpropaganda programmes were created. Another group singled out for attention consisted of merchant seamen and fishermen, held to be particularly vulnerable because they spent long periods at sea, visited foreign ports, and often met citizens of other nations. A conference on "Ideological Struggle and Counterpropaganda" was, for example, held in November 1983 in the Pacific port of Vladivostok, located close to the Soviet border with China. The secretary of the Party organisation of the Far Eastern Shipping Line described the perils of life at sea. It was not, he said, storms and typhoons that made seafaring so hazardous; far more threatening were the dangers of life "in the front line of psychological warfare":

> Soviet [Pacific] seamen are drenched by a downpour of false and specially cooked-up information emanating from fifteen hostile radio stations.... Our seamen must be vigilant when they find themselves in foreign ports....They often encounter missionaries of various religious denominations...who strive to instill in them the idea that the Soviet system needs a bit of correcting, that it should be brought closer to capitalism.... Moreover, our vessels are often visited by guests who suffer from forgetfulness and leave behind ...various books, magazines and leaflets of an anti-Soviet or religious content, both of which are harmful.[40]

It appears, to sum up, that the Polish events, combined with deteriorating East-West relations and a decline in popular living standards caused by a slowdown in Soviet economic growth, greatly alarmed the Brezhnev leadership. Fear of popular discontent prompted the authorities to seek new and differentiated means of countering the attraction exerted by foreign influences over broad sections of the Soviet population. To the extent that the counterpropaganda campaign gradually led, as Vera Tolz has suggested, not only to more vivid descriptions of the ills of Western society but also to some criticism of Soviet social problems, the campaign may even be seen as contributing to the policy of openness (*glasnost'*) later introduced under the leadership of Mikhail Gorbachev.

FOOTNOTES TO CHAPTER 11

1. The same argument, coming to slightly different conclusions, is to be found in an interview with Richard Pipes published in *Time Magazine*, 1 March 1982.
2. See, for example, *Sovetskaya Rossiya*, 22 June 1982.
3. *Pravda*, 28 November 1978.
4. *Ibid.*, 6 May 1979.
5. *Ibid.*, 12 and 13 November 1981.
6. *Pravda*, 24 February 1981.
7. *Za vysokoe kachestvo i deistvennost' ideologicheskoi raboty*, Moscow, Politizdat, 1981.
8. *Ibid.*, p. 7.
9. *Ibid.*, pp. 59, 63, 65-66.
10. *Ibid.*, p. 488. The conference split up into a number of workshops; that which seems to have dealt most directly with the subject of counterpropaganda heard speeches from, among others, the ideology secretaries of the Party committees of Primorsky krai (in the Far East, adjoining the Chinese border, and containing the major seaport of Vladivostok), Kaliningrad oblast on the Baltic, L'vov oblast in Western Ukraine, and Brest oblast in Western Belorussia; the last three areas all adjoin

the Polish border (*ibid.*, pp. 570-71).

11. FBIS Trends, "New Book Confirms Leadership Concern Over Public Discontent," 6 January 1982.

12. *Za vysokoe kachestvo...*, pp. 12-33.

13. *Trud*, 15 May 1981.

14. FBIS Trends, "Conferences Signal New Stress on Ideology, Internal Discipline," 10 June 1981, and "Moscow Fights Polish Spillover with Ideology, Reform," 5 August 1981.

15. *Sovetskaya Latviya*, 19 July 1981.

16. *Pravda*, 27 May 1981.

17. *Molodoi kommunist*, No 4, 1981, pp. 28-34.

18. *The Times*, 9 June 1981.

19. *Pravda*, 31 July 1981.

20. *Slovo lektora*, No 3, 1982, pp. 1-11.

21. *TASS*, 14 October 1982.

22. Quotations are taken from reports on the conference published in *Partiinaya zhizn'*, No 21, 1982, pp. 12-20, and *Voprosy istorii KPSS*, No 2, 1983, pp. 96-108.

23. *TASS*, 14 June 1983.

24. *TASS*, 15 June 1983.

25. *Pravda*, 15 October 1983.

26. V.I. Lenin, *Sochineniya*, fifth edition, Vol. 42, p. 116; quoted in RL 124/85, "Counterpropaganda: A 'New Weapon' of Soviet Ideologists," by Sergei Voronitsyn, 18 April 1985.

27. *Za vysokoe kachestvo...*, p. 488.

28. *Sotsiologicheskie issledovaniya*, No 3, 1983, pp. 36-44.

29. *Sotsiologicheskie issledovaniya, loc. cit.*

30. *Ibid.*

31. RL 126/87, "Soviet Media Coverage of the United States and the Campaign for *Glasnost'*," by Vera Tolz, April 6, 1987.

32. *Partiinaya zhizn'*, No 14, 1983, pp. 65-68.

33. *Moscow Radio*, 13 September 1983.

34. *Partiinaya zhizn', loc. cit.*

35. *Slovo lektora*, No 1, 1984, pp. 28-35.

36. *Kommunist*, No 4, 1984, pp. 27-36.
37. *Sovetskaya Rossiya*, 30 September 1983.
38. *Partiinaya zhizn'*, No 16, 1983, pp. 39-42.
39. *Kommunist*, *op. cit.*
40. *Vladivostok Radio*, 28 November 1983.

Chapter 12

ATTEMPTS TO TIGHTEN LABOUR DISCIPLINE

As soon as he was elected Party leader, Andropov launched a vigorous campaign to improve discipline in the workplace. His aim was to raise the morale of the Soviet population which had sunk, during Brezhnev's last years, to dangerously low levels. A related and equally important aim was to boost labour productivity and reverse the decline in the rate of Soviet economic growth.

As has already been mentioned, Soviet GNP grew from 1979 to 1982 at less than 2.0 percent per annum. Therefore, the Polish crisis erupted at a time when Soviet economic growth was barely keeping pace with the rate of growth of the population, and the "social compact" between leaders and led--dependent as it is generally understood to be upon the ability of the authorities to maintain a slow but nonetheless perceptible rise in the standard of living of the general population--was beginning to show signs of strain. Seen against this background, the Polish events could not fail to alarm the Soviet leaders. Their initial response, as has been seen, was to make "consumerist" policy adjustments. Then, as they regained confidence, they shifted instead to a policy of "discipline."

Opinions differ as to the reasons and, accordingly, the remedies for the Soviet Union's economic slowdown. While the view is widely held among Western specialists that the root cause lies in the inherent inefficiency of the USSR's overcentralised economy, systemic factors are not solely to blame for the deterioration of the country's economic performance.

In the past, the USSR was able to achieve rapid growth by mobilising its seemingly inexhaustible supplies of land, labour and raw materials, but such a strategy of "extensive" economic growth can be maintained no longer. First, cheap and easily attainable reserves of mineral and fuel resources have been exhausted. Even more importantly, the Soviet Union's working population has almost stopped growing. Whereas the labour force grew in the 1960s at a rate of over 4.0 percent per annum, its growth slowed to an annual rate of 1.9 percent in the first half of the 1970s, and to 1.5 percent in the second. Now, in the 1980s, it is growing at less than 1.0 percent a year.[1]

The shortage of labour is particularly acute since the USSR has already achieved high, almost maximum, rates of labour force participation. In 1970, 93 percent of males aged between 20 and 59, and 89 percent of females aged between 20 and 54, were already employed in the official economy. In addition, about one in four persons of pensionable age is still working. Accordingly, there are virtually no surplus reserves that can be drawn into the workforce.[2]

But the problem is not simply one of absolute numbers. Nearly all the growth of the labour force in the 1980s and 1990s is set to come from the populations of the Central Asian and, to a lesser extent, the Caucasian republics, where birthrates are high. Birthrates in the Soviet industrial heartland--the RSFSR, Ukraine and the Baltic states --are, in contrast, actually declining. Not only do Central Asian and Caucasian youngsters tend to be relatively low in skills, with a poor mastery of the Russian language; they are also, by and large, extremely unwilling to leave their native areas in search of work. These areas are, however, predominantly rural; they are not ones in which an industrial base already exists or where newly discovered natural resources await exploitation. The central authorities face a dilemma: either these young people will have somehow to be lured from their native villages and persuaded to move to the established manufacturing areas in the European part of the USSR and to the inhospitable areas of Siberia where natural resources are still abundant, or scarce resources will have to be invested to create new industries in Central Asia--threatening a transfer of economic power to the area which Moscow would be very unlikely to welcome.

Many observers argue that the real cause of the USSR's labour shortage is not demographic, but systemic.[3] They point out that labour hoarding--the tendency of managers to keep more workers on the payroll than strictly necessary--is a characteristic feature of Soviet industry. Managers tend to hoard labour to cushion themselves against chronic supply bottlenecks and to ensure that enough spare manpower will be on hand to enable the enterprise to meet plan targets. (Managers' incentive payments depend partly on whether or not the enterprise meets its targets on time.) Managers hoard labour, too, because enterprises may be required at any moment to send a detachment of workers to the countryside to help with seasonal tasks, such as harvesting, for which state and collective farms lack adequate manpower. Furthermore, managerial bonuses and pay scales are both determined to some extent by the size of the wage fund, that is, by the size of the enterprise as measured by the number of workers it employs. Underlying all these motives for hoarding labour is, finally, the absence of competitive pressure to induce the enterprise to economise on labour costs. From the point of view of the Soviet manager, any addition to his labour force is "free" so long as he has or can get a planned wage-bill allocation to cover it.

The USSR can compensate for its geographic and demographic constraints only by making a decisive shift from "extensive growth"--economic growth achieved as a result of putting to work ever greater supplies of labour, capital and land--to "intensive growth"--economic growth achieved by raising factor productivity growth and making more efficient use of raw materials. Measured total factor productivity is predominantly determined by labour productivity; any significant improvement in factor productivity performance would, therefore, require faster growth of labour productivity.

By comparison with that of other industrialised countries, Soviet labour productivity is low.[4] More importantly, in recent years the USSR has seen a steady slowdown in the rate of growth of labour productivity, which decelerated in the 1970s even more markedly than the overall rate of economic growth. According to official Soviet data, labour productivity rose in 1966-70 at an average annual rate of 6.8 percent; in 1971-75 at 4.6 percent; in 1976-80 at 3.3 percent and in 1981-83, again, by 3.3 percent.[5]

There are several explanations why Soviet labour productivity is low. The first is the comparatively low level of automation in Soviet industry and agriculture. According to one of the USSR's most influential economists, Abel Aganbegyan, every second worker or collective farmer is engaged in manual labour.[6]

A second reason for low labour productivity in the USSR in the early 1980s was the paucity of incentives. In the first place, economic stagnation curtailed the opportunities for upward social mobility that had abounded during the early years of the Soviet state. Young workers interviewed in 1981 at a plant in Tula oblast complained:

> We've grown up as workers here, started our married lives here, been assigned apartments, raised our professional skills to the highest level.... But sometimes we

> ask ourselves, what happens next? The more we think about it, the more sharply we feel we've reached the limit and have no further prospects for growth.[7]

Even more important, perhaps, was the lack of monetary rewards to encourage effort. The Brezhnev period saw a marked tendency toward the equalisation of wages, as a result of which workers found themselves with little incentive to work hard. Productivity suffered as people idled on the job or simply failed to show up for work. Such behaviour tended to go unchecked because, given prevailing labour shortages, managers were more interested in attracting and keeping any available manpower than in punishing even unproductive workers. In any case, a worker threatened with disciplinary action had little difficulty finding another job elsewhere. At the same time, the failure of the Soviet economy to provide high-quality consumer goods adequate to meet popular demand, as well as the fact that such consumer goods as were available through official retail outlets tended to be offered for sale at below-equilibrium prices, deprived ordinary workers of the incentive to increase their purchasing power by means of hard work. In such circumstances the black market, or "second economy," flourished, while access to high-quality goods was skillfully manipulated by the authorities to secure the loyalty of the elite.

This problem was highlighted in a letter published by *Komsomol'skaya pravda* in 1984. Tanya Agapova, a 22-year-old lathe operator from the seaport of Rostov-on-Don, wrote to complain about the poor quality of consumer goods available in the shops. Her monthly take-home pay, she wrote, was 200 rubles. She could earn a good deal more if she wanted, but saw no reason to do so because there was so little to spend her earnings on:

> Yes, I understand that our society cannot yet afford for everyone to dress well and fashionably. That's not the point. The point is that those who deserve them should receive the most benefits, and by that I mean the workers, who deserve more than other people.[8]

In the USSR, low labour productivity is often attributed to "violations of labour discipline." This catch-all phrase describes a wide range of actions on the part of the workers that impair production and output. It embraces absenteeism, poor time-keeping, shoddy workmanship, consumption of alcohol during working hours and, because of the harmful effect that alcohol abuse has on work performance, drunkenness in general. It also includes unacceptably high levels of labour turnover.

Over the years, the Soviet authorities have used a wide variety of methods in their attempts to improve labour discipline. These may be divided into educational measures, material incentives, and legal sanctions. Though the authorities have tended to use a combination of all three simultaneously, one specific means has generally predominated at any particular time.

During the industrialisation of the 1930s, for instance, severe legal sanctions were enacted that made felonies of even minor workplace infractions. The official line was that labour discipline violations were the acts of malicious individuals, "wreckers" and "saboteurs" conspiring against the interests of the state. Truancy and absenteeism became criminal offences.

Legislation introduced in 1932 decreed that truancy would be punishable by the loss of trade union food rationing, housing, and social welfare benefits; as the result, "the price for one lost day of work became the loss of access to most goods and services."[9] In 1938 it was made illegal for an industrial worker to change his place of employment without official permission, while regulations introduced in 1939 defined arriving twenty minutes late for work as "unjustifiable absence," subject to criminal prosecution. Since management, Party and trade union officials often failed to enforce these regulations, a law was introduced in 1940 that made supervisory personnel equally liable to criminal proceedings.[10]

After the death of Stalin, his successors began to dismantle the apparatus of terror with which he had ruled the Soviet population. In labour policy, the Khrushchev and Brezhnev periods saw a shift away from coercion and toward education.[11] The negative impact wrought on workers' morale and motivation by social factors such as poor living and working conditions, low wages and ineffectual material incentives began to be openly discussed. Labour discipline, it was argued, could best be improved by the creation and maintenance of a "healthy psychological climate" in the workplace. Labour discipline infractions were decriminalised and workers' job security was enhanced. Legislation was introduced according to which a worker could be sacked only if he or she presented a serious discipline problem. Even then, no worker could be dismissed without the prior approval of the enterprise trade union committee. In the opinion of the American scholar Blair Ruble, the result was that "by the late 1960s, Soviet workers were beyond the reach not only of the judicial system for labor discipline violations but of their managers as well."[12]

Birmingham University's Nick Lampert disagrees with this conclusion. Lampert concedes that Soviet managers may, and often do, turn a blind eye to labour discipline infractions; in this respect, he says, employees' job security may be "more protected than the legislation intended." But he argues that this happens not because managers are unable to sack errant workers, but because they do not always see it as in their interests to enforce the letter of the disciplinary code. In fact, Lampert states, managers can and do sack employees, but often they do so less to uphold the law than to get even with a troublesome subordinate, such as a worker who has attempted to "blow the whistle" on managerial malpractice. Lampert argues that, in this respect, workers' job security is "less protected than the law intends" while, as was seen in Chapter 2, trade unions lack the independence to oppose managerial decisions that infringe workers' rights.[13]

Although the USSR now has a mature workforce, with only a small proportion of new entrants still coming from the country into the towns in search of work, labour discipline problems persist. For example, the results of a nationwide public opinion poll published in 1985 revealed that only 25 to 35 percent of the more than 10,000 workers questioned claimed they made a consistent effort to do their jobs as well as they could.[14]

Since comprehensive statistics relating to workplace infractions are not published in the USSR, it is difficult to gain more than an impressionistic idea of how serious the problem really is. Mikhail Gorbachev claimed in January 1987 that the level of labour discipline infractions had been rising since the 1960s.[15] The constant attention devoted to the problem in the Soviet press in the early 1980s also indicated that, in the eyes of the authorities, the problem was a serious one.

Alcohol abuse is generally considered one of the most serious "violations of labour discipline." Alcoholism is a major cause of disease and death among Soviet males, especially among men of working age, and the evidence available in the early 1980s suggested the problem was growing. In particular, alcoholism was increasing among women and adolescents.[16] Its negative impact in the workplace was of course considerable. According to the USSR deputy procurator general, Sergei Shishkov:

> One of the chief reasons for absenteeism is people coming to work in a state of intoxication, or not coming at all for the same reason. Unfortunately, one can quote many examples of alcohol consumption even in factories. Pitenko, a punch operator at the Frunze heavy electrical engineering works, got so drunk at work that he fell into a pit in the carpentry shop.... There are many cases where drunkenness leads not only to a drop in labour productivity and plan targets not being met, but to outrageous violations of safety regulations and even to serious accidents.[17]

Aganbegyan wrote despairingly in 1981:

> Drunks are to be found on the shop floor more and more often. At some enterprises, special brigades have been formed to "grab" those who have drunk too much and stop them getting to their machines, in order to prevent accidents. They drink during working hours, they drink after work.... This is the ultimate in lack of respect for work, the ultimate negative attitude toward it.[18]

And *Pravda* wrote on 11 December 1982 that, as a result of alcohol abuse,

> machinery stands idle, building sites come to life on Tuesdays instead of Mondays and are deserted again by Friday; while on payday the women wait for their husbands

at the factory gates to prevent them from drinking their paypackets away.

Low labour productivity is frequently blamed, too, on absenteeism. This is a violation of labour discipline of which women are said most often to be guilty though, as a general rule, women are reported to be less likely than men to infringe labour discipline.[19] A significant cause of absenteeism is the inconvenient opening hours kept by shops and other consumer service outlets. Many such businesses keep the same working hours as factories and offices: they shut in the lunch-hour, and then in the evening they close just when their potential customers are leaving their offices and factories to go home. Since in the majority of Soviet families both husband and wife are in fulltime employment, many people--women in particular--are left with no alternative but to slip out during working hours if they are to keep their families fed and clothed. Visits to the doctor, to get shoes mended or to have household appliances serviced must all be fitted in during working hours.

The result, according to Soviet statistics, is that for every 100 workers there are 30 incidents of absenteeism every day. Each period of absence is said to average 1.6 hours.[20] An investigation in Moscow oblast found that in some factories and offices "no more than 10 percent of the workers were at their workplaces during the final hour of the shift," and that throughout the region, "73 percent of the workforce regularly took time off during working hours to attend to personal business."[21]

Shishkov stated in 1983 that absenteeism was on the rise. He laid the blame on lenient managers who, "trying to paint a rosy picture, often cover up slipshod work and thereby indulge wrong-doers."[22] *Sovetskaya Rossiya* explained that, "because the foreman is held responsible for cases of absenteeism, and not the absentees themselves, 90 percent of absenteeism is concealed."[23] As a result, Shishkov complained, "persistent violators of labour discipline are paid wages--and even bonuses--for days when they were absent from work."

Of all the phenomena included under the general term "violations of labour discipline," the rate of labour turnover is considered the most damaging to the economy.[24] "Labour turnover" includes workers who leave their jobs voluntarily and those sacked for violations of work regulations. (It does not include those whose reasons for leaving are regarded as "acceptable," such as those who are drafted into the armed forces, leave work to have a child, are transferred to another place of employment by their superiors, or retire on a pension.)

A wide range of labour turnover rates has been cited for various sectors of the Soviet economy. Clearly, the rate varies from industry to industry and from area to area. An authoritative source reported in 1981 that at that time over 20 million Soviet workers (collective farmers excluded)--that is, one out of every five workers and employees--were changing their jobs every year. Two-thirds of this total (that is, just under 14 percent) were said to come under the heading of "labour turnover," with the remaining third accounted for by young men being called up into the army, pensioners taking retirement, and so on.[25]

An annual rate of around 14 percent is not particularly high by international standards; it appears, too, to mark a drop from previous rates recorded in the USSR.[26] What seems chiefly to concern the Soviet authorities about even a turnover rate of 14 percent is the resulting frictional unemployment, or time lost between jobs. This is reported to be an average of 24 days for every worker who changes jobs.[27] The authorities also express concern at the fact that a worker's productivity tends to be lower than average both in the period immediately before he or she leaves the old job and in the first three months in the new one.[28]

Given the authorities' preoccupation with labour shortages, the millions of working hours lost to the economy through frictional unemployment are bound to be a source of concern. The Soviet press never tires of reminding its readers that the loss of just one minute of working time, spread over the whole of the national economy, adds up to a shortfall in industrial production of more than one million rubles.[29] Workers who change their jobs are berated in the media for fecklessness and lack of consideration for their fellow workers. During the discipline campaign of 1982, the media lambasted the *shabashniki*, or moonlighters, who work in the official economy during the winter and take off during the summer to work for higher wages as unofficial contract labourers, returning to their original place of work only when winter comes again.

As to whether some categories of workers are more prone than others to violate labour discipline, there seems little doubt that young, inexperienced workers are more likely culprits than are older, experienced ones. At a factory in Krasnoyarsk, it was found that young workers who had spent less than one year in their jobs were guilty of 70 percent of the infractions recorded,[30] while surveys in Ivanovo and Novgorod revealed that there every third worker found guilty of a discipline offence had been in paid employment less than three years and was still in his or her first job.[31]

In particular, young people (that is, those aged under 30) change jobs more frequently than veteran workers do.[32] According to V.A. Yadov, deputy head of the Institute for Social and Economic Problems of the USSR Academy of Sciences, this can be explained by the fact that:

> changes in labour conditions at the workplace do not progress as fast as the rising demands and aspirations of the workers, especially the young ones.... A young worker is far less tolerant of rush work and poor conditions.[33]

Such "lack of tolerance" seemed to be growing. Comparative studies conducted in 1962 and 1976 among young workers in Leningrad revealed that:

> some young people are undergoing a so-called instrumentalisation of their attitude toward work, that is, the basic values of labour are shifting from the sphere of its content to the area of working conditions and remuneration. People are affected by the kind of work they do, but they are affected even more by the conditions in which they work and what they receive for it. At the beginning of the 1960s the content of work, the possibilities for advancement, and interest in the work process itself were of greater significance than working conditions or earnings. Today one might say that they have become equal with respect to motivational significance.[34]

The secretary of the Moscow city Komsomol committee reported in 1983 that, nationwide, 60 percent of those quitting their jobs were young people. "In effect," he wrote, "such people are voting with their feet," for "many new workers are simply not ready to work in modern assembly line conditions."[35] The director of a Vladivostok factory wrote in 1980 that 80 percent of those leaving his factory every year were aged under 30; as a result, veteran workers were demanding that young workers should not be taken on at all.[36] But, he went on, many young people left their jobs in order to improve their working conditions. Charging that veteran workers gave all the dirty, boring tasks to the new recruits, he concluded that "it might be argued that the primary cause of high turnover is dissatisfaction on the part of the worker with the enterprise, that is, a form of spontaneous protest."

This indictment is borne out by the findings of a survey conducted by the Komsomol among young infringers of labour discipline in the central Siberian city of Tomsk, where dissatisfaction with repetitive manual labour was found to be the complaint most frequently voiced by young people.[37] In an article published in 1982, a Kiev newspaper also blamed the fact that young workers were given the worst jobs to do. It cited an Odessa plant at which, of 285 young workers recruited in 1981, only 45 were given work in the specialties for which they had trained. As a result, the newspaper commented, "only about 80 percent of the young entrants remain each year at the enterprises to which they have been assigned."[38] Of the youthful infringers of labour discipline interviewed in Tomsk, 44.7 percent said they were unhappy with their work or, at best, indifferent to it.

Soviet data such as these bear out the claims of Western scholars who argue that those who are for some reason dissatisfied with their working or living conditions are the most likely to violate labour discipline. These scholars divide dissatisfied workers into two broad groupings. In the first place, it is argued that those most likely to feel dissatisfaction are unskilled or semi-skilled manual workers with low educational levels. According to the American academic Charles Ziegler, these are likely to be "young workers, or migrants from the countryside with limited aspirations. The frustrations of this segment of the working class find an outlet in drunkenness, violations of labor discipline, and high levels of turnover."[39] The survey conducted by the Komsomol in Tomsk also found that violations of labour discipline were most likely to occur among those with the lowest professional qualifications. Only 20 percent of those interviewed in connexion with their poor work records were in charge of any kind of machinery or equipment; the remainder were engaged in unskilled, manual labour.

A second group likely to feel dissatisfaction with their working conditions are, according to the British scholars David Lane and Felicity O'Dell, those "whose education and qualifications are superior to the kind of work they do."[40] While surveys carried out in Vladivostok found that the better educated a Soviet worker, the less likely he or she was to commit violations of discipline,[41] this may not hold true for those overqualified for the work they do. Lane and O'Dell state that "the average educational level of those dissatisfied with their work is usually somewhat higher than for workers doing the same job but happy with their work," and conclude that "education may sometimes make young workers more demanding of the work they have to do."[42]

The fact that opportunities for upward social mobility have shrunk for the average Soviet worker seems to be the culprit here. As avenues for promotion narrow, the frustration felt by workers with high educational and skill levels who find themselves trapped in jobs for which they are overqualified is likely to be reflected in negative work attitudes. The West German specialist Wolfgang Teckenberg reports that "workers with a high education in unqualified positions are likely to be among the most frustrated." This, he adds, is "especially often the reason for dissatisfaction of younger workers in the USSR."[43]

It is widely recognised that the USSR has trained and is continuing to train more engineering and other technical specialists than its economy can absorb. As a result, a substantial number of specialists fail to find jobs corresponding to their training, and employment below skill level is a common phenomenon.[44] It was reported from Estonia in 1980, for example, that 17.6 percent of those who had graduated from secondary-specialised schools in 1975-77 were occupying blue-collar jobs not requiring secondary specialised education at all.[45]

The fact, too, that white-collar workers earn relatively low wages as compared with blue-collar ones has led a substantial number of qualified specialists to move into more remunerative jobs that do not exploit their expertise. Many engineers, for example, have taken jobs as industrial workers (so-called worker-intellectuals).[46] Others drift into such jobs as taxi-driving or working in shops, which offer greater freedom and the chance to earn some money on the side.[47] *Pravda* described the disillusion of a bright young engineer recruited to work in a research institute. Not only was he paid only two-thirds of the average state wage, but he found his colleagues playing chess and table tennis, or going shopping, when they were supposed to be working. After a few days' absence on sick leave, he found he had been registered as present, which suggested that nobody much cared whether he was there or not. He turned instead to working as a floor polisher, at which he earned more money and gained some independence, but where his training was wasted.[48]

MEASURES TAKEN UNDER THE BREZHNEV LEADERSHIP

At the end of 1979, the Brezhnev leadership adopted a major decree aimed specifically at reducing labour turnover and infringements of labour discipline.[49] The decree threatened tougher penalties for those who violated labour discipline, but stopped short of introducing fresh penalties and relied in reality more on carrot than on stick. Improvements were promised in consumer services and child care. Housing was to be provided for factory workers with work tenure of over five years (or two years for young workers). Up to three days' extra holiday was awarded to workers with three to seven years' uninterrupted service. Increases of between 10 and 20 percent were made in the retirement pensions of workers with 25 years' uninterrupted service; female workers with children would receive the same privilege after 20 years. Those guilty of labour discipline violations would be denied such privileges. In particular, a worker who changed jobs "without good reason" more than once in the course of a year would lose his uninterrupted service record, or *stazh*--which determines the scale of various social welfare benefits such as retirement pensions.[50]

The concrete changes made by the decree were minimal, the most significant being the extension from two weeks to one month of the length of written notice a worker had to give of his intention to quit. The impression created was that the authorities felt existing regulations were severe enough and needed only to be more strictly enforced.

The decree had some initial impact. In 1980, labour turnover in industry and construction fell "by as much as it had during the whole of the preceding five-year period." However, the effect was of only short duration and, "as early as 1981-82, the process slowed abruptly."[51] Perhaps this was because the material benefits and incentives promised by the decree were bound to take time to come into effect: improvements in housing and child care could obviously not be realised overnight. During the 1982-83 campaign it was asserted that the provisions of the 1979 decree had amounted to no more than "half-hearted measures" that "bypassed the causes leading to various violations of labour discipline." "There was a time," Radio Moscow commented,

> when we thought it was possible to fight discipline violations only by means of persuasion, encouragement and, of course, punishment for those guilty of absenteeism, bad timekeeping, and so on.... But it turned out that it is impossible to strengthen discipline by incentives and punishments alone.[52]

As a result, reports of the period suggest that labour discipline showed no improvement, and very probably deteriorated, during Brezhnev's last years --subsequent, that is, to the introduction of the 1979 decree.

Writing early in 1983, Yadov reported that:

> According to our data, the level of labour discipline has declined by some 5.0 to 6.0 percent during the past few years.... a portion of the workers are becoming less accurate and less efficient, and the instructions of the management are being violated more frequently.

He went on to offer striking personal testimony to support his contention that the overall situation had deteriorated:

> I remember that 15 years ago a foreman would characterise a good worker as follows: "golden hands," "a rationaliser," and so forth. Today, the same foreman will distinguish the one who "won't let him down," that is, the one who won't be

> late, who won't refuse to exert himself toward the end of the month. Such exaggerated appraisal of altogether elementary requirements of behaviour clearly reveals a shortage of such qualities.[53]

Soviet press reports from the late 1970s and early 1980s suggested a perturbing increase not only of labour discipline violations but of social problems such as theft, vandalism, marital breakdown and juvenile crime. There seemed in particular to be an increasing awareness on the part of ordinary working people that the gap was widening between their aspirations and the realities of everyday life. The gap was particularly stark between public and private morality--between the tenets of the official ideology and the practices in which people at all social levels were forced to indulge if they wished not merely to survive but to prosper under the existing system. These practices included crimes such as bribery, speculation, report-padding and moonlighting.

The gulf between private and public morality was graphically described by the American author George Feifer, who visited the USSR in 1980 after an absence of ten years.[54] Feifer found a "collapse of civic morale" which he attributed to "the virtual disappearance of commitment to Marxism-Leninism." It was, he wrote, "as if the American Bible Belt had lost its belief in God." Feifer attributed the disillusionment of the general population not to a real but to a perceived decline in living standards:

> Falling consumer satisfaction and the collapsing belief in socialism have dragged down shopfloor morale to an all-time low.... The ordinary Russian has lost his optimistic belief that his life will get better, and is losing faith in

what he now calls his "unworkable" system.

Feifer quoted one of his friends as saying, "Soviet society in its middle levels is becoming a society of thieves.... The assumption that 'everybody steals' is erasing the nation's sense of right and wrong."

Concern at the blurring of moral values could also be found in the Soviet press. On 13 April 1983, for example, the newspaper *Sovetskaya Belorossiya* described cases of petty theft in the town of Slutsk. The culprits, the newspaper wrote, did not consider their actions to be stealing, but instead said things like "I took a couple of oxtails along with me," "I walked out with a ball of yarn," "I found some sugar and took it home."

An editorial published in *Kommunist* that same month also complained of a decline in moral values:

> Displaying indifference and lack of exactingness to themselves and to others, people gradually stop seeing this as a moral and social evil and grow accustomed to the soothing thought that it is not reprehensible to behave in this way....

As a result, *Kommunist* declared, many Soviet citizens had come to approach their work "without proprietary interest, uncreatively, without enthusiasm, and without putting their heart into its results." This was causing "not only economic but moral damage" and "deforming public and private consciousness."[55]

Several Soviet writers tried to get to the root of this moral malaise. The most incisive analysis was offered by the sociologist, Tat'yana Zaslavskaya, in her confidential "Novosibirsk report"--a document presented in April 1983 at a closed Moscow seminar, but later leaked to the

Western press.[56] Zaslavskaya argued that the excessive centralisation of the Soviet economy generated laziness, neglect of quality, a low level of morality, and social inertia. An economic system that treated workers like cogs in a machine worked well enough in the 1930s, she said, when the labour force was passive, obedient and poorly educated, but such a system was no longer appropriate when the workforce was better educated and materially more secure. In other words, as Philip Hanson has remarked, "the Stalinist economic system could be made to work during a reign of terror, but not after the terror ended."[57]

ANDROPOV'S CAMPAIGN TO RAISE DISCIPLINE

Yurii Andropov gave every sign that, as a former head of the KGB, he was well aware of the moral malaise of Soviet society. But while Andropov adopted "discipline" as his byword, his leadership displayed far clearer understanding of the seriousness of the problems to be tackled and a greater receptivity to ideas of economic reform than had that of Leonid Brezhnev.

At a plenary meeting of the CPSU Central Committee in November 1982, Andropov promised "a resolute struggle against all infractions of Party, state and labour discipline." Shoddy work, idleness and irresponsibility must, he said, be made to have "a direct impact on the financial earnings, status and moral authority of the workers."[58]

The groundwork for Andropov's campaign seemed to have been laid before the November plenum, perhaps at the time of his election to the Central Committee Secretariat in May 1982. The results of the surveys carried out in Ivanovo and Novgorod into the problem of worker absenteeism were discussed, for example, in *Sovetskaya Rossiya* on 23 July 1982. The newspaper published readers' responses on 15 August, and these may be seen as having provided the authorities with an indication of the state of public opinion on the topic prior to the full-scale launching of the campaign. Its readers, *Sovetskaya Rossiya* reported, were unanimous: "the escapades of drunkards and shirkers have been endured long enough; effective ways must be found to keep them in check."

It was announced in September 1982 that the State Committee for Labour and Social Problems had been charged with drawing up proposals for new measures to deal with labour discipline violations.[59] At the beginning of January 1983, a high-level Party, government and trade union meeting took place in the Central Committee of the CPSU. Attended by Central Committee secretary Mikhail Gorbachev, the meeting called for the elaboration of practical measures to "strengthen labour and production discipline and reduce losses of work time."[60] Pointing out that the introduction of new labour discipline regulations was not envisaged in the legislative plan for the years 1983-85 adopted under Brezhnev in 1982, the American specialist on Soviet law, Robert Sharlet, has convincingly argued that the impetus for fresh legislation came from Andropov.[61]

Andropov's campaign was notable for its sharpness of tone. Although agreement still failed to emerge over what steps were necessary to improve worker morale and discipline, the letters and articles that appeared in the press under Andropov's leadership took a consistently harsher line than those published before his accession to power. Calls were heard both for less leniency in the application of legal sanctions to offenders and for the introduction of sterner legislation to punish the guilty. The impression created by the media was that those advocating a tougher approach were in the majority, and that they were expressing the opinions of the workers themselves. Those who contended that existing legislation was adequate, and that what was needed was either more education or more generous provision for social needs, were presented as a minority. They tended, too, to be members of the intelligentsia such as lawyers, teachers and sociologists.

A survey conducted in 1980 among workers in Gor'ky and Moscow had come up with evidence suggesting that few of the workers there had much faith in the power of punitive measures to deter labour discipline violations. Only 17 percent of the workers interviewed favoured the application of administrative measures in such cases, while 46 percent said "social means" were a more effective way of influencing behaviour.[62] During the campaign of 1982-83, however, it was the workers who were portrayed by the press as calling for the toughest measures.

Outraged workers wrote to the press demanding that those guilty of producing shoddy goods should be fined; that staff in one enterprise should have the right to veto the hiring of any workers who had earlier been sacked for violating labour discipline elsewhere, or to insist on their being hired at reduced rates of pay; that feckless workers should be deprived "wholly or in part" of their annual vacation rights and their bonus payments, lose their places on the waiting list for housing, or be expelled from trade union membership--so losing the privileges that union membership brings; that young workers should be required to sign contracts for not less than two to three years; that the law should be changed to make it easier for management to dock workers' pay packets as a way of compensating the state for losses incurred through absenteeism; that workers should be made to pay for any damage they had caused to machinery when in a state of intoxication; that persistent slackers should have their salary levels downgraded or be transferred to lower-paid work regardless of their skills and qualifications; that those who went absent without leave should subsequently be allowed to change jobs only through a central labour bureau; and that details of a person's work record should be entered in his or her internal passport (which cannot be so conveniently "lost" as the workbook all Soviet workers carry, because of the greater difficulty involved in its replacement).[63]

Pravda editorialised:

> Workers themselves are proposing that such people [drunkards, shirkers, "rolling stones"] should be allowed to give in their notice only with the agreement of a workers' meeting.... This procedure is being followed, for example, in many enterprises in Tula.[64]

At an "Open Letter Day" on the subject of labour discipline held in December at an industrial association in Kursk, a resolution was adopted that included the following proposals: that any worker found guilty of infringing labour discipline would for one year be deprived of the right to move to a new job in another enterprise, to receive a voucher for a sanatorium or a tourist trip, or to take a vacation at any time other than between November and February; and that he or she should be moved to the bottom of the housing list (a new apartment being the most prized of Soviet commodities).[65]

One article in particular--a survey of readers' letters published in *Pravda* in December 1982--seemed designed to whip up popular resentment against purported slackers.[66] A truck driver wrote:

> We drivers begin our mornings with chit-chat about who spent the night where, how

> much we drank yesterday, what personal errands we have to do that day.... Toward evening, with the trucks back in the garage, we drivers set up a do-it-yourself restaurant. Each of us picks up a little something extra wherever we can--at railway stations, airports, hotels, shops. The bosses know about our "under-the-counter" earnings, but they don't say anything because they're using the repair shops illegally to fix private cars.

Pravda also cited the complaint of a worker from Ufa: "Young people hang about the city streets with nothing to do. We must put every parasite, drunkard and hooligan to work." A personnel manager from Zhdanov denounced the *shabashniki*: "They move around the country at will--no-one controls these people." And a reader from Kirov oblast complained about "the knights of the market place":

> At markets in cities all over the country one can find, at almost any time of the year, healthy men who have come from Central Asia and Transcaucasia. They live for weeks by selling flowers, dried apricots, mandarin oranges and other gifts of the south. It turns out that they don't work anywhere, and no-one cares.

Throughout December 1982, the Soviet press was full of such material. The new year brought a number of developments in the campaign. That which attracted the greatest attention in the Western press--though it went unmentioned in the Soviet media--was the sudden introduction in January of "Operation Trawl."[67] Teams of vigilantes began to conduct raids in Moscow and other major cities. They carried out spot checks in department stores, hairdressing salons and cinemas, asking everyone for their identification papers and their reasons for not being at work. The *International Herald Tribune* described a raid at a Moscow bath-house:

> According to various reports, the vigilantes and police sealed off the bath at midday and found hundreds of persons, including some high-ranking bureaucrats, who were unable to provide a convincing explanation for absence from their desks. People caught were not arrested, but their names were taken for forwarding to their superiors.[68]

The clampdown was said to have aroused fear among many citizens. For a short while, it led to a drop in the number of people to be seen on buses, in shops, and at steam baths during working hours. "I don't dare to try to go shopping during my work any more," one young mother was quoted as saying, "but when am I supposed to buy groceries if I get home 15 minutes before the stores close?"[69] According to numerous reports, the raids gave rise to a good deal of resentment on the part of ordinary citizens and, early in February, they halted as suddenly as they had begun.[70]

Throughout the spring the press maintained what was clearly a coordinated campaign, publishing an unremitting flood of denunciations of feckless "slackers," "spongers" and "idlers." Even *Pravda* was moved to comment, on the suggestions it was receiving from some of its readers, that "it is possible that some of them are too categorical, too harsh."[71] In April, when the campaign was still in full swing, *Pravda* reported cheerlessly that the main topics being raised in readers' letters were "discipline, order and duty."[72]

Gradually, however, more moderate views began

to make an appearance. It is impossible to say whether this change reflected a change in a centrally-decreed policy or a genuine shift in public opinion. There may even have been some limited divergence between the editorial policies of the different national newspapers. Reporting on its postbag in April 1983, for example, *Izvestia* managed to strike a subtler note than *Pravda* and to convey a clear impression of a lack of consensus. It was, *Izvestia* told its readers, receiving "a flood of letters of support for the Party's course toward the all-round strengthening of state, production and labour discipline." However, the newspaper went on,

> ...stronger discipline is unimaginable without correct organisation of work and reliable supplies of raw materials and spare parts. We are receiving many interesting letters on this topic. And truly, what's the use of coming to work on time if there's nothing to do when you get there? I. Nikitin writes from the Berdsk radio factory to complain that "We fulfill 45-48 percent of the plan in the first three weeks of each month, and in the last week to ten days we produce everything else." The practice of storming [rush work], he says, explains why what is produced is of poor quality, why faulty goods are dispatched instead of good ones, and why the workers have to put in "massive amounts of overtime."[73]

Izvestia added that this idea was to be found in the majority of letters the paper was receiving.

Other commentaries drew attention to the fact that, for many Soviet citizens, the only solution to chronic shortages and inconvenient opening hours was to run errands during working hours. Other articles stressed that crowded public transport was often to blame when workers arrived at work late or went home early.[74] In mid-January it was announced that, at its latest meeting, the Politburo had discussed the question of more flexible opening hours for shops and other service outlets, and ordered steps "to impose the necessary order."[75] Soon after, a decree of the USSR Council of Ministers called for the extension of opening hours in shops, and for services such as dry-cleaning and shoe repair to be made directly available in farms and factories.[76]

Meanwhile, articles appeared that argued that sanctions against labour discipline violations were already in existence, and needed only to be properly enforced.[77] Workers' letters began openly to ask whether the attention being paid to discipline would have any lasting impact.[78] In one, published in *Trud* in March, a trade union activist complained that officials in the Ukrainian city of Dnepropetrovsk saw it all as "just another campaign," ordered by Moscow, that could safely be disregarded at the periphery. Of course, such suggestions were strenuously denied by the central press.[79]

A worker from a Moscow automobile plant protested in *Pravda* that merely demanding discipline was not enough. Order was also essential. It wasn't, he said, just a matter of coming to work on time and staying there until it was time to go home: the workforce must be provided with adequate tools and supplies to enable them to work efficiently while on the job.[80] A workers' meeting at a Chelyabinsk factory indicted inefficient managers for the fact that workers often found themselves obliged to stand around during working hours with nothing to do.[81]

Sociological research in Georgia bore out these claims, showing that "most" of the losses of working time were caused not by laziness on the part of the ordinary worker, but by machinery going down during a shift or even "for entire days," and by bottlenecks and shortages of essential equipment and raw materials. "After all," *Zarya Vostoka* summed up, "is the worker who comes to work on time with the intention of doing a conscientious job to blame if a tool is defective or not in its place, or if the necessary raw materials have not been delivered to the enterprise? Of course not."[82]

Despite such arguments, the general tone of the campaign throughout the spring and summer of 1983 and, in particular, the frequency of calls for harsher measures to punish idle workers, left little doubt that many top policymakers favoured tighter controls. It appeared that the ground was being prepared for the introduction of tougher punitive measures. It therefore came as no surprise when it was announced in August 1983 that new legislation relating to labour discipline was being adopted.[83]

The new provisions represented a significant reinforcement of the existing legislation.[84] At the same time, they seemed to reflect a degree of compromise between harder and more conciliatory approaches to labour policy. Not only could they not be compared with Stalin's draconian measures; they were considerably milder than many of the sanctions that had been put forward, ostensibly by the workers themselves, during the preceding media campaign. For example, the proposal frequently voiced during that campaign--that workers should be allowed to leave their jobs only with the permission of their workmates--was not, in the event, adopted. The main changes announced in August 1983 were as follows:

Increased sanctions against absenteeism. Thus, a worker absent "without a valid reason" would lose one day's holiday for every working day missed (though a worker's annual leave must not be reduced to less than two weeks, that is, twelve working days).

A worker absent "without a valid reason" for more than three hours in any one day would be regarded as having been absent the entire day and be docked a full day's holiday.

A worker guilty of shoddy work would be liable to be demoted or transferred for a period of up to three months to lower-paid or less responsible work. While demotion was already one of a number of possible punishments for shoddy workmanship, a worker could previously be demoted only to work in line with his qualifications. The new law made it possible for a worker to be transferred to *any* work; for example, an engineer or office worker could be demoted to physical labour.

During such a three-month period of demotion, a worker would lose the right to tender his resignation. A worker who refused to accept the penalty and who left his job regardless, would forfeit any benefits he had earned as reward for uninterrupted service: his place in the queue for housing, his sick-leave benefits, and any percentage increments to his pension benefits.

A worker sacked from one enterprise for slacking or drunkenness would be eligible to receive only one half the normal monthly production bonus for the first three to six months in his new job. Any worker found directly responsible for shoddy output or wasted materials would in future be required to pay compensation of up to one-third of his average monthly salary, deductible at source.

Here there were two important changes. First, a worker could previously be fined only one-third of his monthly *normed* salary, which is generally lower than the average net salary since many workers regularly overfulfill the norm. The amount that could be levied on the worker therefore increased. Second, a worker could previously be required to pay this fine only if he gave his written consent. Not surprisingly, this was not always forthcoming and, if the management wanted to pursue the matter, it had to take the worker to court. If the sum of money involved was small, the management often did not bother to follow the matter through. Under the new legislation the worker's consent would no longer be required before his salary could be docked. If he objected, the onus would be on him, not on the management, to lodge an appeal with the court. Damage caused by a worker when in a state of intoxication would, moreover, be liable to be repaid in full, with no upper limit on the sum.

In an attempt to reduce labour turnover, the period of notice of termination of employment required from a worker was raised from one month to two months, one month's notice being retained only for those wishing to leave for "valid reasons." And, if he wished to retain his "uninterrupted service" record and, therefore, his full pension and social security benefits, a worker would in future have to find himself a new job within three weeks (not, as previously, one month) of leaving his old one.

Diligent workers would be eligible to receive two extra vacation days each year, instead of only every second year as stipulated by the 1979 legislation. Additional privileges and bonuses were promised for conscientious workers, but were not elaborated upon.

Managers who proved unable to maintain discipline among the workforce would be "deemed to have failed in their duties" and would (though this was not spelled out) presumably be liable themselves for demotion. Later in August, *Pravda* announced the adoption of a decree making managers of plants that turned out poor-quality goods, fell behind with plan schedules, or failed to meet production targets, liable to lose "at least" 25 percent of their bonuses; cash benefits over and above those already in existence were, however, promised to enterprises that performed well.[85]

Andropov's campaign to raise labour discipline seemed to have an initial shock value and to give a temporary boost to productivity. Industrial output for 1983 as a whole was 4.0 percent up on that of 1982--which had reached an all-time low of 2.8 percent growth. This represented a significant increase over growth rates achieved during the final years of Brezhnev's rule, which had averaged around 3.0 percent. Labour turnover also fell.[86] Of course, coercion and exhortation were able to increase output wherever there was organisational slack. But the nature of the increase meant that it could be only temporary, and that it lacked the potential to create a base for sustained growth. By the beginning of 1985, growth rates had resumed their earlier tendency to slow down.

This was partly because the adoption of fresh legislation put a stop to the campaigning. Once new measures were decided upon and adopted, the purpose of public discussion disappeared and the campaign inevitably lost saliency in the public imagination. Much more important however was the fact, clearly shown in much of the press discussion, that many of the problems laid at the door of "poor labour discipline" were in reality beyond the control not only of the workers but even of their managers. They were, in short, systemic, and nothing but a radical reform of the economic mechanism could be expected to put them right.

The question arises, therefore, whether or not Andropov intended to introduce such a reform. On the one hand, much of the discussion initiated in the press under his leadership tacitly recognised that merely frightening workers into working harder was not enough. Andropov himself acknowledged that: "All our efforts will be in vain if the drive for discipline remains on the surface and is reduced to trivia, such as reprimanding a worker for being five minutes late."[87] Nor was it long before the emphasis of the campaign began to shift from "labour discipline" pure and simple to "planning and production discipline," that is, to the management of the economy.

Some Western observers point to the lack of real initiatives under Andropov's leadership and argue that he set out less to reorganise the economy than to mobilise available reserves in an attempt to make the existing system work better. Others argue that Andropov saw his discipline campaign as a short-term measure to restore public morale and give a temporary boost to economic growth, and that he understood as well as anyone that more radical measures were essential if social and economic decline were to be reversed. What Andropov was trying to do, according to this analysis, was to stimulate debate that would eventually lead to general recognition that labour discipline problems were only symptoms of larger defects in the system of central planning.

Arguments in favour of economic reform were voiced more openly under Andropov's leadership than at any time since the days of Khrushchev. In February 1983, for example, Vladimir Kostakov of Gosplan's Economic Research Institute wrote in *Literaturnaya gazeta*:

> The acuteness of the problem connected with labour discipline requires us soberly to acknowledge that all the measures so far taken to counter the habit of last-minute rush work have proved ineffectual and should not be relied upon in future. What seems to be the problem is that all these measures left the existing mechanism untouched--above all, the system of material and technical supply. There is an ever more urgent need for fundamentally new solutions:

> correlation of central planning and local initiative; genuine freedom and genuine responsibility in the operation of enterprises and associations.[88]

In retrospect, it seems probable that Andropov was planning to introduce some kind of decentralisation of decision-making in both industry and agriculture. He lost no time upon election as Party leader in calling for practical measures to "extend the independence of associations and enterprises, and of state and collective farms."[89] A joint Party-government decree published in July 1983 instituted an "economic experiment" whereby enterprise managers in certain industries were given increased latitude in using investment and wage funds. Workers' and managers' rewards were both to be tied more closely to enterprise performance, while contract fulfillment was made a key success indicator.

At the same time, a new law on work collectives was introduced. Its purpose appeared to be to create a new level of control--at grass-roots, shop-floor level--to dovetail with the decision-making powers tentatively being extended to enterprise managers. But though the law on work collectives called for increased worker participation in management, it turned out to be so hedged about with restrictions that workers did not receive a significant managerial role. Many observers were accordingly left wondering whether the real purpose was not to create the illusion rather than the reality of worker participation.[90]

Andropov's leadership encouraged wider use of small work teams, or brigades, in industry, construction and agriculture. This policy seemed aimed at increasing workers' participation in decision-making at the lowest level of production, as well as at boosting productivity by making workers' wages and bonuses more dependent upon final results. Andropov's frequent denunciations of the evils of wage-equalisation suggested, moreover, that his leadership was dedicated to the introduction of wider wage differentials as a means of encouraging harder work.

Whether or not Andropov harboured serious intentions of economic reorganisation may never be known, since his health began to fail a bare three months after his appointment as Party leader. The most that can be stated with any certainty is that his election was the result of a general recognition within the Soviet elite that the country needed strong and decisive leadership to check and reverse a long-term process of social and economic disintegration. The example of Poland's labour unrest seems to have made the Soviet leaders more aware of the threat posed to the stability of their own system by the moral malaise in Soviet society.

FOOTNOTES TO CHAPTER 12

1. CIA, *Handbook of Economic Statistics 1984*, Washington DC, 1984, p. 68; *Vestnik statistiki*, No 8, 1984, p. 75.

2. Gertrude E. Schroeder, "Managing Labour Shortages in the Soviet Union," in Jan Adam (ed), *Employment Policies in the Soviet Union and Eastern Europe*, London, 1982, p. 4.

3. Philip Hanson, "The Serendipitous Soviet Achievement of Full Employment: Labour Shortage and Labour Hoarding in the Soviet Economy," in David Lane (ed), *Labour and Employment in the USSR*, Brighton, 1986, pp. 83-111.

4. Schroeder, *op. cit.*, p. 5.

5. Derived from *Narodnoe khozyaistvo SSSR v 1979 g.*, p. 46, and *Narodnoe khozyaistvo SSSR v 1983 g.*, pp. 38, 39 (indices of the productivity of

social labour). Concealed inflation in the output figures tends to bias these growth rates upward. CIA estimates of the growth rates of Soviet labour productivity over the same periods of time are 3.2, 2.0, 1.4, and 1.7 percent, respectively.

6. *Trud*, 17 October 1981.

7. *Pravda*, 22 April 1981.

8. *Komsomol'skaya pravda*, 29 September 1984.

9. Blair A. Ruble, *Soviet Trade Unions: Their Development in the 1970s*, Cambridge, 1981, p. 19.

10. *Ibid.*

11. *Ibid.*, pp. 5-6.

12. *Ibid.*, p. 2. *Literaturnaya gazeta* on 12 January 1983 quoted a letter from a worker in Kiev describing how his collective had tried to get an idle worker sacked and how, in the end, the miscreant was merely transferred to another section of the same factory. The letter continued: "And what happens if the management does sack someone? Then all hell breaks loose: the commission for labour disputes, the factory trade union committee, the courts.... You end up wasting so much time and energy going to all these different agencies that you think twice before ever crossing swords with an idle worker again."

13. Nick Lampert, "Job Security and the Law in the USSR," in Lane (ed), *op. cit.*, pp. 256-77.

14. *Izvestia*, 3 May 1985.

15. *Pravda*, 28 January 1987.

16. See RL 321/84, "Soviet Concern About Alcoholism among Women," by Dana Townsend, 24 August 1984; and RL 307/84, "Alcoholism among Children and Teenagers," by Yuliya Voznesenskaya, 13 August 1984.

17. *Radio Moscow*, 17 January 1983.

18. *Trud*, 22 October 1981.

19. G.M. Podorov, *Tekuchest' kadrov i bor'ba s nei*, Gor'ky, 1983, reviewed in *Referativnyi zhurnal "Obshchestvennye nauki v SSSR,"* No 4, 1984, pp. 76-80, reports that in the city of Gor'ky male

workers make up 55-60 percent of the workforce but perpetrate 66.7 percent of the labour discipline violations; *Kyrgyzstan kommunisti*, No 11, 1984, pp. 85-9, asserts that, in the USSR overall, men are guilty of 68.5 percent of all labour discipline infractions.

20. *Trud*, 29 December 1982.

21. *Pravda*, 28 December 1982.

22. *Radio Moscow*, 17 January 1983.

23. *Sovetskaya Rossiya*, 5 January 1983.

24. David E. Powell, "Labor Turnover in the Soviet Union," *Slavic Review*, June 1977, pp. 268-85.

25. A. Kotlyar and M. Talalai, "Puti sokrashcheniya tekuchesti kadrov," *Voprosy ekonomiki*, No 5, 1981, pp. 33-44 at p. 34; these figures were later cited in *Kommunist*, No 4, 1983, p. 6.

26. *Cf.* the figures given by Murray Feshbach and Stephen Rapawy in US Congress Joint Economic Committee, "Labor Constraints in the Five-Year Plan," *Soviet Economic Prospects for the Seventies*, Washington DC, 1973, p. 559; reproduced in Powell, *op. cit.*, p. 269.

27. *Pravda*, 25 March 1982; *Radio Moscow*, 24 August 1983. A worker who goes through a labour exchange, *Pravda* added, takes an average of only ten days to find a new job.

28. Kotlyar and Talalai, *loc. cit.*

29. *Pravda*, 24 February 1981.

30. *Ibid.*, 5 August 1983.

31. *Sovetskaya Rossiya*, 23 July 1983.

32. See Kotlyar and Talalai, *op. cit.*, p. 37, S. Lenskaya and V. Gobareva, "Stabil'nost' trudovykh kollektivov i podvizhnost' kadrov," *Politicheskoe samoobrazovanie*, No 6, 1981, pp. 34-40 at p. 36; *Zarya Vostoka*, 3 August 1984.

33. *Sovetskaya kul'tura*, 5 April 1983.

34. M. Levin, "Molodezh' i trud," *Ekonomika i organizatsiya promyshlennogo proizvodstva* (*EKO*), No 8, 1983, pp. 110-28.

35. *Komsomol'skaya pravda*, 29 March 1983.

36. Yu. N. Udovichenko, "Sotsiologichesky lokator rukovoditelya," *EKO*, No 10, 1980, pp. 31-37.

37. *Molodoi kommunist*, No 7, 1981, pp. 13-16.

38. *Rabochaya gazeta*, 18 September 1982.

39. Charles E. Ziegler, "Worker Participation and Worker Discontent in the Soviet Union," *Political Science Quarterly*, Summer 1983, pp. 235-53, at pp. 245-46.

40. David Lane and Felicity O'Dell, *The Soviet Industrial Worker*, Oxford, 1978, p. 136.

41. Udovichenko, *op. cit.*, p. 36.

42. A.G. Zdravomyslov, V.P. Rozhin and V.A. Yadov (eds), *Chelovek i ego rabota*, Moscow, 1967, cited in Lane and O'Dell, *op. cit.*, p. 86.

43. Wolfgang Teckenberg, "Labour Turnover and Job Satisfaction: Indicators of Industrial Conflict in the USSR," *Soviet Studies*, No 2, 1978, pp. 193-211, at p. 207.

44. See Eduard Gloeckner, "Underemployment and Potential Unemployment of the Technical Intelligentsia: Distortions Between Education and Occupation," in Lane (ed), *op. cit.*, pp. 223-36.

45. *Sotsialistichesky trud*, No 7, 1980, p. 66.

46. *Ibid.*, No 1, 1980, pp. 88-97.

47. *Pravda*, 7 and 29 June 1981.

48. *Ibid.*, 20 July 1982.

49. Decree of the Central Committee of the CPSU, the USSR Council of Ministers, and the All-Union Central Council of Trade Unions, "On the further strengthening of labour discipline and the reduction of personnel turnover in the national economy," *Pravda*, 12 January 1980.

50. Since 1956, a Soviet worker has had the right to quit his job on giving the appropriate amount of written notice (originally two weeks, this period was extended in 1979 to one month, and in 1983 to two months). In 1960, a worker leaving his job at his own request was given the right to retain

his record of uninterrupted service as long as he found other work within one month. In 1983, this period was reduced to three weeks.

51. *Izvestia*, 26 April 1985.

52. *Radio Moscow*, 29 September 1983.

53. *Sovetskaya kul'tura*, 5 April 1983.

54. George Feifer, "Russian Disorders: The Sick Man of Europe," *Harper's Magazine*, February 1981, pp. 41-55.

55. *Kommunist*, No 6, 1983, pp. 58-67.

56. AS 5042.

57. RL 356/83, "Discussion of Economic Reform in the USSR: The 'Novosibirsk Paper'," by Philip Hanson, 23 September 1983.

58. *Pravda*, 23 November 1982.

59. *Ibid.*, 3 September 1982.

60. *Ibid.*, 8 January 1983.

61. Robert Sharlet, "Law and Discipline in the USSR: The Early 1980s Under Brezhnev, Andropov, and Chernenko," paper presented at the National Convention of the American Association for the Advancement of Slavic Studies, New York, November 1984, pp. 13-4. Sharlet cites *Vedomosti Verkhovnogo Soveta SSSR*, No 39, 1982, pp. 667-71.

62. *Sovety narodnykh deputatov*, No 11, 1980, pp. 19-26.

63. See, in particular, the proposals made in *Trud* on 15 December 1982 and in *Pravda* on 27 December 1982. Not all the proposals cited here were adopted, but they played a role in establishing the parameters of the debate and of future policy.

64. *Pravda*, 13 December 1982. A lawyer writing in *Literaturnaya gazeta* on 12 January 1983 countered that it would be a "scandalous illegality" if enterprises took it on themselves to deprive workers of their right to terminate their contracts at will.

65. *Sovetskaya Rossiya*, 25 December 1982.

66. *Pravda*, 17 December 1982.

67. *Financial Times*, 17 January 1983; *UPI*, 18

January 1983; *Christian Science Monitor*, 19 January 1983; *Baltimore Sun*, 25 January 1983.

68. *International Herald Tribune*, 31 January 1983.

69. *AP*, 18 January 1983.

70. *New York Times*, 7 February 1983.

71. *Pravda*, 23 March 1983.

72. *Ibid.*, 4 April 1983.

73. *Izvestia*, 2 April 1983.

74. See *Trud*, 29 December 1982; *Komsomol'skaya pravda*, 4 January 1983; *Literaturnaya gazeta*, 5 January 1983; *Pravda*, 11 January 1983.

75. *Radio Moscow*, 14 January 1983.

76. *Pravda*, 18 January 1983. On 28 August 1983, *Sovetskaya Rossiya* reported the results of a series of raids to check whether the new timetables had been put into operation. It found implementation to have been patchy and that, after a good start, shops slipped back to their old, inconvenient opening hours.

77. See, for example, *Izvestia*, 17 December 1982 and *Komsomol'skaya pravda*, 11 January 1983.

78. *Trud*, 16, 17 and 23 March 1983.

79. *Pravda* of 23 March 1983, *Sovetskaya kul'tura* of 5 April 1983, and *Pravda* of 7 August 1983, all stressed that discipline was not "the object of a temporary campaign, but a long-term social goal."

80. *Pravda*, 18 April 1983. *Pravda* had already commented on 23 March 1983 on the need for "production discipline," saying, "it's quite possible for a worker to turn up for work on time and stay for the required length of time, to come back from lunch at the appropriate time and still to spend his working day doing nothing at all."

81. *Sovetskaya Rossiya*, 26 April 1983.

82. *Zarya Vostoka*, 15 January 1983.

83. *Pravda*, 7 August 1983.

84. Compare *Kodeks zakonov o trude RSFSR*,

Moscow, 1974, as amended by the 1979 legislation.

85. *Pravda*, 28 August 1983.

86. Z. V. Kupriyanova, "Tekuchest' kadrov: perelomit' nezhel'atel'nye tendentsii," *EKO*, No 5, 1984, pp. 18-26.

87. *TASS*, 31 January 1983.

88. *Literaturnaya gazeta*, 2 February 1983, p. 13.

89. *Pravda*, 23 November 1982.

90. See Elizabeth Teague, "The USSR Law on Work Collectives: Workers' Control or Workers Controlled?" in Lane (ed), *op. cit.*, pp. 239-55.

Chapter 13

THE CAMPAIGN AGAINST CRIME AND CORRUPTION

Andropov's efforts to raise discipline in the workplace were accompanied by energetic measures against crime and, in particular, against economic crime, or corruption. In both instances, his aim was to restore public confidence in a society that had become dangerously demoralised.

The former Moscow lawyer Konstantin Simis has described the Soviet Union of the Brezhnev era as "a land of corrupt rulers, ruling over a corrupted people." According to Simis:

> the Soviet Union is infected from top to bottom with corruption--from the worker, who gives the foreman a bottle of vodka to get the best job, to Politburo member Mzhavadnadze, who takes hundreds of thousands of rubles for protecting underground millionaires; from the street prostitute, who pays the policeman ten rubles so that he won't prevent her from soliciting clients, to the former member of the Politburo, Minister of Culture Ekaterina Furtseva, who built a luxurious suburban villa at the government's expense --each and every one is afflicted with corruption.[1]

This phenomenon is already the subject of a sizable body of scholarly Western literature.[2] Like Simis, Western specialists reject any suggestion that corruption flourished in the Brezhnev period because Soviet citizens were naturally immoral and inclined toward deceit. Instead, they argue that the causes lay in the nature of the Soviet system.

The economy that took shape under Stalin was highly centralised and extremely inefficient. Output targets were determined at the centre and handed down to enterprises, for which they had the force of law; the system of material supply was also centrally-administered and far from perfect. Managers were often obliged to go outside the official economy and to make their own arrangements:

> During the Brezhnev era this increasingly engendered the growth of a system of pervasive corruption in which plant, factory and construction representatives found it necessary to bribe officials at various levels in the different ministries, planning agencies and committees, and in assorted Party organs, in order to get the delivery of supplies they needed in sufficient quantities and on time, which otherwise could simply not be obtained through officially sanctioned channels.[3]

Even so, bottlenecks and shortages occurred with monotonous regularity. Chronic shortfalls in the supply of consumer goods--and the generally low quality of those goods that were available--gave rise to a flourishing second, or parallel economy which supplied those goods and services most in demand at whatever price the market would bear. It was even suggested that the official Soviet economy was so inefficient that, had it not been for the "lubricating" role played by the second economy, the first might have collapsed. In other words, the USSR might be a society whose political economy required corruption in order to function at all.[4]

The irony or, rather, the tragedy of the situation was that people were all but driven by the system to engage in corrupt practices--bribery, speculation, petty pilfering--to obtain goods they would willingly have bought had they been available for purchase. It was difficult for even the most ordinary and law-abiding Soviet citizen to go about his or her daily business without having to grease somebody's palm, engage in some deal on the black market, or bribe an official simply to do his job. There were, British journalist Michael Binyon wrote, so many rules and regulations that almost everyone broke one or another in the course of daily routine and, Binyon argued, "public respect for all laws and for the principle of legality" was thereby diminished.[5]

The Soviet leaders appeared well aware of the corrosive effect that corruption, bribery and black marketeering were having upon the population as a whole. In the words of the former Party first secretary in Azerbaidzhan, Geidar Aliev:

> In an atmosphere of abuse of official position, corruption, whitewash, and contempt for honest labour, the initiative of the masses cannot fail to diminish; moral indignation holds sway and gives rise, among many social strata, to a state of despondency and apathy.[6]

This was exactly what happened in Poland, where revelations of corruption among the elite led to a rejection of the Party by the mass of the people. An official poll conducted in Poland in mid-1981 showed that, in response to a question asking which of fourteen national institutions people trusted most, first place went to the Church, and second to Solidarity. The Party came fourteenth, and last.[7]

Both Zhores Medvedev--a biologist and former Soviet dissident now living in Britain--and the American scholar Robert Sharlet have argued that the Polish events of 1980-81 played a direct role in persuading the Soviet authorities of the need for steps to curb corruption in the USSR.[8] In particular, the resentment of ordinary Poles at their leaders' privileged lifestyles alerted Soviet leaders to the danger that, unless precautionary measures were adopted, the existence of corruption on a comparable scale in the USSR might provoke similar feelings among the Soviet population. In September 1980, the CPSU Central Committee adopted a resolution outlining measures to be taken against corruption in Soviet official circles.[9] This was distributed to regional and district Party organisations in the form of a secret circular, but was not published. "The top leadership," Medvedev states, "clearly realised how widespread the trouble was and how sensitive an issue, and hoped to improve the situation without causing serious embarrassment."[10] Gradually, however, the campaign spread to other levels of society.

Changes made in September 1981 to the Criminal Code of the RSFSR,[11] and subsequently incorporated into those of the other Union Republics,[12] substantially toughened existing legislation relating to corrupt practices in the retail trade and consumer service sectors. In any society, of course, people employed in shops or warehouses tend to have opportunities for petty pilfering and illegal trading, but such behaviour is likely to be especially common in a society plagued, like the USSR, with chronic shortages of consumer goods. (The Soviet media frequently lament the number of smart young school leavers and even qualified specialists who take jobs as shop-assistants or waiters because of the rich pickings such theoretically low-paid and unskilled jobs command.[13])

The legal changes introduced in September 1981 extended the range of penalties that could be enforced against personnel in the light and food industries, restaurants, warehouses, shops and other consumer service outlets. In future, anyone found guilty of selling directly from warehouses, withdrawing goods from sale in order to create a deliberate shortage, or demanding under-the-counter payments for selling a scarce item or providing a service, would be liable to a range of punishments that included fines, corrective labour for a period of up to one year, or imprisonment for a period of up to three years.[14]

The the All-Union Fundamental Principles of Legislation on Criminal and Corrective Labour Law were amended in July 1982.[15] With the exception of one liberalising change--an extension of the use of suspended sentences for first offenders--these amendments meant that convicted persons serving sentences other than imprisonment, parolees and recidivists were to be brought under tighter control by the authorities while serving their sentences or probation. New provisions were added, according to which convicted persons who shirked serving corrective labour sentences, or who failed to pay fines, became liable to imprisonment. The maximum corrective labour sentence was raised from one to two years, meaning that people who would previously have been sent to jail for short terms could now be sentenced to longer terms of corrective labour.

Hardly a day passed after the adoption of these provisions without the publication in the media of details of the fining, imprisonment and even sentencing to death of officials, shop-assistants and others found guilty of speculation or black marketeering. Articles in the press attempted to lay the blame for consumer goods shortages on small- and large-scale speculators. In an interview on Radio Moscow on 3 February 1982, for example, first deputy minister of internal affairs Yurii Churbanov charged that black marketeers were "creating an artificial deficit of industrial goods and foodstuffs" with the deliberate aim of lining their own pockets.

On 27 April 1982 *Pravda* published an article by the USSR's senior legal officer--procurator general Aleksandr Rekunkov--in which the Soviet public was officially notified for the first time that a former deputy minister of fisheries, Vladimir Rytov, had been sentenced to death for economic crime.

Although well known, the story of the "Great Caviar Scandal" bears repeating. The operation was discovered in 1979, but details were not made public inside the USSR. The essence of the operation, in which some 200 officials of the ministry of fisheries were involved, was that black Russian caviar was packed in tins labelled "smoked herring." These were either distributed to specially selected restaurants in the Black Sea resort of Sochi, or exported to the West. In Sochi the contents of the tins were resold as caviar, with the difference in price between herring and caviar going into the pockets of the syndicate members. Exported tins were relabelled in the West and sold as caviar. Again, the profits were split between the members of the syndicate, with the hard currency earnings of the Soviet officials involved being banked in the West for their personal use during business trips.

The swindle was discovered by chance. Some of the tins were mistakenly released for general sale, and one happened to be bought in a Moscow store by a police detective who, on finding caviar inside a tin sold as "herring," launched an investigation.

Rytov, who had allegedly masterminded the operation, was executed; several of his accomplices received prison sentences.[16] As the result of a campaign by a small group of Sochi residents, who sent hundreds of letters to the press and to the Central Committee in Moscow, the chairman of the Sochi town Soviet, Vyacheslav Voronkov, received thirteen years' imprisonment for his part in the affair.[17] But Voronkov's superior, the Party first secretary of Krasnodar krai, Sergei Medunov, was shielded from investigation by the fact that he was a close friend of Leonid Brezhnev and of Brezhnev's son Yurii, first deputy minister of foreign trade.

This was the first time since capital punishment for economic crime was introduced in the Soviet Union in the early 1960s that the death sentence had been passed on so high an official as a deputy minister at all-Union level.[18] In the past, top state or Party officials found guilty of abusing their positions had got away with administrative punishments or Party reprimands. Coming when it did --early on in the campaign against corruption--the revelation of Rytov's fate seemed designed both to warn corrupt senior officials not to expect immunity from retribution, and to show the general public that their leaders would spare no-one in their efforts to punish corruption wherever it occurred.[19] Last but not least, corruption charges served as a convenient pretext on which a new generation of leaders was able to rid itself of an older one.

The American journalist Dusko Doder has described Andropov as an ascetic man who "lived for the last 16 years of his life with his wife in a one-bedroom apartment." A few floors below Andropov lived Brezhnev, "whose palatial apartment occupied the entire floor," and Brezhnev's close associate, minister of internal affairs Nikolai Shchelokov, "whose apartment was equally grand." Doder claims that "even while [Andropov] was in the KGB he had on several occasions expressed anger and disgust over the elite's corruption."[20]

Whatever the truth of such unconfirmed reports, Andropov seemed to appreciate that, with his reputation as one of the few incorruptible members of the leadership, he could exploit popular resentment of the life-styles of the elite to discredit his rivals and enhance his own chances in the struggle for the Brezhnev succession. Andropov's rival in this struggle was Brezhnev's closest associate,

Konstantin Chernenko.

Brezhnev began to cut down on his workload in 1975, following his first stroke. His health continued to decline until, in the last year of his life, he was almost completely incapacitated. While Chernenko was clearly Brezhnev's own favourite to succeed him as Party leader, his chances of securing the post were slight. Chernenko's only real source of support was Brezhnev: he had virtually no power base of his own. In Andropov, meanwhile, Chernenko faced a formidable opponent. In making his bid for the leadership, Andropov showed no compunction in using knowledge gained during his years at the KGB to discredit Brezhnev and, by extension, members of his entourage.

In his account of his fourteen months as a correspondent in Moscow, Andrew Nagorski recalls that the campaign against corruption that began in late 1980 was shortlived. Nagorski was told by one knowledgeable Muscovite that the authorities soon found that cracking down on black market activity hindered rather than helped the economy:

> "During an anti-corruption campaign like this, you can get five years in prison for taking a $70 bribe and a lot of people are hurt. But the authorities discovered that without bribes and the second economy the system doesn't work at all." ... Within a couple of weeks, ... complaints were so widespread that the government had begun quietly backing away from the entire campaign.[21]

Early in 1982, the campaign suddenly revived. But this time its focus shifted from small-scale speculators toward those at the very pinnacle of Soviet society. As the succession struggle entered its decisive stage, Andropov used the corruption issue to hit, through Brezhnev and his associates, at his rival Chernenko.

In January rumours began to circulate in Moscow that implicated Brezhnev's daughter Galina, wife of the first deputy minister of internal affairs, in a spectacular scandal. It was whispered that two of her friends--circus manager Anatolii Kolevatov, and a singer from the Bolshoi Theatre known as "Boris the Gypsy," believed to be Galina's lover--were engaged in a multimillion dollar diamond and hard-currency smuggling racket.

What was interesting about these rumours was not whether they were true, but why they were being so freely bandied about at that time. Though the private lives of prominent Soviet personalities are usually closely guarded secrets, allegations of wrong-doing may, on occasion, be used as a political weapon.[22] The significance of the rumours that circulated in January 1982 was, first, that they implicated Brezhnev's family; second, that they seemed to originate from the KGB; and third, that they served Andropov's purposes. Nagorski recalls:

> As other correspondents and I pieced together what had happened, it was evident that we were engaged less in investigative reporting than in following tracks that had been intentionally left uncovered. The speed with which the scandal broke and reports about it spread left little doubt that somebody high up wanted things that way.... That "somebody," I was convinced, had to be Andropov....[23]

A further twist was added to the story when, on 19 January, the first deputy chairman of the KGB, Semen Tsvigun, died in mysterious circumstances.

Tsvigun held responsibility for internal security; he was a full member of the CPSU Central

Committee; and he was said to be married to a sister of Brezhnev's wife. What was most mysterious about his death was that his obituary was signed neither by Brezhnev--who as general secretary of the Central Committee would normally sign the obituary of every deceased member of the Central Committee--nor by the Party's unofficial "second secretary" or "chief ideologist," Mikhail Suslov.[24] Western reporters were told Tsvigun had committed suicide.[25] Some reports maintained he had been involved in a cover-up of Galina's misdemeanours and that, when his boss Andropov faced him with documentary proof of her guilt, he shot himself. Other rumours held that, on the contrary, it was Tsvigun who ordered the arrest of Boris the Gypsy. This action supposedly led to a furious confrontation between Tsvigun and Suslov--the guardian of Kremlin rectitude who protected the reputations of the elite and ensured that their scandals were hushed up. Suslov reportedly told Tsvigun he had overstepped his authority in seeking to arrest someone close to Brezhnev's family and, his career in ruins, Tsvigun shot himself.[26] Moreover, the rumours added, the confrontation proved too much for the elderly Suslov. Whatever the truth of these stories, Suslov died of a stroke on 25 January.

Suslov, the king maker, had "held the ring" within the Kremlin leadership for nearly twenty years. It was with his death that the Brezhnev succession really began.

On the day of Suslov's funeral--ten days after Tsvigun's death--Boris the Gypsy was taken into police custody. Andropov was serving notice on the aging leaders of the Brezhnev generation that their days of carefree ease were numbered.

As the next step in their contest for the Party leadership, Chernenko and Andropov both bid for Suslov's mantle as Party ideologist. In April 1982, Chernenko published a theoretical article in the

Party journal *Kommunist*,[27] while Andropov was chosen to deliver the keynote speech at the annual Kremlin ceremony marking the anniversary of Lenin's birth.[28]

Andropov seemed in this speech deliberately to project himself as a sterner disciplinarian than Chernenko, whose article was complacent by contrast. Andropov stressed that any further development of "socialist democracy" must be dependent upon prior "successes of socialist construction," suggesting that in his view the achievement of sound economic growth was a more vital task at the current stage than any increase in popular participation. In an apparent reference to the scandals that had sullied the image of the Brezhnev family, Andropov said:

> The justified indignation of the Soviet people is aroused by cases of theft, bribery...and other anti-social phenomena. ... As long as such phenomena exist, they hinder our progress.

Chernenko seemed in his article to be asserting that the economy was on course and that the ills of Soviet society should not be exaggerated. "It is sometimes possible," he wrote, "to hear people asking whether we do not already have too much democracy in our society, and whether it is not leading to a weakening of discipline." Chernenko rejected such views as "witting or unwitting confusion of democracy with petty-bourgeois notions."

Andropov's views carried the day. He left the KGB in May and was promoted to membership of the Central Committee Secretariat. According to unconfirmed rumours, the Politburo session at which Andropov's transfer was discussed was a heated affair. Brezhnev supposedly suggested Chernenko for Suslov's slot but was overruled. Politburo members Dmitrii Ustinov, Mikhail Gorbachev, Andrei Gromyko and Andrei Kirilenko backed Andropov's candidacy.[29]

Jockeying for position was to continue between Chernenko and Andropov throughout the summer and autumn, until Brezhnev's death in November 1982.

Evidence that Andropov's power was growing came with the removal in July of Sergei Medunov from his post as Party first secretary in Krasnodar krai. The downfall of Brezhnev's personal friend, and his replacement by an ally of Andropov, was a clear sign that Brezhnev had grown too weak to protect those who had relied upon him in the past, and that he had lost his former power of appointment. Gradually, a series of exposes in the Soviet press revealed what had been going on in the Krasnodar region. Farm accounts had been systematically falsified and agricultural produce siphoned off for sale on the black market. Local Party officials had demanded bribes before they would allocate hotel rooms at resorts along the Black Sea coast, or before ordinary residents could obtain housing, jobs, or promotions. Those who dared to complain faced harsh retribution: some lost their jobs, others were imprisoned, some were confined in psychiatric hospitals.[30]

Andropov's election as general secretary saw the campaign against corruption broaden into an all-out battle against crime. No crime statistics were published, but reports published at the time in the official press implied that, under Brezhnev, law and order had become dangerously lax. Moreover, as the former head of the KGB, Andropov seemed determined to bring a rival law enforcement agency, the ministry of internal affairs (MVD), to heel.

The MVD controls the uniformed police, or militia. It is responsible for criminal investigation and crime prevention; maintenance of public order (which includes the detention of vagrants, beggars and drunks, and the supervision of persons "avoiding socially useful work and leading an anti-social or parasitic way of life"); administration of the internal and external passport system, including the granting of residence permits to Soviet citizens; licensing of fire-arms, explosives and photocopiers; supervision of the fire service; and traffic control (including the licensing and inspection of motor vehicles). The MVD also has its own military organisation, in the form of regular troops who keep order at football matches and public parades, and who stand by in case any unexpected trouble, such as unauthorised demonstrations or strikes, should break out.

Under the leadership of Brezhnev's associate, Shchelokov, the MVD acquired a reputation for laxity and venality. It was rumoured at the end of 1982, for example, that the MVD had been obstructing the KGB's attempts to clamp down on economic crime--a field in which the two law enforcement agencies had overlapping responsibilities.[31]

Problems of crime and public order were clearly matters of concern to the general population at this time. One of Andropov's first acts as general secretary was to authorise the publication of brief weekly reports summarising the topics discussed by the Politburo at its regular Thursday sessions. The first report, published in *Pravda* on 11 December 1982, revealed that the Politburo had discussed letters from the public complaining about corruption and crime. The Politburo, the report said,

> has drawn the attention of the USSR procurator general and the ministry of internal affairs to the necessity of taking proper measures to improve socialist legality in towns and villages.

A few days later, *Izvestia* devoted a frontpage editorial to the topic, saying that readers were writing to the newspaper "protesting against cases of bureaucracy and red tape and violations of Soviet laws.... Questions concerning the need to strengthen law and order in our cities and towns are pointedly raised in these letters."[32] Noting the role played here by letters to the authorities, Zhores Medvedev comments that:

> the new initiative against corruption cannot be explained entirely as emanating from the top. It was also the result of great pressure from below, expressed in the letters: the same kind of force which brought Solidarity to life in Poland so quickly in August 1980 and made the organization ten million strong. In the Soviet Union mass dissatisfaction cannot yet find expression in such an open form. However, its leaders were forced to take serious notice of the public mood and public expectations.[33]

Within days, the first personnel change of Andropov's leadership was announced: Shchelokov was replaced as minister of internal affairs by General Vitalii Fedorchuk, Andropov's former deputy at the KGB.[34] Six months later, it was announced that Shchelokov had been stripped of his membership in the CPSU Central Committee for "mistakes in his work."[35] The implication was not only that he had been lax in fighting corrupt practices, but that he had himself been guilty of corruption. Shchelokov is believed to have committed suicide to escape criminal prosecution on corruption charges.[36]

Fedorchuk, who had gained a tough reputation during his years as head of the KGB in Ukraine, set about cleaning up the mess Shchelokov had left behind, and lost no time in launching a major shake-up of police activity. His appointment was widely interpreted as a move to assert KGB influence over the MVD and to coordinate the activities of the two agencies in the fight against crime. It was a victory for the KGB in its longstanding struggle for turf with the MVD.

A further stage of Andropov's new campaign was marked by the publication in *Pravda* on 9 January 1983 of another article by the USSR procurator general. On this occasion, Rekunkov described the law-and-order situation in Soviet cities in terms (as the *Economist* put it) "reminiscent of New York or Detroit,"[37] and spoke of citizens' concern over "the unsatisfactory state of affairs in certain towns and villages." In some places, he said, people hesitated to go out on the streets at night for fear of being attacked. Theft of state property was rampant; criminals went unpunished because the police were turning a blind eye. The most urgent task, Rekunkov implied, was to clean up the police force itself. What was striking about Rekunkov's article was his (for that time) unusually frank admission both that crime was widespread in the USSR, and that it had tainted the ranks of the MVD.

Less than a month after his appointment, Fedorchuk addressed a meeting of the Presidium of the USSR Supreme Soviet at which the work of both the police and the procuracy (which supervises the investigation of criminal cases, authorises arrests and prosecutes offenders) came in for criticism. Fedorchuk called for greater coordination of the activity of the law enforcement agencies in the struggle against crime.[38] A fortnight later, Fedorchuk summoned an all-Union conference which, meeting in Moscow, discussed "ways of preventing crimes against socialist property" (bribery, speculation, theft, embezzlement) and approved "concrete measures for eliminating shortcomings in the work of the organs of internal affairs."[39]

On 17 March, *Pravda* reported that the MVD's police patrol service had been "restructured" to put more policemen back in the streets and parks, on buses and suburban trains, "particularly in the evenings." But, *Pravda* went on, "quite a few serious omissions are still to be found in the work of the law enforcement bodies"; this was "giving rise to justified criticism on the part of the general public." The purpose of the reorganisation of the MVD, Fedorchuk told *Pravda* on 10 August 1983, was to free police officers from paperwork so that they could spend more time on the beat. Police officers had been told to get to know their neighbourhoods and to identify potential "hot spots." Police patrols and document checks would, Fedorchuk promised, be stepped up during the hours of darkness. Finally, the minister promised a crackdown on corrupt policemen: "The personnel of the internal affairs organs are being purged of slackers and of those who are ideologically and morally immature," he stated.

Fedorchuk's militia launched a campaign to encourage citizens to inform on their neighbours. Western newsmen reported in March 1983 that police officers were visiting Moscow homes, leaving calling cards with the address and telephone number of the nearest police station, and asking citizens to tell them "if they noticed anybody drunk, rowdy or otherwise breaking the law."[40] Similar cards were said to have been distributed in Krasnodar in January. There, an informer was requested merely to underline one or more of a list of twelve offences and to return the card with the name and address of the offender; he was "not required" to reveal his own identity. The offences included: being a loafer and refusing to find work; refusing to pay alimony or fines imposed by the courts; failing to raise one's children responsibly; getting drunk or taking drugs; living off "unearned income"; or simply "violating public order and the rules of communal living."[41] The distribution of similar cards had been reported from Kiev in 1981--that is, when Fedorchuk was heading the KGB in Ukraine.[42]

In July 1983 the Politburo announced the creation of new bodies--"political organs"--in the MVD.[43] Their task was to "organise and guide Party political, ideological, cultural and educational work in the MVD, and to enhance the responsibility of personnel for the discharge of their duties." The move was clearly designed to tighten Party control over the MVD. The new system resembled that in the Soviet armed forces, where political officers act as the Party's agents within the military and as the means whereby political control is exercised over the rank-and-file. Interviewed in *Izvestia* on 25 November 1983, the head of the MVD's freshly created political administration, Major-General Viktor Gladyshev, stated that a stronger political presence was needed in the militia because policemen were coming into greater contact with the public in the fight against crime and because an increasing number of civilians (Party and Komsomol volunteers) were serving in auxiliary police units. There were, Gladyshev said, "still shortcomings" in the work of the police force.

Interviewed in *Pravda* on the first anniversary of his appointment, Fedorchuk claimed that the drive against corruption, hooliganism and alcoholism was showing positive results.[44] There had been many arrests of "speculators, thieves and bribe-takers," he said. Black market rings had been broken up in Georgia, Ukraine, Armenia, the Kalmyk autonomous republic and Krasnodar krai. Crooked car dealers had been exposed in Leningrad, "plunderers of cereal products" in Kaliningrad and, in Astrakhan oblast, corrupt officials who had pocketed the profits from the sale of state-owned cattle, sheep, fish and caviar. It had also been necessary, Fedorchuk asserted, to stamp out corruption in the MVD. Police officers guilty of laxity or corruption had been weeded out, and the militia had been "replenished" with new staff.[45]

The campaign against corruption was accompanied by a stiffening of legal penalties for a wide range of crimes, including theft or embezzlement of state property, abuse of office for mercenary gain, and speculation (the purchase of goods, for the purpose of resale, by an unauthorised individual). These provisions were announced on 18 December 1982 and came into force on 1 January 1983.[46] The maximum sentence for black marketeering was upped to ten years' imprisonment, while the maximum fine for "mercenary crimes" was raised to 1,000 rubles. Corrective labour terms were introduced for a number of offences previously punishable only by fines. The powers of the courts to confiscate the personal property of those found guilty of embezzlement or extortion were extended. At the same time, penalties were reduced for a number of less serious offences by expanding the use of corrective labour, conditional and deferred sentences, and other alternatives to imprisonment. For example, a prison sentence of less than three years could in future be deferred for a first-time offender if the court decided he or she could be reeducated through corrective labour and "without being isolated from society."[47] These changes were intended to make the punishment of criminals more flexible and therefore more effective.

In October 1982, that is, while Brezhnev was still alive, changes to the law on "parasitism" were adopted in the RSFSR. They came into effect shortly after Brezhnev's death, on 1 January 1983.[48]

Although Soviet citizens are guaranteed the right to work by the 1977 Soviet constitution, they do not enjoy any corresponding right to choose *not* to work. On the contrary, the duty to "work conscientiously" is the first of the duties of Soviet citizens listed in the constitution. The "right to work" is therefore not a right at all, but a legal obligation, and any able-bodied citizen of working age who "follows a parasitic way of life," that is, who does not hold a job within the official economy and is found to be living on "unearned income," is liable to criminal prosecution.

Originally drawn up to control the activities of gypsies and vagrants, the Soviet parasite laws have also been brought to bear against members of the dissident community such as religious activists and would-be emigres. The law operates in the following way. A Soviet citizen who is unemployed for a period of three consecutive months is supposed to receive an official warning from the local branch of the MVD that he or she must find work within one month. The local Soviet, alerted by the MVD, is obliged to find a job and to make "living arrangements" for the person in question within 15 days of receiving an application for assistance. (The instructions of the local Soviet are mandatory upon the enterprise to whom the offending citizen is assigned, though plentiful evidence attests that enterprises are often reluctant to accept such "problem" workers onto their staff.) A citizen who fails to take up employment within one month of receiving a police warning becomes liable to criminal prosecution.[49]

Until January 1983, the offence in question was described as "systematically engaging in vagrancy or begging, or leading a parasitic way of life for a protracted period of time." From the beginning of 1983, however, the words "systematically" and "for a protracted period of time" were deleted. The range of people liable to prosecution was thereby widened, and the law became applicable not only to a person who had been unemployed for four consecutive months, but also to anyone who had been unemployed for a total of four months in the course of any one year. The maximum penalty for a first offence was raised from one year's imprisonment to two, and for a repeat offence from two years' imprisonment to three. The new legislation provided, in addition, for the establishment of "educational prophylaxis centres" for those found guilty of parasitism.[50]

The alterations to the parasite laws seemed to have a dual purpose. On the one hand, they reflected the authorities' general drive for tougher labour discipline, and sought to encourage idle workers to find jobs. Equally importantly, they seemed to be intended to curb the USSR's thriving black market.

The parasite laws were aimed not only at those living by vagrancy and begging, but also at anyone for whom "unearned income" was the principal, or one of the principal, means of support. Unearned income was defined as "money obtained through gambling, fortune-telling, solicitation, petty speculation and other illegal means."[51] Thus, a "parasite" might be someone who lived by scrounging money from friends and relations. The term might also refer to someone who did not hold a job in the official economy, but earned his or her living on the second economy. In the early 1980s the term "parasite" was applied to migrant workers; to people who earned money from the sale of garden produce (particularly of illicitly distilled alcohol); and to those doing private household repairs such as plumbing, electrical work and home decorating. The income of such people was considered "unearned" because it almost always involved the purloining of state property (tools and raw materials) unavailable for purchase through normal channels. It might also involve the use of an official position as cover for private activity --for example, a dentist might use his official surgery and its equipment to do private dental work.

It could be argued that official efforts to reduce the role of the black market strike a blow at the standard of living of the average Soviet citizen. After all, the second economy may be said to perform a "lubricating" function in improving the performance of the chronically inefficient official economy. In the words of Harry Gelman,

> In a sense, the regime's toleration of the unplanned "second economy" is tacit recognition that more concessions must be made to consumer services than the official allocation of resources would otherwise permit. Attacks on "corruption" thus threaten to shrink this extra margin usurped from the planners for the consumer by the "second economy."[52]

According to this interpretation, the attempts to crack down on corruption and the black market made by the Brezhnev leadership in 1981, and again in 1982 by that of Andropov, ran counter to the consumer-oriented policies that characterised the Soviet leaders' initial response to the events in Poland. For this reason, the campaign was soon abandoned by Brezhnev. It was relaunched under Andropov's leadership partly as a means of tightening social controls, and partly because it served Andropov as a weapon against political opponents.

Robert Sharlet has remarked upon the large amount of new legislation introduced under Andropov's brief leadership, which he describes as "one of the most prolific periods of legislative activity in recent Soviet history."[53] Much of this legislation falls outside the scope of the present discussion, but it would not be an exaggeration to say that much of it was repressive both in tone and in effect. The first law adopted under Andropov's aegis, for example, was a new law relating to the Soviet border. Introducing this legislation at a session of the USSR Supreme Soviet on 24 November 1982, the then KGB chief Vitalii Fedorchuk painted a grim picture of the Soviet Union as under permanent siege from hostile Western enemies. The new law, he told his audience, reflected the "worsened international situation." "Our class enemy," Fedorchuk went on, "is conducting, more actively and more massively than ever before, all-out espionage and ideological subversion against our country."[54] The new law did not, in fact, differ in any substantial way from the law on the state border, adopted in August 1960, that had been in effect until that time. However, its adoption was given wide coverage in the mass media, and appeared designed as a warning to the population at large and as reinforcement of a "Fortress Russia" mentality.

Other laws adopted under Andropov's leadership had an openly repressive character. On 1 October 1983 a new law--"On Malicious Disobedience of the Demands of the Administration of a Corrective Labour Institution"--was added to the Criminal Code of the RSFSR. This meant that, upon completion of his or her sentence, any prisoner who had displayed opposition to the prison or camp administration could--virtually at the administration's whim--be resentenced to a fresh term of up to three years' imprisonment. In the case of a "particularly dangerous recidivist," the maximum term was five years' imprisonment. In effect, the authorities gained the right to prolong the imprisonment of prisoners of conscience who took part in protests--as many of them did--or who refused to recant. The penalty for trying to escape from a place of administrative surveillance (that is, a place of internal exile) was also stiffened. Such attempts were previously punishable by detention for a period of six months to a year, after two warnings had been given; the new punishment was one to three years, and no prior warning was required.[55]

In January 1984, when Andropov was already on his death-bed, the law "On Criminal Liability for Crimes Against the State" was amended. Harsher penalties were provided for "anti-Soviet agitation and propaganda" where offenders were found to have "used monies or other valuables obtained from foreign organisations or persons acting in the interests of those organisations." To supplement existing laws on divulging state and military secrets, penalties of up to eight years' imprisonment were added for "passing on to or gathering in order to pass on to foreign organisations or their agents...information constituting a professional secret"--something that had not previously been defined as a crime.[56] One purpose of this law was presumably to discourage Soviet citizens from providing foreign journalists with information that might prove embarrassing to the authorities.

On the basis of the large amount of new legislation introduced under his leadership, Sharlet describes Andropov as "a believer in the efficacy of law to remedy social problems," and suggests that Andropov saw "implacable law" as "his instrument for social engineering."[57] In the same vein, the British sociologist George Kolankiewicz summed up Andropov's approach as "the legalistic road to communism."[58] At the same time, it should be borne in mind that much of the legislation adopted under Andropov's leadership was criticised by Western legal specialists for the tendency it showed, not toward greater legality, but toward increased arbitrariness.

This point was forcefully made by Anthony Williams, head of the British delegation to the CSCE (Conference on Security and Cooperation in Europe) human rights conference held in Ottawa in May 1985. Williams expressed concern that laws introduced by the Soviet authorities since the holding of the CSCE review conference in Madrid in September 1983 "define rights and crimes so loosely or vaguely that even the most innocent cannot be sure that they are not getting on the wrong side of the law." Such "open-endedness," the British representative said, "gives an opportunity to even low-level officials to pursue and persecute individuals whose only real offence is to claim rights which these authorities find inconvenient." Turning to the law on "malicious disobedience," Williams commented:

> I must be frank and say that there is a good deal of apprehension that this new law could be applied to essentially non-violent "criminals" by the Soviet state, serving sentences for actions which would not be regarded as crimes in most of the states here represented. Many of the individuals to whom I refer are in detention in the first place because they have been convicted under articles of criminal legislation which...are worded in what seems to us a dangerously vague and open-ended manner. I am thinking, in particular, of the well-known articles concerning "anti-Soviet agitation and propaganda" and the circulation of "anti-Soviet fabrications."

Williams went on:

> Perhaps even more perturbing is a new law headed "The transmission to foreign organisations of information constituting a work-related secret."... As we all know, there are quite a few people wishing, for one reason or another, to leave the Soviet Union for elsewhere, who have been refused permission to do so because of past--in some cases rather surprisingly long past--acquaintance with what, in that country, is regarded as very secret. However, this new category of "work-related secrets" seems to us to go even further and to be

> so open-ended as to be almost limitless ....This legislation, with its vagueness and obscurity, seems to be yet another development ... calculated, like the increasing interference with private communications from abroad, to inhibit the kind of contacts between ordinary people which is one of the cornerstones of the Helsinki Final Act.[59]

To sum up, the Andropov leadership introduced a large amount of new legislation intended to tighten social controls. The impression conveyed was that the authorities were stepping up still further the reduction of contacts with the outside world that began under Brezhnev with the launching of the crackdown against dissent in 1979, gathered momentum under the impact of the Polish events of 1980, when jamming of Western broadcasts was resumed, and continued into 1982 with the cutting off of direct-dial telephone links between the USSR and the USA, Western Europe, and Japan. The Polish example, it appeared, had served the Soviet authorities as a dreadful warning of what might happen in a socialist country that became too open to foreign capital and ideas. It had shaken their confidence and encouraged the emergence of a tougher line in domestic policy.

FOOTNOTES TO CHAPTER 13

1. Konstantin M. Simis, *USSR: The Corrupt Society*, New York, 1982, p. 297. The notoriously corrupt Vasilii Mzhavadnadze, Party first secretary in Georgia from 1953-72, "retired at his own request on grounds of age" (*Pravda*, 30 September 1972). Ekaterina Furtseva, the only woman ever elected to the Politburo, lost her post in 1961, allegedly on grounds of corruption.

2. See, for example, A. Katsenelinboigen, "Coloured Markets in the Soviet Union," *Soviet Studies*, January 1977, pp. 62-85; Gregory Grossman, "The 'Second Economy' of the USSR," *Problems of Communism*, September-October 1977, pp. 25-40; Konstantin Simis, "The Machinery of Corruption in the Soviet Union," *Survey*, Autumn 1977-78, pp. 35-55; Aron Katsenelinboigen, "Corruption in the USSR: some methodological notes," in Michael Clarke (ed), *Corruption: Causes, Consequences and Control*, London, 1983, pp. 220-38; Stephen Shenfield, "*Pripiski*: false statistical reporting in Soviet-type economies," in Clarke (ed), *op. cit.*, pp. 239-58; Gerald Mars and Yochanan Altman, "How a Soviet economy really works: cases and implications," in Clarke (ed), *op. cit.*, pp. 259-67; Nick Lampert, "The whistleblowers: corruption and citizens' complaints in the USSR," in Clarke (ed), *op. cit.*, pp. 268-87; *idem*, "Law and Order in the USSR: The Case of Economic and Official Crime," *Soviet Studies*, July 1984, pp. 366-85; *idem*, *Whistle-blowing in the Soviet Union: Complaints and Abuses under State Socialism*, London, 1985.

3. Elliot R. Goodman, "The Brezhnev-Andropov Legacy," *Survey*, Summer 1984, pp. 34-69 at pp. 36-7.

4. This point is made by Nick Lampert in "Law, Order and Political Power in the USSR," a paper delivered at the annual conference of the British National Association for Soviet and East European Studies, Cambridge, March 1984; and by Katsenelinboigen in his contribution to Clarke (ed), *op. cit.*

5. Michael Binyon, *Life in Russia*, London, 1985, p. 365.

6. *Literaturnaya gazeta*, 18 November 1981.

7. *Kultura* (Warsaw), 21 June 1981, as cited by Richard Pipes in *Survival is not Enough*, New York, 1984, p. 157.

8. Zhores Medvedev, *Andropov*, New York, 1983,

p. 135; Robert Sharlet, "Law and Discipline in the USSR: The Early 1980s Under Brezhnev, Andropov and Chernenko," a paper presented at the annual convention of the American Association for the Advancement of Slavic Studies, New York, November 1984, p. 5.

9. Medvedev, *loc. cit.* See also *AP*, 5 November 1981, and *Washington Post*, 28 November 1981.

10. Medvedev, *loc. cit.*

11. *Trud*, 3 November 1981.

12. *Izvestia*, 15 January 1981.

13. See, for example, *Komsomol'skaya pravda*, 29 May 1980; *Pravda*, 7 and 29 June 1981; *Sotsialisticheskaya industriya*, 30 October 1982; *Pravda*, 10 June 1982.

14. *Vedomosti Verkhovnogo Soveta RSFSR*, No 38, 1981, pp. 763-4. See also Sharlet, *op. cit.*, pp. 6-7, and RL 464/81, "New Legislation against Under-the-Counter Trading," by Allan Kroncher, 19 November 1981.

15. *Vedomosti Verkhovnogo Soveta SSSR*, No 30, 1982, pp. 505-8; *Sotsialisticheskaya zakonnost'*, No 10, October 1982, pp. 17-19; *Izvestia*, 19 December 1982; Sharlet, *op. cit.*, pp. 7-9.

16. Medvedev, *op. cit.*, p. 140.

17. Andrew Nagorski, *Reluctant Farewell*, New York, 1985, pp. 71-3.

18. See RL 300/77, "Capital Punishment in the USSR," by Sergei Voronitsyn, 22 December 1977.

19. RL 182/82, "Execution of Deputy Fisheries Minister Revealed in Soviet Press," by Sergei Voronitsyn, 29 April 1982.

20. *International Herald Tribune*, 30 July 1985.

21. Nagorski, *op. cit.*, p. 176.

22. Stories began to circulate in 1979, for example, according to which Politburo member Grigorii Romanov, Party first secretary in Leningrad oblast, had ordered Catherine the Great's dinner service to be brought to his country house from the

Hermitage Museum for use at his daughter's wedding party. Drunken guests were said to have followed the old Russian tradition and to have smashed the antique glasses. Although the incident was not treated as a crime and there was no investigation, outside observers concluded that rumours of the incident had been spread deliberately to scotch Romanov's ambition of moving to the central Party apparat in Moscow; Medvedev, *op. cit.*, p. 139.

23. Nagorski, *op. cit.*, p. 182-3.

24. *Pravda*, 21 January 1982.

25. Jonathan Steele and Eric Abraham, *Andropov in Power*, Oxford, 1983, p. 141.

26. Nagorski, *op. cit.*, p. 181.

27. K. U. Chernenko, "Avangardnaya rol' partii kommunistov," *Kommunist*, No 6, 1982, pp. 25-43.

28. *Pravda*, 23 April 1982.

29. Zhores Medvedev, "Yuri Andropov and His Ways," *Labour Focus on Eastern Europe*, Winter 1982-83; Myron Rush, "Succeeding Brezhnev," *Problems of Communism*, January-February 1983, p. 4.

30. See for example *Pravda*, 11 December 1982, 29 January and 15 March 1983; *Sovetskaya Rossiya*, 20 May 1983.

31. *Reuters*, 17 December 1982.

32. *Izvestia*, 14 December 1982.

33. Zhores Medvedev, *Andropov*, New York, 1983, pp. 143-4.

34. *TASS*, 17 December 1982.

35. *Pravda*, 16 June 1983.

36. *UPI*, 15 December 1984.

37. *Economist*, 15 January 1983.

38. *Radio Moscow*, 12 January, *TASS*, 16 January 1983.

39. *Pravda*, 26 January 1983.

40. *UPI*, 3 July 1983.

41. *AP*, 3 July 1983.

42. *UPI*, 3 July 1983.

43. *Pravda*, 30 July 1983.

44. *Ibid.*, 20 December 1983.

45. Fedorchuk wrote in *Pravda* on 29 May 1985 that, in all, 55,000 communists had been drafted into the MVD in order to strengthen law and order "strictly and decisively."

46. *Vedomosti Verkhovnogo Soveta RSFSR*, No 49, 1982, pp. 1093-1108; Paul B. Stephan III, "Comrades' Courts and Labor Discipline Since Brezhnev," University of Virginia School of Law, Working Paper Series No 1, 1985, pp. 12-13.

47. *Izvestia*, 19 December 1982.

48. *Vedomosti Verkhovnogo Soveta RSFSR*, No 41, 1982, pp. 935-7; RL 519/82, "Campaign against 'Parasitism' Likely to be Stepped up in RSFSR," by Sergei Voronitsyn, 27 December 1982; *Sovetskaya Rossiya*, 19 January 1983.

49. *Vedomosti Verkhovnogo Soveta RSFSR*, No 51, 1984, pp. 1261-3. This is not, apparently, a duty that the militia always takes very seriously. A study of court cases in Kirgizia in 1984 revealed that "only 8 percent of loafers received official warnings about their obligation to work during the first six months of their 'vacation,' and 50 percent had not received one even after they had been out of work for more than six months"; *Sovetskaya Kirgiziya*, 27 June 1985.

50. *Vedomosti Verkhovnogo Soveta RSFSR*, No 51, 1984, pp. 1261-3.

51. *Ibid.*

52. Harry Gelman, "Soviet Vulnerabilities and Advantages: An Attempt at a Balance Sheet," Santa Monica, Calif., 1985, p. 14.

53. Sharlet, *op. cit.*, p. 25.

54. *Pravda*, 25 November 1982.

55. *Vedomosti Verkhovnogo Soveta RSFSR*, No 37, 1983, p. 796. See also RL 430/83, "New Law on 'Malicious Disobedience' in Soviet Camps," by Julia Wishnevsky, 14 November 1983.

56. *Vedomosti Verkhovnogo Soveta SSSR*, No 3,

1984, pp. 91-3. See also RL 78/84, "New Additions to the Law on Crimes against the State," by Julia Wishnevsky, 16 February 1984.

57. Sharlet, *op. cit.*, pp. 12 and 36.

58. George Kolankiewicz, "The Polish Question: Andropov's Answer?" in Leonard Schapiro and Joseph Godson (eds), *The Soviet Worker: From Lenin to Andropov*, second edition, London, 1984, p. 272.

59. RFE/RL Special by Roland Eggleston, Ottawa, 24 May 1985.

Chapter 14

IDEOLOGICAL DEBATES SPARKED BY THE POLISH CRISIS

Marx and Lenin, who devoted all their energies to considering how recurring crises could be used to promote class war and revolutionary change in the societies into which they were born, were supremely confident that the communist system they foresaw--a classless society without rulers, police or army --would be free of crisis and conflict. The history of "really existing socialism" has not lived up to these expectations. From the Kronstadt uprising of 1921, through the strikes by East German workers of 1953, the Hungarian revolution of 1956 and the Prague Spring of 1968, to the frequent outbreaks of social unrest in Poland that led in the summer of 1980 to the establishment of Solidarity, socialist societies of the Soviet type have proved as chronically crisis-prone as capitalist ones.

Under Brezhnev's leadership, Soviet ideologists denied the possibility that an internally-generated crisis could occur in the USSR. Indeed, Soviet society in the second half of the twentieth century emitted an air of considerable stability. Yet, as Ernst Kux has demonstrated, the belief of Soviet ideologists that "socialism contains the possibility of a crisisless and progressive development in an ascending line" was profoundly shaken by the unrest that erupted in Poland in 1980.[1] A debate began in official circles over the causes of the Polish crisis; at the same time, Soviet theoreticians began to ask themselves: "Could it happen here?"

The Soviet authorities were concerned not only that the example of Poland's unrest might spill over to the Soviet population. An examination of the debate over the "lessons of Poland" betrays a deeper fear: that the Polish crisis might not be attributable merely to the peculiarities of Polish socialism, but be symptomatic of a general weakness afflicting all socialist societies of the Soviet type. If Poland was subject to periodic bouts of social conflict, did that mean that the USSR might one day find itself facing similar crises? And if, as Brezhnev stated at the Twenty-sixth Congress of the CPSU in February 1981, "a threat has arisen in Poland to the foundations of the socialist state,"[2] did that imply that socialism in the USSR was also potentially reversible?

The debate was the sharper in that the Soviet Union in the 1980s was facing an important turning point. In the first place, a major generational shift was under way within the leadership. Secondly, this change of leadership was taking place at a moment when the loss of dynamism of the Soviet economy had generated a deep moral malaise among the population. As the Brezhnev era drew to a close, there was general agreement within the elite that urgent remedies were needed to halt and reverse the decline both of economic growth rates and of popular morale. Completely lacking, however, was any consensus as to how this feat was to be accomplished. In the circumstances, the search for an ideologically acceptable explanation of what had gone wrong in Poland inevitably became entangled in a debate over the future of the Soviet system. While a reformist wing advocated decentralising and liberalising reforms to ward off social unrest, a "purist" group of Party ideologists warned that the Polish example showed the need for the enforcement of greater conformity and homogeneity among the Soviet population.

Official interpretations of the Polish crisis have been skillfully classified by Ray Taras.[3] Taras divides them first into explanations that see Poland's various crises as having been either (a) socio-economic or (b) political in character. Then he distinguishes a further official set of variables which he describes as "the determinants of crises"; these are (a) systemic, (b) structural, (c) functional, and (d) voluntaristic determinants. Taras goes on to suggest that explanations that emphasise "systemic" or "structural" causes tend to show a closer correlation with reformist solutions than do those that stress "functional" or "voluntaristic" ones. In particular, Taras argues that what he terms "characterological" explanations ("Gierek's mistakes," "the excesses of Solidarity extremists") represent "an attempt to discredit the need for structural reform."

Taras found the two explanations most commonly offered by official Polish sources to be:

> (1) one that is in origin economic in character (falling living standards resulting in social discontent) and caused by functional failures of the system (erroneous policies, distorted implementation) and (2) one that is primarily of a political nature (factional struggle, the existence of illegal political groups) and caused by voluntaristic factors (the autocratic personality of a ruler, the reactionary consciousness of much of society).

Such explanations, Taras comments,

> stress micropolitical or microeconomic factors and, accordingly, exonerate the system and its basic structures of responsibility. They minimise, moreover, the need for reform.[4]

Discussing the causes of the crisis at the Twenty-sixth Congress of the CPSU, for example,

Brezhnev stressed the voluntaristic and the political, alleging that "in Poland, the enemies of socialism, supported by outside forces, are stirring up anarchy in an attempt to channel events in a counterrevolutionary direction." The Polish events, Brezhnev went on, "convince us once again how important it is for the Party...to lend a sensitive ear to the voice of the masses, to struggle resolutely against all manifestations of bureaucratism and voluntarism, actively to develop socialist democracy, and to pursue a balanced and realistic policy in foreign economic relations."[5] Addressing the same Congress, Polish Party leader Stanislaw Kania likewise complained of the activity of "counterrevolutionary forces, supported by centres of imperialist aggression" and of the mistakes of the Gierek leadership: "voluntaristic disrespect for the economic laws of socialism and for Leninist norms of Party life; failure to appreciate class contradictions in society; and neglect of ideological work."[6]

CONTRADICTIONS IN SOCIALISM

During the 1970s, Soviet and Polish ideologists declared that Poland had, as the other industrialised socialist countries of Eastern Europe were held to have done, completed the transition from capitalism to socialism and embarked upon the construction of a developed socialist society.[7] Faced in 1980 with the spectacle of widespread worker unrest, Soviet theoreticians revised this view and announced that Poland was still in the pre-socialist, transition stage. To appreciate the practical significance of these formulations, it is necessary briefly to review their theoretical underpinnings.

Marx saw "the history of all hitherto existing society" as determined by economic conditions, played out (from a certain point in time) in a succession of class struggles between the haves and the have-nots.[8] According to Marx, human beings are fixed into classes by forces over which they have no control. These forces, which Marx dubbed the "forces of production," refer to the level of technological development reached by a society at any one time. Marx used the term "relations of production" to describe the relationship of each class within society to the dominant system of productive forces. Each class has its own interests; these are by definition opposed to those of other classes. Conflicts between classes in pre-socialist society are accordingly known, in Marxist terminology, as "antagonistic" while, under capitalism, workers and capitalists are held to be locked, willy nilly, in deadly struggle.

Marx believed, too, that the productive forces are in a constant state of change. As they develop, they outgrow the existing relations of production. Eventually, the productive forces come into outright conflict with the established system of productive relations. This clash results in an economic and social crisis which is resolved only by means of a revolutionary upheaval, which ushers in a new set of productive relations and a new ruling class.

Building on Hegel's philosophy of the dialectic --that is, the process of change which occurs as a result of "a struggle between contradictions" and in which there exists a constant tension between any present state of affairs and that into which it is developing--Marx saw the "contradiction" between the forces of production and the relations of production as the "fundamental antagonism," that is, the motor force of social progress.

Finally, Marx saw the Europe of the nineteenth century as on the verge of a violent revolution in which the oppressed proletariat would rise up and overthrow the bourgeoisie. The proletariat he saw as the last of the classes: its self-liberation would lead to the establishment of a classless society.

Marx saw "antagonisms and contradictions" as the motive force behind all social change and historical development. Lenin distinguished between antagonisms and contradictions, asserting that, under socialism, antagonisms would disappear, while contradictions would remain.[9] "Life," Lenin stated, "moves forward by contradictions."[10]

Contemporary Soviet ideology adheres to the formulation elaborated by Stalin which further distinguishes "antagonistic" and "nonantagonistic" contradictions.[11] "Antagonistic" contradictions are said to characterise pre-socialist, that is, class societies. (That includes not only capitalist societies but also those making the transition from capitalism to socialism.) Antagonistic conflicts (graphically summed up by Lenin as a question of "*kto kogo?*"--"who defeats whom?") cannot be resolved peacefully, but only by means of revolutionary upheaval.

"Nonantagonistic" contradictions, on the other hand, typify socialist society. They are supposedly amenable to rational resolution by means of friendly cooperation between the various groups involved. Thus, the development of Soviet society from socialism to communism is considered a dialectical process whereby nonantagonistic contradictions are gradually resolved by political means and the question "*kto kogo?*" loses all relevance. Just as in other phases of historical development, the fundamental internal contradiction of socialist society--which provides the motor power for the transition to communism--is held to be that between the constantly growing productive forces and the lagging relations of production.

Lenin's formulations notwithstanding, the sharpness of the struggle that erupted in 1980 between the Polish workers and their Communist Party leaders caused Soviet ideologists to ask themselves whether, in some circumstances, antagonistic contradictions might not also arise under socialism. Why did such bitter social conflicts still occur? Richard Kosolapov, chief editor of *Kommunist*, revealed in an interview with a Greek communist newspaper in 1984 that "Consideration of the problem of contradictions was rekindled [in the USSR] three years ago. The spark was the Polish crisis."[12]

Writing in *Pravda* in November 1981--only a month before the declaration of martial law--a leading Soviet Party philosopher, Academician Petr Fedoseev, warned that "the development of world socialism should not be regarded as a continuous, undeviating progress, a triumphal procession." Social progress, Fedoseev went on, "has always been contradictory and accompanied by ebbs and flows." Turning to the Polish events, Fedoseev wrote:

> The historical experience of the USSR and the fraternal countries teaches us that without combating private property habits, nationalism, religious fanaticism, and petty-bourgeois thinking it is impossible to build and perfect a new way of life.... Where the struggle is waged with insufficient determination, ideas hostile to socialism imperceptibly penetrate the tiniest pores of the way of life, threatening to corrupt social institutions from within. It is no accident that the present crisis in Poland was preceded not only by a worsening of the economic situation, but also by a sharp deterioration in the ideological climate, the spread of philistine, consumerist sentiments and nationalist prejudices, and the weakening of class vigilance.[13]

Fedoseev wrote that, while in Russia the "class enemy" was defeated in "open battle," in other countries (which by implication included Poland) the transfer from capitalism to socialism took place by "more or less peaceful means." As a result, "the remnants of the exploiting classes and anti-proletarian parties still retain quite significant forces." Exploiting the "errors and weaknesses" of the Party and state authorities, these forces had launched an attack "against the foundations of socialism." Socialism, Fedoseev warned, "cannot secure complete and final victory without curbing counterrevolutionary elements."

Fedoseev's article was one of the first official attempts to provide the Soviet public with an explanation of what had gone wrong in Poland. It appeared at a crucial moment, on the eve of the declaration of martial law and, with its stress on the need for unrelenting struggle against the "enemy within," at a time when (as has been argued in previous chapters) the Soviet authorities were switching from a "softer" to a "harder" approach in domestic policy.

Fedoseev was also the author of a pioneering article that appeared in September 1981 in the international communist journal *Problemy mira i sotsializma.*[14] The article sought to draw conclusions from the events in Poland that would have relevance for the whole socialist community. In it, Fedoseev broke new ground by saying that it would be a "methodological simplification" to maintain that in socialist society "all contradictions always and in all circumstances are nonantagonistic." On the contrary, he wrote, "history shows that in certain circumstances, as a result of serious and prolonged errors,...nonantagonistic contradictions may acquire the features of antagonistic contradictions" even in a country "that has established itself on the socialist path."

Did that mean that the socialist system in the USSR might also come under threat? Here Fedoseev was cautious. "It seems possible," he wrote, that "only with the attainment of such a level of mature socialism that the reconstruction of the entirety of social relations is being achieved on its own already existing collectivist bases ... does the transformation of nonantagonistic contradictions into antagonistic contradictions become objectively impossible."

Brezhnev had specifically stated at the Twenty-sixth Congress of the CPSU that this was the stage reached by "developed socialism" in the USSR. On the face of it, therefore, Fedoseev was implying that a Polish-type crisis was not a possibility for the Soviet Union. Given what is known of Fedoseev's opinions, however, it is likely that what he really meant was something different.

Along with Kosolapov, Fedoseev belonged to what might be termed a "purist" wing of official Soviet opinion whose members advocated an accelerated restructuring of Soviet society that would, by merging the collective farm sector into the state sector, "integrate" the peasantry into the working class and lead to the long-awaited creation of the classless society. Bitterly opposed to any idea of decentralising, market-oriented reforms, this group perceived the peasants' private plots as a vestige of private enterprise and a potential threat to the socialist system; they were, of course, appalled by proposals for expansion of the private sector of the Soviet economy. Borrowing a phrase from Marx, Kosolapov extolled the "integrity of socialism" to urge the elimination of what he termed the "bifurcation" of Soviet society into two forms of ownership (state and cooperative) and two classes (the working class and the collective farm peasantry).[15]

Theoreticians like Fedoseev and Kosolapov saw the Polish events as a dreadful warning of the dangers awaiting any socialist state that tolerated "privately-owned agriculture" and a "capitalist sector." To secure Soviet society against a similar fate, they redoubled their calls for the merger of state and cooperative property, the "industrialisation" of agriculture, the "socialisation" of labour, and the establishment of what Kosolapov dubbed an "economy of the whole people."[16] Fedoseev in his article of September 1981 adopted an obscure reference of Lenin's to "integral socialism" (*tsel'nyi sotsializm*) and, from then on, he and Kosolapov used this term to denote the collectivist society toward which they thought the USSR should be moving.[17]

Fedoseev's implicit warning that, unless structural changes were made in the Soviet social system, the USSR might experience the same kind of unrest as Poland, clearly touched a vital nerve. It met opposition from reform-oriented members of the intelligentsia who, also citing the Polish example, called not for "integration" of the economy but for its decentralisation. It ran into resistance, too, from the "conservative" trend then dominant within the leadership. This group, represented by Brezhnev and Chernenko, took a complacent view of the development of Soviet society. The USSR, they argued, had built a developed socialist society and was well advanced along the road to the final goal of full communism. To be sure, there were several areas of Soviet life where improvements were needed, but the Party's policy was basically correct and not in need of fundamental change.

The subject was controversial and gave rise to keen disagreements. In an article published in *Kommunist* in April 1982, Chernenko reiterated the orthodox position that, under socialism, "contradictions are fundamentally different from the antagonisms of bourgeois society and are soluble." Nonetheless, he added, it was a matter of paramount theoretical and practical importance to study "the nature and types of contradictions characteristic of the contemporary stage of development of Soviet society, and the objective and subjective factors that cause them."[18] Andropov, on the other hand, began his tenure as general secretary by making what was, for a Soviet leader, a truly extraordinary admission. "We have not," he stated, "yet made a proper study of the society in which we live and work, and have still not fully revealed the laws governing its development...."[19] With these words, the new Party leader gave the green light to discussion of areas of social policy taboo during the Brezhnev years.

The chief editor of the USSR's main philosophy journal, *Voprosy filosofii*, Vadim Semenov, threw its pages open to the debate, to which he himself contributed.[20] In an article published in September 1982, Semenov examined the conditions in which, even in socialist societies, "nonantagonistic contradictions may grow into antagonistic ones." He listed Hungary in 1956, Czechoslovakia in 1968, and Poland in 1980-81 as examples of socialist countries in which nonantagonistic contradictions were allowed to escalate into antagonistic ones. "By its very nature," Semenov asserted, "socialism provides the possibility of crisis-free, progressive development." However, Semenov went on, this was not an automatic process but one that required purposeful direction by Party and state authorities.[21]

In a series of articles published in the wake of the Polish crisis, Anatolii Butenko, a sector head at the USSR Academy of Sciences' Institute of the Economics of the World Socialist System (Moscow's leading research institute dealing with Eastern Europe), went even further.[22] Writing in *Novoe vremya* early in 1982, Butenko argued that reform-oriented leadership was essential to forestall the outbreak of crises caused, he said, like that in Poland, by "socialist deformations." Citing the "distortions...that occurred in Hungary in the late 1950s, in Czechoslovakia in the 1960s and of late in Poland," Butenko went on:

> It is an obvious deformation when the bilateral ties between the managers and the managed, i.e., the ties from above downward and from below upward, are reduced to relations of commanding from above. Incompatible with scientific socialism are attempts to supplant the power of the working people themselves with the exclusive activity of the state apparatus in the name of the working people, but not in their interests.[23]

"If these deformations are not rectified in time," Butenko warned, "they may and sometimes do result in some degree of dislocation of social development." "Life shows," he continued,

> that as soon as a ruling party or its leaders become divorced from the masses, fail to see their own mistakes, or engage in voluntarism, discontent appears among the people. They can sense by infringements of social justice that the policy is erroneous, that the principles of socialism have been departed from.... That is when a political crisis breaks out...[24]

Writing in *Voprosy filosofii* in October 1982, Butenko expressed even more unorthodox opinions, arguing that the Polish crisis of 1980-81 was the result not just of mistakes made by the Polish leaders, but of essential contradictions in Poland's socialist society. Contrary to the claims of certain Soviet theoreticians, Butentko stated, the Polish crisis could not be adequately explained merely by reference to "residuary antagonisms," that is, to "holdovers" from Poland's earlier, capitalist phase. Poland's socialist system, Butenko stated, had failed to adapt to changing individual and group interests, and it was this lag that had led to the alienation of the workers from the political system. If prolonged economic and political stagnation were tolerated and the interests of the workers were neglected, Butenko warned, dissatisfaction and "political tension" would inevitably mount.[25]

Butenko refuted the "theory of conflictlessness" which, he said, assumed that socialism develops free not only of antagonisms but even of contradictions, and concluded that the nonantagonistic contradictions inherent in socialist society might, if ignored by the leadership, "take on the character of antagonistic contradictions."[26]

Scholastic as these arguments about "antagonistic" and "nonantagonistic" contradictions might appear, they had important political implications. As Ernst Kux has pointed out, they called into question the orthodox view of socialist society as crisis-free and immune to revolutionary upheaval. If the Soviet Union proved to be, like Poland, vulnerable to disruptive social conflicts, then the Soviet leaders must be prepared to take drastic measures to ward off popular unrest.

Warnings that, even under socialism, nonantagonistic contradictions might develop into antagonistic ones provoked a sharp reaction. Kosolapov emerged as the chief spokesman for the orthodox view, arguing in a series of articles that those who challenged it were "divorced from reality" and guilty of "outmoded dogmatism." The proper view, he stated, was that while contradictions continued to exist under socialism, they were nonantagonistic in nature.[27]

It was particularly misleading, Kosolapov wrote, to try to apply the experience of a country like Poland--still in the transition stage from capitalism to socialism--to more developed socialist countries. Kosolapov acknowledged the existence, in pre-socialist Poland, of "objective causes for antagonistic class contradictions," but said they were to be explained by "the existence there for several decades, alongside the socialist structure, of stable, privately-owned agriculture and a capitalist sector." This gave rise to "strong anti-socialist ideological tendencies."[28] But Kosolapov denied that Poland's experience could be applied to more developed socialist societies and, in particular, to the Soviet Union, with its state-owned industry and relatively mechanised agriculture. There was in the USSR virtually no private sector and therefore no basis for antagonistic contradictions. "We cannot," Kosolapov protested, "discuss the Soviet Union on the basis of Poland's different reality."[29] "Experience has shown," he went on, that

> in fraternal countries where the building of socialism's foundations is not yet complete and where the question "*kto kogo?*" has not been finally resolved, exacerbations of class struggle and manifestations of social antagonism are sometimes possible. I mention this because misunderstanding here can lead and has already led to serious errors.[30]

Kosolapov distinguished between what he called "social antagonisms," which were not to be found under socialism, and "individual antagonisms," which might occur under socialism and which were "evidence either of differences *between individuals* or of the counterposing of the selfish interests of an *individual or group of individuals* to the interests of society as a whole." Kosolapov dismissed the idea that "social antagonisms" might be found under socialism as "poor assessment of Marxism-Leninism."

Class and national antagonisms disappeared after the full and final victory of socialism, he said, and contradictions took on an exclusively nonantagonistic character because "they are no longer the expression of the struggle of one class against another or of hostility between nations."[31]

While denying the possibility of "social antagonisms" in modern Soviet society, Kosolapov recognised the existence of "individual antagonisms," that is, of "phenomena diametrically opposed to communist morality." He pointed to "pilferers and bribetakers, speculators and scroungers, drifters and parasites," and reminded his readers that Lenin considered such people to be just as dangerous as "class enemies." "Wherever they are able to install themselves," Kosolapov wrote, "they make holes, like moths, in the fabric of socialist social relations"; they were, he went on, "individual carriers of the germ of antagonism."[32]

Tat'yana Zaslavskaya, on the other hand, made approving mention of Butenko's ideas in her "Novosibirsk report"--the confidential document, written in 1983, which was cited in Chapter 12. A significant feature of Zaslavskaya's argument was the stress she laid on the strength of potential opposition to economic reform in the USSR. By refusing to recognise the possibility that antagonistic interests might exist under socialism, Zaslavskaya warned, orthodox Soviet doctrine precluded all possibility of dealing with such opposition which, in her opinion, had its roots in those social interests that would suffer if a reform were carried out. A realistic analysis of the sources of resistance to change was indispensable, she wrote, if an effective way of overcoming it was to be devised:

> ...the perfecting of productive relations under socialism is a more complicated task

> than is commonly supposed, for reorganisation of the existing system of productive relations has to be entrusted to social groups that occupy rather high positions in that system and who accordingly have a vested interest in its maintenance.... Therefore, a radical reorganisation of economic management has a direct impact on the interests of many social groups.

As examples of antagonistic relationships within Soviet society, Zaslavskaya cited "real contradictions between vertically dependent groups: workers and foremen; foremen and managers; managers and ministers."[33]

The Party line was laid down by Andropov. Both shortly before and shortly after his election as Party general secretary, Andropov declared that antagonistic contradictions could not occur under socialism--quoting Lenin's dictum that "in socialist society...antagonisms do not arise."[34] Andropov nonetheless showed some flexibility. In an article published in February 1983, he candidly admitted the USSR was experiencing both difficulties and contradictions and warned that, if they were ignored, "contradictions that are not by nature antagonistic may provoke serious collisions."[35] Even more important, Andropov advanced a new thesis, according to which the Soviet Union was only at the very *beginning* of the phase of developed socialism, and substantial changes would be necessary before it advanced further.[36] He warned against "exaggerating the level of the country's progress toward the higher stage of communism," and stated that the USSR faced "problems left over from yesterday" as well as "difficulties of growth." It would, Andropov cautioned, "take some time to draw up the straggling rear and forge ahead."[37] Andropov's stress on the existing shortcomings of

Soviet society distanced him from both the "purists" and the "conservatives," tending instead to align him with the "reformers."

Once Andropov had laid down the official line, Fedoseev retracted the views he had expressed in 1981 in *Problemy mira i sotsializma.*[38] Butenko on the other hand was unrepentant, and forcefully defended his opinions in an article published in *Voprosy filosofii* in February 1984. Taking issue with Kosolapov's contention that conflicts under socialism were "residual social antagonisms" and "vestiges of capitalism" (that is, that they were merely hangovers from earlier social formations and not specific to socialism), Butenko began openly to discuss the interconnexions which, he said, existed between contradictions and interests. Citing such "ugly, negative phenomena" as "bureaucratism, formalism, conservatism, localism and nationalism," Butenko stressed that they reflected "interaction between living individuals and social groups with specific interests." "We are not," he asserted,

> dealing with some featureless excrescence on the social organism, but with real people who are the bearers of a particular social evil and with their actions, which are harmful to socialism. Who are they, these bearers of evil, and where do they come from? ... Obviously, specific people and their interests lie behind [negative social phenomena]. Which people, and what interests?[39]

Were these clashing interests, Butenko asked rhetorically, "antagonistic or nonantagonistic?" Were the interests behind them "mutually exclusive, or not?" As an example of a clash that might occur under socialism but which was neither a vestige of capitalism nor a residual or individual antagonism,

Butenko cited the relationship between managers and managed. He argued that:

> If managers lose contact with the managed, if they begin to use their position to implement their own selfish group interests at the expense of public interests and those of the working people, ... then it can hardly be denied that these interests become mutually exclusive and acquire the nature of an antagonistic contradiction.[40]

Butenko rejected the idea that social conflicts under socialism were "residual" or "individual," and could be explained away as mere "vestiges of capitalism." Such arguments, he said, distracted attention from socialist society's own contradictions and their solution, and threatened thereby to lead to "grave social collisions."[41]

To sum up the argument so far: if, as Kosolapov claimed, Poland's crisis was to be blamed on specifically Polish features such as the retention of private agriculture and the influence of the Catholic Church, then the solution was, as Fedoseev had argued in *Pravda* in November 1981, to take firm steps to socialise property and counter the influence of religion among the population. If, on the other hand, the origins of the Polish crisis were, as Butenko suggested, common to societies of the Soviet type and rooted in the "deformation of certain links of the system" and in "the inept solution of contradictions inherent in socialism,"[42] then it was only to be expected that, in the absence of radical systemic reforms, these symptoms would continue to recur and that they would eventually provoke similar crises in other socialist countries.

A conservative reaction set in with the accession of Chernenko to the Party leadership following Andropov's death in February 1984. Butenko's article was singled out for criticism when, in June 1984, the work of *Voprosy filosofii* came under review at a special session of the Scientific Council of the Institute of Philosophy of the USSR Academy of Sciences.[43] That month, Fedoseev coauthored an article with another veteran Party ideologist, Leonid Il'ichev. The initiative of *Voprosy filosofii* in tackling burning theoretical issues deserved support, they wrote, but in some articles the question of contradictions "had unfortunately been dramatised to an excessive degree." The contention that differences between various social groups under socialism might be antagonistic in character did not, they said, take into account the fundamental unity of interests between the toiling classes in the socialist system. Fedoseev and Il'ichev did however concede that, even under socialism, contradictions might in certain circumstances prove "not progressive, but regressive and even destructive."[44]

The editorial board of *Voprosy filosofii* was obliged to make a public admission that its publication of Butenko's unorthodox views had been a "serious error."[45] But the editorial in the journal's issue for October 1984, in which this admission appeared, went on to justify the action in a manner that sounded less than wholly repentant. It pointed out that Soviet theoreticians were constantly being called upon by the Party to make deeper analyses of the nature of socialist society. This was what it had been trying to do, wrote the editorial board of *Voprosy filosofii* in an aggrieved tone, and what it would continue to do in the future. The person who never made a mistake, the journal seemed to be saying, never made anything. Besides, it went on, there was still no unanimity among Soviet social scientists as to the precise nature of the "essential contradiction underlying the developed socialist phase"--that is, the fundamental moving force behind the transition of Soviet society from socialism to communism. In those circumstances, the journal implied, it could hardly be blamed for reflecting varying shades of opinion.

CALLS FOR ECONOMIC REFORM

The dispute triggered among Soviet theoreticians by the Polish crisis was by no means restricted to hair-splitting squabbles over terminology, but also involved discussion of economic reform--a debate that gave every sign of being tolerated and even encouraged by Andropov's leadership, though it became rather more muffled under that of Chernenko. Reference has already been made to an article by Butenko that appeared in February 1982 in *Novoe vremya*, which praised the way in which "Lenin acted in a crisis" and cited the launching of the New Economic Policy (NEP) in 1921.[46]

The NEP--Soviet Russia's experiment with a mixed economy--was introduced to repair the ravages of the preceding period, known as "War Communism." Launched soon after the Revolution, War Communism tried to effect the immediate transition of the young Soviet state to full communism. It was characterised by nationalisation of land and stringent economic centralisation of industry, and it led to virtual guerrilla warfare in parts of the country, economic collapse, and enormous suffering for the population through death, famine, disease, and civil war,[47] culminating in the mutiny that broke out at the Kronstadt naval base early in 1921. Lenin's response was to relax central controls on peasant farmers, craftsmen and small-scale traders, and to permit the temporary reemergence of a private sector alongside the public one.

Discussion of the NEP period has long loomed large in Soviet debates over the desirability of economic reform, being commonly invoked as a symbol by those who advocate political pragmatism and flexibility. Those who favour a "liberal" interpretation of the period depict the NEP in a positive light and stress its continuing relevance to the USSR even in modern conditions. Such writers assert that it is legitimate to use the market mechanism to increase the efficiency of the socialist economy--that is, that the plan and the market are not incompatible.[48]

Butenko was only one of a number of reform-minded Soviet economists and Party theoreticians who were at this time advocating a limited revival of private enterprise along the lines of the NEP, and who pointed to the existence of the private sector in Eastern Europe as a model for the Soviet Union itself. In an article in *Novy mir* in April 1982, Fedor Burlatsky, long the Soviet Union's most outspoken proponent of economic and political reform, outlined a reform blueprint that stressed the need for decentralisation and envisaged a much expanded role for the private sector, particularly in the provision of consumer goods and services.[49]

A particularly controversial article appeared in April 1984 in the journal *Voprosy istorii*. Its author, Evgenii Ambartsumov, like Butenko a sector head at the Institute of the Economics of the World Socialist System, had already made a name for himself as one of the USSR's most vocal advocates of an extension of private enterprise in the Soviet economy. Citing the Polish events of 1980-81, Ambartsumov now tried to identify the reasons why "socio-economic crises" occurred in socialist countries. Defining a crisis in this context as "a conflict within the system between authority and a part of its social base, ... a process of accumulation and exacerbation of contradictions in all important spheres of the functioning of society," he advocated as an "anti-crisis strategy" the adoption of political and economic measures modelled on those of the NEP.[50]

Ambartsumov complained that Soviet literature had failed to provide a general theory of the causes of crises under socialism. Socialism's ideological opponents accused it of being incapable of crisis-management but, he said, this charge could be refuted by the example of Lenin's analysis of the causes and remedies of the crisis that gripped Soviet Russia in 1921. Instead of blaming the Kronstadt mutiny on the activities of "counter-revolutionaries" in the pay of hostile foreign powers, Lenin recognised that its primary cause was the fact that the Soviet leaders had been pursuing mistaken policies and neglecting the needs of the masses. The lessons of Kronstadt, Ambartsumov went on, "retain their significance to this day." Echoing Butenko, he said that crises in socialist systems arose as a result of "bureaucratic distortions," that is, when the leaders lost touch with the led, and when

> contradictions, even conflicts, erupt between the revolutionary power and its policies, on the one hand, and the vital interests of certain members of the working masses, on the other, leading to sharp demonstrations of discontent.

Extending his argument to crises in the East European socialist states, Ambartsumov argued that, while foreign interference undoubtedly played a role in the development of such conflicts, the decisive role belonged to internal factors. Counterrevolutionary forces, he said, could whip up popular discontent only if domestic causes for dissatisfaction were already present and were being neglected by the leaders. Crises in socialist countries could be overcome only if their domestic causes were frankly recognised and if Party leaders had the courage to take the necessary corrective measures.

Five months after its appearance in *Voprosy istorii*, Ambartsumov's article came under heavy attack from a well-known conservative ideologist. Writing in *Kommunist* in September 1984, Evgenii Bugaev castigated Ambartsumov for "a lack of academic rigor" and "a shallow approach to Leninist theory," and took the editors of *Voprosy istorii* to task for their failure to exercise proper editorial control. Bugaev rejected Ambartsumov's claim that the lessons of 1921 retained their relevance in the modern world. The class basis of the young Soviet state was, Bugaev asserted, quite different from that of the USSR today; and Ambartsumov was therefore wrong "to superimpose Lenin's analysis of the events of 1921 on completely different phenomena that took place under totally different socio-economic and political conditions."[51]

In his criticism of Ambartsumov, Bugaev echoed Kosolapov's argument that the Polish crisis was attributable to the fact that Poland was at a much earlier stage of social development than the USSR. Poland, Bugaev reiterated, was still in the transitional period between capitalism and socialism--a period characterised by antagonistic class contradictions, when the question "*kto kogo?*" was still unresolved. The Soviet Union, Bugaev went on, had on the other hand reached the stage of "developed socialism" and possessed "reliable guarantees" against "negative tendencies of a crisis nature." Bugaev reproached Ambartsumov for focussing on "contradictions between leaders and led" and underestimating the role played by foreign interference in the Polish events. Internal contradictions alone, Bugaev asserted, were not sufficient to provoke counterrevolution.

CONCLUSION

The Polish events shattered the accepted Soviet

orthodoxy, according to which the political systems of Eastern Europe and the USSR were inherently more stable than those of the Western democracies and socialist rule was unchallengeably established in all the states of the area. The ensuing ideological debate left its mark on official Soviet thinking. The period of conservative retrenchment ushered in in February 1984 with the election of Konstantin Chernenko proved as short-lived as its mentor; Chernenko died in March 1985 and was replaced as Party general secretary by Mikhail Gorbachev. Several of the ideas given official recognition during Gorbachev's first two years in power seemed to reflect the "lessons of Poland."

Gorbachev came to power as a young, energetic, and pragmatic leader, determined to revitalise Soviet society and to inject fresh life into the ailing economy. Professing unswerving loyalty to the Soviet Union's Leninist heritage, Gorbachev was nonetheless impatient with dogmatic approaches wherever these threatened to impede his goal of modernising the Soviet system. The Lenin upon whom he modelled his leadership was not the Lenin of the period of War Communism; Gorbachev chose instead the Lenin of the NEP years.[52] For while Lenin never abandoned his ultimate goal--the building of communism--his advocacy of the NEP did mark a rejection of doctrinaire tactics and a victory, however short-lived, for pragmatism and common sense. In this respect, Gorbachev aligned himself with members of the reform lobby--in particular, the sociologist Tat'yana Zaslavskaya--whose ideas were discussed in this chapter. Gorbachev shared their opinion that, as a result of the stagnation of Brezhnev's last years, the needs of the general Soviet population had been neglected and that ordinary citizens had become dangerously alienated from the leadership. Addressing a plenary meeting of the CPSU Central Committee in January 1987, Gorbachev went so far as to speak of "crisis phenomena" threatening Soviet society. The system, he said, was "deaf to social issues." People's needs for housing, food, health care and education had all been ignored. People had grown cynical, callous, and sceptical; they had lost both their "enthusiasm for work" and their "Soviet patriotism." The frequency of labour discipline infringements and industrial injuries, Gorbachev asserted, had been rising since the 1960s.[53]

Gorbachev's leadership showed incomparably more readiness than those of Brezhnev, Chernenko, or even Andropov openly to discuss these and other shortcomings of Soviet society. Not only were social problems aired in the mass media; it was officially recognised for the first time that social difficulties could not be dismissed as mere "vestiges of capitalism" but were rooted in structural faults of the existing social and political system. The new edition of the Party Programme adopted in March 1986 was, in the words of the chief editor of *Pravda*, "the first Party document on such a level to speak not only of carryovers from the distant past, but also of 'acquisitions' that have appeared as a result of our own errors."[54]

The Gorbachev leadership lost no time in abandoning Brezhnev's triumphalist concept of "developed socialism"; "integral socialism," as interpreted by Kosolapov and Fedoseev, vanished from the Party's vocabulary; and the doctrine according to which, in a socialist system, state property took automatic precedence over cooperative property was dropped.[55] Instead, the new leadership encouraged family farming and the setting up of small cooperatives; measures were also introduced to legalise certain forms of private enterprise. Although these and other measures were not adopted without resistance from the Party's conservative wing, Kosolapov relinquished his post as chief editor of *Kommunist* to an appointee in the Gorbachev mould, Bugaev retired from the editorial board and, almost overnight, the journal became interesting reading for the first time in many years.

Once in power, too, Gorbachev revised the official Soviet interpretation of the Polish events, citing the Polish example in support of his calls for economic and social reform in the USSR. Speaking in Warsaw in June 1986, the Soviet leader stated that the workers' protests in Poland in 1980 were aimed not against socialism itself but against "subjectivist distortions of the socialist system." Only later, he implied, were the workers' legitimate grievances exploited by "forces hostile to socialism." The Polish events, Gorbachev said, were a warning that the establishment of a socialist system "does not mean that from then on progress is automatically guaranteed, or that production relations have been brought into line with the productive forces once and for all." In other words, socialist governments must adapt in response to changing circumstances. Otherwise, Gorbachev warned, stagnation could set in and economic and social problems grow to "dangerous proportions." This lesson, Gorbachev added, applied to the Soviet Union as much as to the other socialist states. The USSR, he claimed, was "learning from the errors and miscalculations of the past."[56]

This is not to claim that the Polish events were the main stimulus to the reform policies of the Gorbachev leadership. Credit for that should go to the dangerous decline in the rate of economic growth which the USSR experienced in the early 1980s. But the shock of Poland's worker unrest did open the eyes of a new generation of Soviet leaders to the dangers of continuing the policies of the Brezhnev leadership, and alerted them to the need for a change of course in Soviet social policy. The Polish events served, in short, to shape the contours of the Soviet reform debate.

FOOTNOTES TO CHAPTER 14

1. Ernst Kux, "Contradictions in Soviet Socialism," *Problems of Communism*, November-December 1984, pp. 1-27 at p. 20.

For other discussions of the materials treated in this chapter, see Astrid von Borcke, "Zwischen Revision und Reaktion: Die Sowjetunion und der Machtwechsel," *Berichte des Bundesinstituts fuer ostwissenschafliche und internationale Studien*, Cologne, March 1983; FBIS Trends, "Leading Ideologists Disagree Over Urgency of Reform," 23 March 1983; *Reuters*, "Soviets Said Debating Ideology," 26 March 1983; Helmut Dahm, "Marx-Lenin-Andropov: Ideologischer Lagebericht nach dem Fuerungswechsel in Moskau," *Berichte des Bundesinstituts fuer ostwissenschafliche und internationale Studien*, Cologne, November 1983.

2. *Pravda*, 24 February 1981.

3. Ray Taras, "Official Etiologies of Polish Crises: Changing Historiographies and Factional Struggles," *Soviet Studies*, No 1, January 1986, pp. 53-68.

4. *Ibid.*, p. 56.

5. *Pravda*, 24 February 1981.

6. *Warsaw Domestic Radio*, 24 February 1981.

7. Kux, *op. cit.*, p. 21; Andrzej Korbonski, "Soviet Policy Toward Poland," in Sarah Meiklejohn Terry (ed), *Soviet Policy in Eastern Europe*, New Haven, Conn., 1984, p. 69.

8. This and following paragraphs draw on: Herbert Marcuse, *Soviet Marxism: A Critical Analysis*, Harmondsworth, 1971; Ernst Fischer, *Marx in His Own Words*, Harmondsworth, 1973; James P. Scanlan, *Marxism in the USSR: A Critical Survey of Current Soviet Thought*, New York, 1985.

9. Kux, *op. cit.*, p. 14.

10. As cited by P. Fedoseev in *Pravda*, 13 November 1981.

11. Kux, *op. cit.*, p. 14.

12. *Rizospastis* (Athens), 9 October 1984.

13. "Sotsial'nyi optimizm kommunistov," *Pravda*, 13 November 1981. See also p. 206, above.

14. Petr Fedoseev, "Dialektika obshchestvennoi zhizni," *Problemy mira i sotsializma*, No 9, 1981, pp. 25-30.

15. Richard Kosolapov, "Metodologicheskie problemy teorii razvitogo sotsializma," *Problemy mira i sotsializma*, No 9, 1984. As the source of this quotation, Kosolapov cited Karl Marx and Friedrich Engels, *Sochineniya*, second edition, Moscow, 1968, Vol. 46, Part I, p. 229.

16. R. Kosolapov, "Vklad XXIV, XXV i XXVI s"ezdov KPSS v razrabotku teoreticheskikh i politicheskikh problem razvitogo sotsializma i perekhoda k kommunizmu," *Kommunist*, No 5, 1982, pp. 54-67.

17. Fedoseev in *Problemy mira i sotsializma*, No 9, 1981, p. 27; see also Kosolapov in *Kommunist*, No 5, 1982, p. 64. Both authors cited V.I. Lenin, *Polnoe sobranie sochinenii*, fifth edition, Moscow, 1958-65, Vol. 36, p. 306.

18. K. Chernenko, "Avangardnaya rol' partii kommunistov. Vazhnoe uslovie ee vozrastaniya," *Kommunist*, No 6, 1982, pp. 25-43 at p. 30.

19. *Pravda*, 23 November 1982.

20. V.S. Semenov, "Problema protivorechii v usloviyakh sotsializma," Parts 1 and 2, *Voprosy filosofii*, No 7, 1982, pp. 17-32, and No 9, 1982, pp. 3-21; "K teoreticheskomy uglubleniyu i konkretizatsii analiza problemy protivorechii v usloviyakh razvitogo sotsializma," *Voprosy filosofii*, No 2, 1984, pp. 130-40; a summary of the whole discussion was published in *Voprosy filosofii*, No 2, 1984, pp. 116-23.

21. Semenov, *Voprosy filosofii*, No 9, 1982, at pp. 11-16.

22. A.P. Butenko, "Sotsializm: formy i deformatsii," *Novoe vremya*, No 6, 1982, pp. 5-7;

idem, "Protivorechiya razvitiya sotsializma kak obshchestvennogo stroiya," *Voprosy filosofii*, No 10, 1982, pp. 16-29. According to Marc Zlotnik (in *Problems of Communism*, November-December 1982, p. 70), Butenko called as early as 1981 for political reform of the Soviet system to forestall a Polish-style crisis.

23. Butenko, *Novoe vremya*, No 6, 1982, p. 6.

24. *Ibid.*, p. 7.

25. *Idem*, *Voprosy filosofii*, No 10, 1982, p. 23.

26. *Ibid.*, p. 19.

27. *Pravda*, 31 July 1981, 4 March 1983 and 20 July 1984; *Literaturnaya gazeta*, 1 February 1984.

28. *Pravda*, 4 March 1983.

29. *Rizospastis*, 9 October 1984.

30. *Literaturnaya gazeta*, 1 February 1984.

31. *Pravda*, 4 March 1983 (emphasis in original).

32. *Ibid.*

33. AS 5042.

34. *Pravda*, 23 April 1982; Yu. Andropov, "Uchenie Karla Marksa i nekotorye voprosy sotsialisticheskogo stroitel'stva v SSSR," *Kommunist*, No 3, 1983, pp. 9-23.

35. Andropov in *Kommunist*, No 3, 1983, p. 21.

36. *Radio Moscow*, 22 April 1982.

37. *TASS*, 15 June 1983.

38. P. N. Fedoseev, "K. Marks i sovremennost'," *Voprosy filosofii*, No 4, 1983, pp. 17-39.

39. A. P. Butenko, "Eshche raz o protivorechiyakh sotsializma," *Voprosy filosofii*, No 2, 1984, pp. 124-9 at p. 128.

40. *Ibid.*, p. 129.

41. *Ibid.*, p. 127.

42. *Ibid.*

43. *Voprosy filosofii*, No 10, 1984, pp. 3-19.

44. P.N. Fedoseev and L.F. Il'ichev, "O nekotorikh metodologicheskikh problemakh istoriches-

kogo materializma," *Voprosy filosofii*, No 6, 1984, pp. 3-22.

45. *Voprosy filosofii*, No 10, 1984, pp. 3-19.

46. A. Butenko, "Sotsializm: formy i deformatsii," *Novoe vremya*, No 6, 1982, pp. 5-7.

47. See Archie Brown *et al.* (eds), *The Cambridge Encyclopedia of Russia and the Soviet Union*, Cambridge, 1982, p. 109.

48. This summary is based on Zenovia A. Sochor, "NEP Revisited: Current Soviet Interest in Alternative Strategies of Development," *Soviet Union/Union Sovietique*, No 9, Part 2, 1982, pp. 189-211.

49. Fedor Burlatsky, "Mezhdutsarstvie, ili khronika vremen Den Syaopina," *Novyi mir*, No 4, 1982, pp. 205-22.

50. E. A. Ambartsumov, "Analiz V.I. Leninym prichin krizisa 1921 g. i putei vykhoda iz nego," *Voprosy istorii*, No 4, 1984, pp. 15-29.

51. E. Bugaev, "Strannaya pozitsiya," *Kommunist*, No 14, 1984, pp. 119-26.

52. See RL 415/86, "Symbolic Role Ascribed to the NEP," by Elizabeth Teague, 3 November 1986.

53. *TASS*, 27 January 1987.

54. Viktor Afanas'ev in *Zhurnalist*, No 12, 1985, pp. 2-4.

55. See RL 314/86, "The Decline and Fall of Developed Socialism," by Elizabeth Teague, 19 August 1986; *idem*, RL 319/86, "A Greater Role for the Cooperative Sector," 22 August 1986.

56. *TASS*, 30 June 1986.

Chapter 15

CONCLUSIONS: IMPLICATIONS FOR GORBACHEV'S LEADERSHIP

How did leaders of the Brezhnev generation perceive their relations with the general population? How much faith did they have in their own security of tenure and in the stability of the Soviet political system? In an attempt to answer these questions, this book has examined the impact of the Polish events of 1980-81 on Soviet domestic policies and traced the reactions of the Soviet leaders, at a time of economic stringency, to a perceived threat to their rule.

Whether or not the threat turned out to be a real one depended in this instance on how susceptible Soviet citizens proved to be to events occurring outside the USSR. Surely, if Soviet popular opinion were at all receptive to external, liberalising stimuli, the example of worker unrest in neighbouring, socialist Poland would not fail to show an effect. To what extent, therefore, was the Soviet public influenced by the Polish events?

This study reached three main conclusions. First, it found that the rise of Solidarity provoked feelings of considerable alarm among the Soviet leaders, who were clearly uncertain how the population would react to the Polish example. They therefore adopted a number of short-term, stop-gap measures to "appease" a workforce they perceived as likely to exhibit a dangerous degree of discontent. The official trade unions were enjoined to take a more active stand in defence of workers' rights; officials began to pay greater attention to public opinion; workers' complaints were aired in the national press; plan priorities were revised to put increased emphasis on consumption; and so on.

This response indicated that the leaders of the

Brezhnev generation were poorly informed about the state of public opinion and that their ignorance made them fearful and mistrustful of the population and, in particular, of the workforce. They displayed, in short, little confidence in their own legitimacy as leaders.

As things turned out, Brezhnev and his colleagues need not have been so anxious. Apart from a few isolated strikes, scattered leaflets, and a fair amount of *samizdat* comment, Solidarity's impact on the Soviet population was small. The vast majority of the workforce remained apathetic. This held true despite the fact that the living and working conditions of the average Soviet worker were not only worse than those of his Polish counterpart but were even, in the early 1980s, threatening to deteriorate.

The book's second finding was therefore that, regardless of the leaders' apprehensions, the Polish crisis did not place the "social contract" between the leadership and the Soviet public at risk. The population at large proved politically quiescent and immune to liberalising influences from outside the country.

However, there was another side to this story. Public passivity might mean the leaders need not fear an imminent popular revolt, with demands for independent unions or freedom of speech, but it imposed other costs and threatened in the long run to prove dysfunctional to the Soviet system. The same passivity which immunised Soviet workers against the Polish "infection" was a source of domestic problems of another kind. These took the form of declining standards of labour discipline and increasing social disintegration. The moral malaise afflicting Soviet society in the early 1980s contributed both to the country's deteriorating economic performance and to the erosion of authority so clearly sensed by its leaders.

The slowdown of economic growth, to which this malaise contributed, represented a long-term threat to the social contract. If the decline was allowed to continue, it would become impossible for the leaders to maintain their side of the bargain, that is, their unspoken pledge to keep popular living standards edging gradually upward.

Even as the members of the Brezhnev leadership heaved a collective sigh of relief that the Soviet population had proved politically immune to the "Polish virus," then, they found themselves facing another danger, that of an impending economic crisis that would force them, willy-nilly, into a renegotation of their relations with the led. From the autumn of 1981, a change could be observed in their behaviour, as they abandoned the "carrot" of appeasement in favour of the disciplinarian "stick." The official trade unions were called upon once again to direct their energies to getting the workers to work harder, and massive if ineffectual campaigns were launched to raise discipline in the workplace and to crack down on crime and corruption. This trend toward tighter social controls reached its peak following the election of Yurii Andropov as Party leader in November 1982. At the same time, calls for a reform of the centrally-directed economy became more insistent.

However, this book reached a third finding, and that concerned a striking exception to the passivity of the mass of the Soviet population. Alone among the Soviet Union's national groupings, the populations of the Western borderlands--Ukraine, Belorussia, and the Baltic states--proved responsive to the example of Poland's labour unrest. These were the areas which, of all the USSR's non-Russian regions, were in the post-Stalin period the object of Moscow's most vigorous policies of assimilation and Russification. Resentment at the political and cultural dominance of the Russians--who make up barely half the Soviet Union's population of 280 million--was particularly acute in these areas, where anti-Russianism frequently took on the character of anti-Sovietism.

ENTER THE "HUMAN FACTOR"

The implications of worker passivity for Mikhail Gorbachev, elected to lead the CPSU in March 1985, were far more serious than they had been for his predecessors. The apathy of the workforce and the general conservatism of the population represented major obstacles to the new leader's plans for economic modernisation.

While still a relatively junior member of the leadership, Gorbachev stood out as one of a number of younger Party and government leaders whose public pronouncements identified them as impatient with the USSR's slow rate of economic growth and innovation.[1] Following his election as general secretary, he showed himself acutely aware that popular demoralisation was a powerful brake on economic development. It was vital, Gorbachev stated over and over again, "to activate the human factor."[2] People must learn "to think and work in a new way"; a means must be found to encourage creativity and reward initiative. Only when "a restructuring of people's thinking" had been achieved, Gorbachev said in September 1986, "shall we be able to tackle our tasks."[3]

By "activating the human factor," Gorbachev meant mobilising the enthusiasm and energy of the population or, in the words of the sociologist Tat'yana Zaslavskaya, bringing about a situation where "exactly the same people using exactly the same material resources learn to achieve a better result."[4] Exploitation of the human factor became an integral part of Gorbachev's policy of "intensification," that is, economic growth achieved by more efficient use of inputs and the application of modern technology.

Looked at from this angle, "activating the human factor" was just another attempt on the part of the authorities to squeeze more out of the long-suffering population. But there were sound reasons why the Gorbachev leadership turned the spotlight on the "human factor." Soviet Marxism proclaims as its goal the creation of the "new man," yet the Soviet workforce of the 1980s conspicuously lacked the qualities of adaptability and creativity essential for the successful running of a complex economy. In a speech in 1984, Gorbachev said that modern production required "the thinking worker," one who was "well-organised, disciplined, educated, and of a new technological caliber." He complained that automated production lines, robots and machine-tools with programmed controls were already being under-utilised because Soviet workers lacked the necessary qualifications.[5]

THE VIOLATION OF "SOCIAL JUSTICE"

A further reason for the preoccupation of the Gorbachev leadership with the "human factor" was its awareness that the corruption and abuse of official privilege that flourished during the Brezhnev years had led to a drastic decline in the confidence felt by the general population in the Soviet system as a whole. In official terminology, people's trust in "social justice" was undermined by the blatant violation of the basic law of socialism--"from each according to his ability, to each according to his work." Graft, bribery and nepotism became seen as the keys to getting ahead, and people found cheating and stealing more profitable than honest labour.

In addition, the chronic tendency of the existing economic system to encourage wage-levelling and labour-hoarding deprived Soviet workers of any incentive to work hard. Enterprise managers were primarily concerned to maximise output; to be sure of meeting production targets comfortably and of fulfilling changing output plan targets, they tried to keep as much spare labour on the payroll as they could. Far from being motivated to economise on labour costs, enterprises competed to attract and retain staff, sharing pay and bonuses more or less equally among workers regardless of quality of output. A manager could not be sure of benefitting in the long run from any improvement in labour productivity secured by sharper wage differentiation because, if he did achieve such an improvement, his future targets were merely likely to be adjusted upward by the central planners. Meanwhile, those of his workers who lost out from greater bonus differentiation because they were lazy or less skilled could easily move on to jobs elsewhere, leaving the enterprise with a smaller labour "reserve" with which to meet periodic demands such as calls for help with seasonal agricultural tasks. For the same reason, managers tended to turn a blind eye to poor workmanship, and sackings for labour discipline offences, as was mentioned in Chapter 12, were relatively rare.

Early on in his leadership, therefore, Gorbachev pledged to streamline the system of economic management. Central planning would be rationalised; the myriad ranks of the middle-level bureaucracy would be pruned; enterprises would be given more independence; wages would be tied more closely to effort. Gorbachev was well aware, however, that even partial decentralisation of the economy would run into substantial opposition from the middle ranks of officialdom. His plan was to neutralise such resistance by appealing to the population over the heads of the bureaucrats, who were to be discredited in the public eye by charges of corruption. "Restructuring," Gorbachev stated repeatedly, "must be carried out from below and from above."[6] As a first step, he resorted to the time-honoured Soviet method of mass mobilisation.

TIGHTENING DISCIPLINE

Gorbachev lost no time, after taking office in March 1985, in reviving the campaign for stricter labour discipline initiated by Andropov. However, his efforts to "mobilise the human factor" by strengthening discipline were not carbon-copies of Andropov's. His leadership appeared to appreciate the inherent weakness of the "campaigning" approach, for, as was seen in Chapter 12, the discipline drives launched under Brezhnev in 1979 and under Andropov in 1983 had an initial impact but rapidly ran out of steam.

Seen against this background, the purpose of Gorbachev's calls for stricter discipline and order seemed to be to give a short, sharp boost to popular morale after a period of drift and uncertainty. "It is sensible," Gorbachev told the Twenty-seventh Party Congress in February 1986, "to begin with those things that do not require major expenditure but which give quick and tangible results."[7]

Gorbachev's "new broom" approach included extensive personnel changes. He focussed, to a much greater extent than Andropov had been able during his short term in power, on sweeping out old, corrupt, and inefficient officials of the Brezhnev generation and replacing them with younger, predominantly technocratic appointees. This process of house-cleaning was partly aimed at restoring popular confidence in the "social justice" of the Soviet system, for wide publicity was given to the misdeeds of some of those who lost their jobs. It also, of course, enabled Gorbachev to lay the foundations of a personal power base.

As far as the vast majority of Soviet citizens were concerned, the most tangible change introduced by the Gorbachev leadership was the widely unpopular campaign against alcoholism.[8] The campaign fitted Gorbachev's attempt to boost economic growth by "activating the human factor," that is, by changing the behaviour of the workforce. Indeed, there were probably some gains for production as a result of the campaign. In 1986, industrial accident rates and the incidence of alcohol-related illness were substantially down from 1985.[9]

However, Gorbachev and his associates seemed well aware that drives to tighten discipline could yield only short-term benefits unless they were combined with further-reaching measures. In particular, it was generally agreed that any attempt to return to the outright coercion of the Stalin era would be counterproductive. In the words of Fedor Burlatsky, "How can you force someone to invent more, to think better, to work more efficiently?"[10] Instead, the Gorbachev leadership recognised that many of the Soviet Union's social and economic problems, of which the declining rate of labour productivity growth was only one, had been caused by longstanding neglect of the interests and needs of the general population.[11]

Following Gorbachev's election, for example, the mass media acknowledged for the first time that sickness, rather than fecklessness on the part of the workforce, was to blame for "the overwhelming majority" of losses of worktime in many branches of the economy.[12] This fact had previously been noted only in specialist journals. Speaking in Krasnodar in September 1986, Gorbachev revealed that a major programme to improve the quality of health care was in preparation.[13] Gorbachev made, too, a striking return to the formulation Soviet leaders used during the "carrot" phase of their response to the Polish events, but which they subsequently abandoned (see p. 194). Addressing a meeting in May 1987, the general secretary admitted that the needs of the population had been neglected. Everybody knows, Gorbachev stated, that "how people live depends on how they work." But, he went on, the equation operates both ways, and how people work also depends on how they live, that is, on how good their living and working conditions are.[14]

Black market activity came under attack in the course of the new leader's campaign to stamp out corruption and restore public confidence in "social justice." This included the adoption of new measures to crack down on "unearned incomes." The term was used to describe a multitude of ill-gotten gains--theft of state property, bribery, speculation, moonlighting--in short, any income not derived from employment in the official economy. Gorbachev's leadership announced the adoption of stiffer penalties for those found guilty of speculation and embezzlement, and sought to close existing loopholes by introducing fresh controls. Any private transaction involving more than 5,000 rubles would have to be made through a bank, while anyone making a purchase valued at over 10,000 rubles, or building a house costing more than 20,000 rubles, would be required to register the deal and provide the authorities with details of the source of his or her income.[15]

At the same time, the new leadership encouraged the development of cooperatives and small family businesses, and legalised certain forms of private enterprise (officially entitled "individual labour"). These moves were clearly controversial. Legislation regulating "individual labour activity" in the fields of domestic crafts, farming, and consumer services came up for discussion by the Politburo in March 1986, at the same time as measures against "unearned income."[16] But while regulations clamping down on unearned income were announced shortly afterward--in May 1986--and came into effect the following July, measures legalising private economic activity were not announced until November 1986, and did not come into effect until May 1987.[17] Moreover, the restrictive character of the measures eventually adopted suggested they were the product of behind-scenes wrangling over how much freedom Soviet citizens should be permitted in this sensitive area. Thus, "individual labour" was to be tolerated only in a worker's free time, housewives, pensioners, and the disabled alone being permitted to engage in it full-time. And the traditional Marxist taboo against "hired labour" held good: private businesses were restricted to single individuals or family members.

REFORMING WAGES AND INCENTIVES

Wage-reform constituted the Gorbachev leadership's medium-term strategy to encourage harder work in return for higher benefits. The new leadership stated its intention of correcting the Brezhnev era's trend toward wage equalisation by widening wage differentials and increasing managerial control over salaries and manning levels. Wage increases were to be paid for only out of enterprise profits. Gorbachev called, too, for wider application of the brigade system of labour organisation, which raises the correlation between output and the pay workers receive for it.[18]

Soviet economists had long argued that real income differentials did not adequately reflect productivity differentials. In other words, people whose work was especially valuable, or who did a particular job more efficiently than their fellow-workers, should be encouraged and rewarded with higher real incomes. This might at first seem redundant advice, for Soviet blue-collar workers were already paid on a piece-rate basis to a greater extent than blue-collar workers in most Western countries, and there was an array of skill grades, bonus payments, and other differentials.

However, several features of the Soviet wage structure were widely seen as discouraging workers from expending effort, improving their skills, and seeking promotion. One was the notoriously low relative pay for certain skilled and professional personnel: junior medical staff, design engineers, teachers, and so on. Another was the tendency of managers--already described above--to practise wage-levelling in payments to their staff. The output norms on which piece-rate calculations were based were kept slack, and bonuses were distributed evenly among the staff, regardless of individual performance. Workers with low levels of skill were often promoted to higher skill grades so that they could be paid more. Since ministry-level officials tended in turn to aim at modest levels of total bonuses, distributed fairly evenly among enterprises, the bonuses related to enterprises' overall "success indicator" performance were themselves not highly differentiated.

Even when there were large differentials in people's money incomes from state employment, the incentive effect was often blunted by differences in access to goods and services and in earnings from the second economy, and in general by the element of rationing, influence and corruption in an individual's command over goods and services. One aspect of this was the lack of differentiation in prices for many items--with standard rental rates for state housing in more or less desirable locations, for example. Thus advocacy of greater incentive payments was accompanied by calls for wider differentials in state pricing. There were suggestions, too, that wage reform should be accompanied by the introduction of differentiated rental rates for housing, private plots and *dachas* (country cottages), a progressive inheritance tax, a graduated income tax and also, perhaps, a wealth tax.[19]

The advocates of greater differentiation in pay and bonuses did not necessarily want greater inequality in real incomes (however that might be measured). But they did want more purposeful inequalities, more closely related to individuals' contributions to output. The economist Natal'ya Rimashevskaya, for example, argued that social consumption should be distributed according to need while incomes from work should become more unequal. (She said that the top ten percent of earners in industry earned three times the income of the bottom ten percent, and that this ratio was "obviously not [large] enough.")[20]

Official endorsements of stronger incentives and denunciations of wage-levelling had been commonplace for years, but under Brezhnev's leadership little was done to correct the situation. After his death, rather more was done. An experiment conducted in 1983 in Leningrad introduced greater differentiation to the pay of research and development (R & D) staff with the aim of encouraging those research engineers who generated new technology and good designs. Judged a success in Leningrad, the scheme was extended more widely, but with mixed results. Gorbachev complained in September 1986:

> You know, we have already adopted a sound decision. Something is not quite working.... These matters are getting lost somewhere. We suddenly discovered that everything we had adopted on the basis of the experiment in Leningrad--where this matter had got off the ground well--was suddenly applied in such a way as to give engineers and technicians five to seven rubles more each. This was not the aim, not the aim at all.[21]

Following Gorbachev's ascent to power, several other measures were introduced that were meant to create more purposeful income differentials. Under a joint decree of the CPSU Central Committee, the USSR Council of Ministers and the AUCCTU adopted in the summer of 1985, pay for R & D and design staff in industry and the USSR Academy of Sciences was made more dependent on variable bonuses and less on fixed pay-scales.[22] Another joint decree published at the end of 1985 sought to raise the relative pay of factory foremen.[23] It was promised that pay-scales for medical personnel would be raised in several stages during 1986-91,[24] while a number of other decrees sought to correct various inter-occupational disproportions.

The most general pronouncement on wages was the joint Central Committee, Council of Ministers and AUCCTU decree of September 1986, "On the improvement of the organisation of wages and the introduction of new pay-scales and appointment salaries for workers in the material production sectors."[25] This was followed by temporary statutes devised by the State Committee for Labour and the AUCCTU to guide its implementation. Piece-rate norms were to be tightened and enterprises encouraged to shed surplus workers (to the benefit of the pay of those remaining). Procedures for retraining and reallocating redundant workers, to be observed by the local Soviets, were also set out.[26]

These revised pay-scales affected 75 million workers. Increases were to be proportionately larger for highly-qualified staff than for others. Piece-rate payments were to vary proportionately with output, rather than less than proportionately, as was previously the case. Differentials between engineers and blue-collar workers were to be increased. Enterprise managers were to have more discretion over the allocation of bonuses, with enterprise directors allowed to receive bonuses of up to 75 percent of their base pay.[27] It is too early to say how effective these measures will be.

RENEGOTIATING THE "SOCIAL CONTRACT"

Increased income differentials are not the only

means of strengthening material incentives. During Gorbachev's first two years in power, proposals were also heard for more effective differentiation in the pricing of consumer goods and services. One possible development on this front was the channelling of a larger part of total food supplies to the non-farm population through the peasant markets and contract selling by consumer cooperatives, at the expense of lower-priced state store sales. The reduction of state subsidies for food and consumer services;[28] the expansion of charges for medical care;[29] and the introduction of greater differentiation in state housing rents[30] were all proposed.

The tendency of such changes would be to enhance the role of personal incomes and to increase the responsibility of the individual to care for himself, while reducing the role of state subventions to that of providing basic protection for members of society unable to take care of themselves. If implemented, these changes would amount to a fundamental renegotiation of the terms of the existing "social contract." As such, they are a matter of considerable political sensitivity, and have so far been approached by the leadership only with the very greatest caution. In spirit, they are somewhat reminiscent of the "wager on the strong"--the land reforms of Tsar Nicholas II's prime minister, Petr Stolypin, who sought to create a new class of prosperous, independent peasants.

A reduced role for state subsidies was not the only controversial proposal. Some writers began to question two other planks of the "social contract": full employment and job security. The social scientist Stanislav Shatalin, for example, argued that enhancing the incentive role of wages was not enough to motivate people to work well; it was also necessary, he stated, to introduce the threat of dismissal. Calling for a shift away from the traditional concept of "full employment" to what he termed "socially and economically effective rational full employment," Shatalin wrote:

> The principles of socialism are not principles of charity which automatically guarantee a job for everyone regardless of his ability to work at it. A person ought to have to wage a daily economic struggle to hold on to a job that suits his abilities.[31]

Other specialists pointed out that, as the economy modernised, workers would have to be ready to undergo retraining or even relocation. The economist Vladimir Kostakov predicted that between 13 and 19 million jobs would be eliminated in the manufacturing sector by the end of the century if targets for labour productivity growth were achieved, and he said that redundant workers should shoulder the responsibility of finding new jobs themselves:

> The need to look for a job--a necessity that many now working in manufacturing and services will certainly face--may also be new and unaccustomed for us. We are used to the exact opposite--work seeking the person.... Obviously, considerable psychological reorientation will be required. We consider it natural and necessary that if, through objective causes, a job slot becomes unnecessary, the worker must immediately be given another job.... Now we shall have to get used to the idea that finding employment is, to a considerable extent, the worker's own responsibility, and that the search may require a certain amount of time--a sufficient, but not an unlimited amount.[32]

Zaslavskaya warned that for some members of society this might prove a painful experience. She seemed to think this would not be a bad thing since it would lead to an overall improvement in labour discipline:

> There is no doubt that the necessity of transferring to branches of production where labour is scarce, and of moving to other areas and cities, will be faced primarily by workers who are the least valuable from the point of view of the work collective, who are indifferent to work and output quality, and who take an inactive part in social life, to say nothing of idlers, drunkards, rolling stones, and so on. Such a situation will lead to ... stronger labour discipline and an increase in the quality of work.[33]

To some extent, the process has already begun. Gorbachev gave his personal approval, for example, to an experiment conducted by the Belorussian railway service, where measures to raise productivity by shedding staff led to the release of 12,000 workers in little over a year.[34] Some 3,200 officials lost their jobs in 1985 as a result of the merger of six agricultural agencies into the State Agroindustrial Committee, and were granted what amounted to unemployment benefit for up to three months while they looked for new posts.[35] And, as noted above, procedures were introduced for retraining workers made redundant in other branches of the economy which included severance payments for those released.[36] The concept of severance pay was previously almost unheard of in Soviet experience.

WIDENING PARTICIPATION AND CONSULTATION

For the first year of his tenure, Gorbachev appeared

to hope that measures such as tightening discipline and increasing incentives for hard work would prove enough to give at least an initial boost to the economy. The population, however, failed to respond or responded negatively. Gradually, the new leader seemed to become convinced that popular apathy was so strong that, until it was overcome, other changes would be impossible. "We must start the reorganisation by reorganising man himself," Gorbachev told a meeting in April 1986.[37] In his efforts to "activate the human factor," Gorbachev shifted the spotlight to political and social reform.

In a major speech delivered in Krasnodar in September 1986, Gorbachev for the first time described the "democratisation" of Soviet society as his main priority. He said that when he was talking to crowds on the city streets earlier in the day,

> I thought of how much our people have grown up, of what intellectual potential they possess, creative potential, and of how, in resolving issues in the country, we still do not make use of this potential, relying on administrative injunction, giving orders, and issuing commands.

"We must," Gorbachev went on, "include the people in the process of restructuring via the democratisation of society."[38] "Our people," he stated the following day, "have matured to the extent that they must be trusted to administer themselves."[39]

Burlatsky described Gorbachev's call for democratisation as a "sensational" departure, because "previously we used only [the term] 'the further development of socialist democracy.'" What Gorbachev was saying, Burlatsky asserted, was that without democratisation--that is, without political reform--the Soviet Union would not be able to attain its economic goals.[40] Burlatsky admitted, however, that it was not clear exactly what "democratisation" entailed in a single-party state. And, he added, "we don't want to change the one-party system."[41]

As it took shape in 1986-87, "democratisation" consisted of three main elements: (1) liberalisation in the cultural sphere and greater openness (*glasnost'*) in the mass media; (2) electoral reform; (3) increased worker participation in management.

The common theme in all these was that the leadership wanted to reduce the passivity and inertia of the population by encouraging popular participation--still, no doubt, guided from above--in the solution of economic and social problems. The Soviet leaders' approach to the relationship between the regime and rank-and-file workers--the subject on which this study is focussed--was therefore being reformulated.

Cultural liberalisation and the introduction of greater openness in the media appealed primarily to members of the intelligentsia, but participation was not restricted to this grouping. At a plenary meeting of the CPSU Central Committee in January 1987, Gorbachev made far-reaching proposals for electoral reform,[42] including the introduction of multiple candidacy in local government elections. Previously, Soviet voters had had no choice at all, being presented with a single, officially-approved candidate in each constituency; the result was widespread indifference on the part of the electorate.[43] As a result of Gorbachev's proposals, multiple-candidacy was introduced on an experimental basis in some local government elections in June 1987. Multiple-candidacy and secret balloting were also introduced in elections to some low-level Party, trade union, and Komsomol posts. These innovations were of considerable potential significance. Some scepticism was nonetheless still in order, for the CPSU showed absolutely no sign of relinquishing its cherished right to preselect candidates for all positions of real power or influence.

Gorbachev also called for the introduction of "self-management" in the workplace. "We want," he said in the summer of 1986, "to activate the human factor by going over to new ways of managing the economy."[44] New legislation (the "Law on the State Enterprise") governing the activities of state-owned enterprises was adopted in June 1987.[45] It called for the workforce to be consulted when an enterprise director was appointed (though his or her election by the workforce was still to be subject to approval by the enterprise's "superior organ," that is, a branch ministry or state committee); in addition, the workforce was given the power to recommend the dismissal of a manager whose performance proved unsatisfactory. The practice of allowing workers to elect their foremen and team-leaders was also extended. Further measures to expand worker participation called for the creation, at enterprise level, of "councils of the work collective." Modelled on the Hungarian experience, these councils were to consist of elected representatives of the workforce, management, trade unions and Party; they were to be endowed with certain consultative powers. They are as yet still in the experimental stage.

A NATIONAL TIME-BOMB?

Gorbachev's encouragement of openness in the mass media struck a responsive chord in the non-Russian republics. Nationalist riots broke out in December 1986 in the Kazakh capital of Alma-Ata, but it was in the Western borderlands that intellectuals spoke out most openly. Writers and historians in Belorussia, Ukraine and the Baltic states seized on *glasnost'* to express long-standing grievances about the loss of cultural identity among the national minorities and, in particular, about the way the teaching of Russian was promoted at the expense of the national languages.[46]

This study found that the populations of the Western borderlands were particularly responsive to the Polish events. It is therefore not surprising that their response to Solidarity was echoed, only a few years later, in their use of *glasnost'* to express resentment at Russian political and cultural dominance. Would the Gorbachev leadership be able to pursue "democratisation" without unleashing pent-up national sentiments? In the long run, the national question might prove Moscow's trickiest problem.

THE "POSTWAR GENERATION"

Western observers have described Gorbachev as a product of the Soviet system, but he and his colleagues differ from their predecessors in at least one significant respect: unlike the Brezhnev generation, they are unburdened by direct experience of the Great Terror of the 1930s. Brezhnev and his colleagues, as Jerry Hough has pointed out, came from the generation born between 1900 and 1906. This was the age-group, as Hough puts it, whose careers spanned the worst period of the Stalin era. Promoted at a young age into the posts of those who perished in the purges of 1937-38, leaders of the Brezhnev generation were the direct beneficiaries of Stalin's terror, and remained indelibly marked by the experience.[47] Gorbachev and his contemporaries, on the other hand, belong to what Hough has termed "the postwar generation" of Soviet leaders: those born in the late 1920s and early 1930s (Gorbachev was born in 1931). These are men who passed their adolescence during World War Two; too young to see wartime military service, they received their college educations in the immediate postwar period.

It was suggested in Chapter 1 that the war years--when leaders and led found themselves united against the common enemy--may have been the only period in Soviet history when the authorities could feel reasonably confident that they enjoyed real popular support. For Gorbachev and his colleagues, too young to have experienced the Great Terror at first hand, Khrushchev's revelation of Stalin's crimes at the Twentieth Party Congress in 1956 was a formative experience. The first Party Congress Gorbachev attended as a delegate was the Twenty-second in 1961, at which Stalin's body was unceremoniously removed from Lenin's mausoleum. This combination of circumstances may perhaps explain why Gorbachev and his colleagues appear to have outgrown at least some of the fear and mistrust of the population that characterised the Brezhnev generation. In other words, Gorbachev and those of his colleagues who are close to him in age may be more likely than their predecessors to believe that the advantages of increased participation by the people in decision-making could outweigh the risks.

POPULAR DISSATISFACTION WITH GORBACHEV'S POLICIES

Members of the Soviet cultural intelligentsia responded warmly to Gorbachev's calls for openness in public life. But what of the ordinary working man or woman, less interested in books and theatres than in housing and food supplies? For the average citizen, the first years of Gorbachev's tenure brought little more than fresh calls for discipline, order and hard work. For many, *glasnost'* went too far and too fast. The campaign to reduce alcohol consumption was widely unpopular, as were Gorbachev's demands for a switch to multi-shift working in industry and the introduction of a new system of quality control that made higher demands of the workforce.[48]

Gorbachev complained bitterly about the strength of resistance to his policies, while a leading Soviet playwright spoke of the Soviet Union's "newly discontented."[49] Gorbachev himself asserted that such people were to be found "among workers, and peasants, and managers, and workers in the Party apparatus.... They are also to be found among our intelligentsia."[50] In short, dissatisfaction existed at every level of society.

The American specialist Peter Hauslohner has argued that part of this dissatisfaction was "normative," that is, based on a fairly widespread belief that "reform would mean the surrender of key values and some of the major accomplishments of Soviet power--that Soviet society would become less 'socialist' and less humane as a result."[51] In 1985, for example, *Izvestia* published a letter from a Leningrad reader who objected in the following terms to the legalisation of some forms of private enterprise:

> It mustn't be allowed! The 7-8 hour working day is our greatest achievement. And to work round the clock without a break is alien to socialism.[52]

The politics of envy also played a role. An office worker, for example, expressed her resentment of a former classmate who had become prosperous through private initiative: "I don't want to live like her. I want her to live like me."[53]

In a mood of seeming despair, Gorbachev told a meeting of writers in June 1986 that "Generations will have to pass before we can really change. Generations!"[54] Popular apathy and entrenched bureaucratic interests were formidable opponents. Gorbachev himself warned a meeting of Party and government officials in Riga early in 1987 that Soviet citizens must be prepared to tighten their belts since the next two to three years would be a "very difficult" period, but he promised that if they did so they would see an improvement in their standard of living in the 1990s.[55] If Gorbachev failed to keep that promise, and if ordinary Soviet people found their daily lives were not getting better, the new Soviet leader might find himself facing an ugly backlash. This study suggests that the risk of such an upheaval is less than past Soviet leaders have tended to think. On the other hand, one of Gorbachev's main objectives is precisely to rouse the Soviet people from the passivity to which they have been so long accustomed.

FOOTNOTES TO CHAPTER 15

1. See RL 104/84, "Election Speeches by Soviet Leaders: An Overview," by Elizabeth Teague, 8 March 1984.

2. This chapter draws extensively on the author's contribution, "Gorbachev's 'Human Factor' Policies," prepared for inclusion in the 1987 US Congress Joint Economic Committee compendium on the Soviet economy, *Gorbachev's Economic Plans*.

3. *Krasnaya zvezda*, 19 September 1986.

4. T. I. Zaslavskaya, "Vybor strategii," *Izvestia*, 1 June 1985.

5. M. S. Gorbachev, "Zhivoe tvorchestvo naroda," Moscow, 1984, p. 23.

6. For example, *Moscow television*, 18 September 1986.

7. *Moscow television*, 25 February 1986.

8. Vladimir Treml, "Gorbachev's Anti-drinking Campaign: A Noble Experiment or a Costly Exercise in Futility?" RL Supplement No 2/87, 18 March 1987.

9. *SSSR v tsifrakh v 1986 g.*, Moscow, 1987.

10. Fedor Burlatsky, "Razgovor nachistotu," *Literaturnaya gazeta*, 1 October 1986.

11. Speaking at the Twenty-seventh Party Congress, Gorbachev deplored the use of what he called "the residual principle" in allocating resources to social needs; *Moscow television*, 25 February 1986.

For assessments of Gorbachev's social policies, see Walter D. Connor, "Social Policy under Gorbachev," *Problems of Communism*, July-August 1986, pp. 31-46; Aaron Trehub, "Social and Economic Rights in the Soviet Union: Work, Health Care, Social Security, and Housing," RL Supplement No 3/86, 29 December 1986; Peter Hauslohner, "Gorbachev's Social Contract," *Soviet Economy*, January-March 1987, pp. 54-89.

12. *Izvestia*, 19 March 1985.

13. *Radio Moscow*, 18 September 1986.

14. *Pravda*, 27 May 1987.

15. *Pravda*, 28 May 1986; *Vedomosti Verkhovnogo Soveta SSSR*, No 22, 1986, pp. 369-73.

16. *Pravda*, 28 March 1986.

17. *Izvestia*, 20 November 1986. Leonid Abalkin, a prominent Soviet economist, confirmed in an interview with Western journalists that legislation on individual labour was originally intended to be enacted at the same time as the measures on unearned income; *Boston Globe*, 28 November 1986.

18. For a fuller discussion of this question see Meredith A. Heinemeier, "The Brigade System of Labor Organization and Incentives in Soviet Industry and Construction," in the 1987 US Joint Economic Committee compendium on the Soviet economy, *Gorbachev's Economic Plans*.

19. V.Z. Rogovin, "Sotsial'naya spravedlivost' i sotsialisticheskoe raspredelenie zhiznennykh blag," *Voprosy filosofii*, No 9, 1986, pp. 3-20 at pp. 17-18; *idem*, *Komsomol'skaya pravda*, 12 November 1985; A. Shokhin, "Otkuda berutsya netrudovvye dokhody?" *Ekonomicheskaya gazeta*, No 1, 1986; L. Velikanova, "Kazhdoi sem'e--otdel'nuyu kvartiru," *Literaturnaya gazeta*, 24 September 1986; T. I. Zaslavskaya, "Taktika peremen," *Izvestia*, 18 April 1986. The measures against "unearned income" called for "greater use of declarations" to check the legality of citizens' incomes and, perhaps, to

facilitate the levying of a graduated income tax; *Pravda*, 28 May 1986.

20. N. Rimashevskaya, "Raspredelenie i spravedlivost'," *Ekonomicheskaya gazeta*, No 40, 1986.

21. *Radio Moscow*, 18 September 1986.

22. *Ekonomicheskaya gazeta*, No 29, 1985.

23. *Pravda*, 12 December 1985.

24. *Ibid.*, 17 October 1986.

25. *Ekonomicheskaya gazeta*, No 43, 1986; *Pravda*, 3 November 1986; *Trud*, 19 December 1986.

26. *Ekonomicheskaya gazeta*, No 44, 1986.

27. *Izvestia*, 26 September 1986.

28. G. Lisichkin, "Razmyshleniya u myasnogo prilavka," *Trud*, 22 August 1986. The state subsidy on meat and dairy products alone in 1986 was projected to be about 50 billion rubles, that is, roughly $70 billion at the official rate of exchange, or more than double the European Community's Common Agricultural Policy total or the US farm subsidy; *Argumenty i fakty*, No 21, 1986.

29. "Platnaya poliklinika: za i protiv," *Izvestia*, 11 July 1986.

30. T. Zaslavskaya, "Chelovechesky facktor razvitiya ekonomiki i sotsial'naya spravedlivost'," *Kommunist*, No 13, 1986, pp. 61-73 at pp. 72-3; Velikanova, *op. cit*.

31. S. Shatalin, "Sotsial'noe razvitie i ekonomichesky rost," *Kommunist*, No 14, 1986, pp. 59-70 at p. 63.

32. V. Kostakov, "Odin, kak semero," *Sovetskaya kul'tura*, 4 January 1986.

33. Zaslavskaya, "Chelovechesky...," p. 70.

34. RL 318/86, "The Belorussian Railway Experiment: A New Shchekino?" by Aaron Trehub, 20 August 1986.

35. *Pravda*, 26 November 1986.

36. *Ekonomicheskaya gazeta*, No 44, 1986.

37. *Moscow television*, 8 April 1986.

38. *Moscow television*, 18 September 1986.

39. *Radio Moscow*, 19 September 1986.

40. Quotations from RL 396/86, "Interview with Fedor Burlatsky," by Henry Hamman, 10 October 1986; and from a talk delivered by Burlatsky at the University of Surrey on 9 November 1986.

41. *Ibid.*

42. *Pravda*, 28 January 1987.

43. V. Vasil'ev, "Vlast', otkrytaya dlya vsekh," *Literaturnaya gazeta*, 17 September 1986; *idem*, "Demokratiya i perestroika," *Pravda*, 31 October 1986.

44. *Radio Moscow*, 31 July 1986.

45. *Izvestia*, 1 July 1987.

46. Numerous articles were devoted to this subject in the research publications of Radio Free Europe and Radio Liberty from the summer of 1986 on. See in particular the work of Roman Solchanyk and Toomas Ilves; for an overview, see Bohdan Nahaylo, "Gorbachev Faces Resurgence of Nationalism," *Wall Street Journal*, 24 December 1986.

47. Jerry F. Hough, "The Generation Gap and the Brezhnev Succession," *Problems of Communism*, July-August 1979, pp. 1-16 at pp. 5 and 15.

48. The average wages of workers at an agricultural machinery plant in the city of Tyumen' were slashed by one-third when their output was rejected under the new system (*TASS*, 4 March 1987).

49. Aleksandr Gel'man, "Chto snachala, chto potom...," *Literaturnaya gazeta*, 10 September 1986.

50. *Moscow television*, 18 September 1986.

51. Peter Hauslohner, "Reforming Social Policy: A Comment," in the 1987 US Congress Joint Economic Committee compendium on the Soviet economy, *Gorbachev's Economic Plans*.

52. *Izvestia*, 30 July 1985.

53. Quoted by Rogovin, *op. cit.*, p. 19.

54. AS No 5785.

55. *Moscow television*, 19 February 1987.

BIBLIOGRAPHY

This bibliography makes no claim to be a complete catalogue of all the available sources relating to Soviet labour policy. It does not even include all the works consulted in the preparation of this book, but only those upon which most reliance was placed. Where minor use was made of an item, it has simply been referred to at the appropriate page in the text or in the footnotes at the end of the relevant chapter, and has not been included in the general bibliography.

SOVIET NEWSPAPERS AND PERIODICALS

The bulk of the material used in the compilation of this book was drawn from the official Soviet press, and the following newspapers and periodicals were screened on a regular basis. Extensive use was made of the daily reports of Soviet radio and television broadcasts issued by the Monitoring Service of Radio Liberty in Munich. Also consulted were the *Summary of World Broadcasts* published by the British Broadcasting Corporation, and the daily reports issued by the Foreign Broadcast Information Service.

Agitator; *Argumenty i fakty*; *Chelovek i zakon*; *EKO (Ekonomika i organizatsiya promyshlennogo proizvodstva)*; *Ekonomicheskaya gazeta*; *Izvestia*; *Kommunist*; *Komsomol'skaya pravda*; *Krokodil*; *Literaturnaya gazeta*; *Molodoi kommunist*; *Nauchnyi kommunizm*; *Novoe vremya*; *Obshchestvennye nauki*; *Partiinaya zhizn'*; *Politicheskoe samoobrazovanie*; *Pravda*; *Problemy mira i sotsializma*; *Sotsialistichesky trud*; *Sotsiologicheskie issledovaniya*; *Sovetskoe gosudarstvo i pravo*; *Sovetskaya Rossiya*; *Sovetskie profsoyuzy*; *Trud*; *Vedomosti Verkhovnogo Soveta SSSR*; *Voprosy ekonomiki*; *Voprosy filosofii*; *Voprosy istorii*; *Voprosy istorii KPSS*.

WESTERN NEWSPAPERS AND PERIODICALS

Extensive use was also made of the following Western publications. The invaluable work of the Central News and Current Information services of Radio Free Europe/Radio Liberty is gratefully acknowledged.

Christian Science Monitor; *Daily Telegraph*; *Economist*; *Financial Times*; *Foreign Affairs*; *Frankfurter Allgemeine Zeitung*; *Guardian*; *International Security*; *Le Monde*; *Los Angeles Times*; *New York Times*; *Newsweek*; *Neue Zuercher Zeitung*; *Problems of Communism*; *Russkaya mysl'*; *Slavic Review*; *Soviet Analyst*; *Soviet Labour Review*; *Soviet Studies*; *Survey*; *Time*; *The Times* (London); *Wall Street Journal*; *Washington Post*.

Dispatches from press agencies including AFP, AP, APN, DPA, PAP, Reuters, Tanjug, TASS, and UPI were also used, and extensive use made of Radio Liberty's Red Archive and Samizdat Archive is gratefully acknowledged.

SOVIET BOOKS AND ARTICLES

Ambartsumov, E.A., "Analiz V.I. Leninym prichin krizisa 1921 g. i putei vykhoda iz nego," *Voprosy istorii*, No 4, 1984.

Andropov, Yu.V., *Izbrannye rechi i stat'i*, second edition, Moscow, 1983.

---"Uchenie Karla Marksa i nekotorye voprosy sotsialisticheskogo stroitel'stva v SSSR," *Kommunist*, No 3, 1983.

---*Leninizm--neischerpaemyi istochnik revolyutionnoi energii i tvorchestva mass. Izbrannye rechi i stat'i*, Moscow, 1984.

Brezhnev, L.I., *Otchetnyi doklad TsK KPSS XXVI s"ezdy Kommunisticheskoi partii Sovetskogo*

Soyuza i ocherednye zadachi partii v oblasti vnutrennei i vneshnei politiki, Moscow, 1981.

Bugaev, E., "Strannaya pozitsiya," *Kommunist*, No 14, 1984.

Butenko, A.P., "Sotsializm: formy i deformatsii," *Novoe vremya*, No 6, 1982.

---"Protivorechiya razvitiya sotsializma kak obshchestvennogo stroiya," *Voprosy filosofii*, No 10, 1982.

---"Eshche raz o protivorechiyakh sotsializma," *Voprosy filosofii*, No 2, 1984.

Chernenko, K.U., *Izbrannyie rechi i stat'i*, Moscow, 1981.

---*Avangardnaya rol' partii kommunistov*, Moscow, 1982.

---"Avangardnaya rol' partii kommunistov. Vazhnoe uslovie ee vozrastaniya," *Kommunist*, No 6, 1982.

---*Narod i partiya ediny. Izbrannye rechi i stat'i*, Moscow, 1984.

---*Izbrannye rechi i stat'i*, second, enlarged edition, Moscow, 1984.

XXVI s"ezd KPSS: Stenografichesky otchet, Moscow, 1981.

Fedoseev, P.N., "XXVI s"ezd KPSS i aktual'nye zadachi razvitiya obshchestvennykh nauk," *Voprosy filosofii*, No 8, 1981.

---"Dialektika obshchestvennoi zhizni," *Problemy mira i sotsializma*, No 9, 1981.

---"Sotsial'nyi optimizm kommunistov," *Pravda*, 13 November 1981.

---"K. Marks i sovremennost'," *Voprosy filosofii*, No 4, 1983.

---and L.F. Il'ichev, "O nekotorikh metodologicheskikh problemakh istoricheskogo materializma," *Voprosy filosofii*, No 6, 1984.

Gorbachev, M.S., *Zhivoe tvorchestvo naroda*, Moscow, 1984.

Kodeks zakonov o trude, Moscow, 1974.

Konstitutsiya (osnovnoi zakon) Soyuza Sovetskikh Sotsialisticheskikh Respublik, Moscow, 1977.

Korshunov, Yu.N., "Sovetskie profsoyuzy: zashchita interesov trudyashchikhsya," *Sovetskoe gosudarstvo i pravo*, No 4, 1981.

Kosolapov, R.I., "Vklad XXIV, XXV i XXVI s"ezdov KPSS v razrabotku teoreticheskikh i politicheskikh problem razvitogo sotsializma i perekhoda k kommunizmu," *Kommunist*, No 5, 1982.

Kostakov, V., "Odin, kak semero," *Sovetskaya kul'tura*, 4 January 1986.

Kotlyar, A. and Talalai, M., "Puti sokrashcheniya tekuchesti kadrov," *Voprosy ekonomiki*, No 5, 1981.

Kupriyanova, Z.V., "Tekuchest' kadrov: perelomit' nezhelatel'nye tendentsii," *EKO*, No 5, 1984.

Levin, M., "Molodezh' i trud," *EKO*, No 8, 1983.

Maslennikov, V.A., "Zakon o trudovykh kollektivakh," *Sovetskoe gosudarstvo i pravo*, No 10, 1983.

Narodnoe khozaistvo SSSR 1922-1982, Moscow, 1982.

Narodnoe khozaistvo SSSR v 1983 g., Moscow, 1984.

Prokhorov, V., "Partiya i profsoyuzy," *Politicheskoe samoobrazovanie*, No 2, 1981.

Petrov, L., "Profsoyuzy--shkola kommunizma," *Partiinaya zhizn'*, No 12, 1981.

Rimashevskaya, N., "Raspredelenie i spravedlivost'," *Ekonomicheskaya gazeta*, No 40, 1986.

Rogovin, V.Z., "Sotsial'naya spravedlivost' i sotsialisticheskoe raspredelenie zhiznennykh blag," *Voprosy filosofii*, No 9, 1986.

Semenov, V.S., "Problema protivorechii v usloviyakh sotsializma," Parts 1 and 2, *Voprosy filosofii*, No 7, 1982, and No 9, 1982.

---"K teoreticheskomy uglubleniyu i konkretizatsii analiza problemy protivorechii v usloviyakh razvitogo sotsializma," *Voprosy filosofii*, No 2, 1984.

Sharapov, G.V., "Leninskie printsipy partiinogo rukovodstva profsoyuzami," *Voprosy istorii*

KPSS, No 11, 1981.

Shatalin, S., "Sotsial'noe razvitie i ekonomichesky rost," *Kommunist*, No 14, 1986.

Shibaev, A., "Samaya massovaya organizatsiya trudyashchikhsya," *Kommunist*, No 4, 1981.

Spravochnik partiinogo rabotnika, Moscow, 1981.

Spravochnik profsoyuznogo rabotnika, Moscow, 1983.

Sotsializm i trud: slovar'-spravochnik, Moscow, 1985.

Torkanovsky, E., "Razvitie demokraticheskikh nachal v upravlenii proizvodstvom," *Kommunist*, No 8, 1983.

Za vysokoe kachestvo i deistvennost' ideologicheskoi raboty, Moscow, 1981.

"Zakon o trudovykh kollektivakh v deistvii," *Sovetskoe gosudarstvo i pravo*, No 6, 1985.

Zaslavskaya, T.I., "Vybor strategii," *Izvestia*, 1 June 1985.

---"Taktika peremen," *Izvestia*, 18 April 1986.

---"Chelovechesky faktor ravitiya ekonomiki i sotsial'naya spravedlivost'," *Kommunist*, No 13, 1986.

WESTERN BOOKS AND ARTICLES

Adam, J. (ed.), *Employment Policies in the Soviet Union and Eastern Europe*, London, 1982.

Alekseeva, L. and Chalidze, V., *Public Unrest in the USSR*, Silver Spring, Maryland, 1985.

Alexeyeva, L., *Soviet Dissent: Contemporary Movements for National, Religious and Human Rights*, Middletown, Conn., 1985.

Alexiev, A.R., *Dissent and Nationalism in the Soviet Baltic*, Santa Monica, Calif., 1983.

Ascherson, N., *The Polish August: The Self-Limiting Revolution*, Harmondsworth, 1981.

Barghoorn, F.C., "Changes in Russia: The Need for Perspectives," *Problems of Communism*, May-June 1966.

Belotserkovsky, V., "Workers' Struggles in the USSR

in the Early Sixties," *Critique*, Nos 10-11, 1979.
Bialer, S., *The Soviet Paradox: External Expansion, Internal Decline*, New York, 1986.
Binyon, M., *Life in Russia*, London, 1985.
Boiter, A., "When the Kettle Boils Over..." *Problems of Communism*, January-February 1964.
Bornstein, M. *et al*. (eds), *East-West Relations and the Future of Eastern Europe*, London, 1981.
Bowker, M.B., "Why People Participate in the Soviet Union," MA dissertation, University of Essex, 1980.
Brown, A., "Andropov: Discipline *and* Reform?" *Problems of Communism*, January-February 1983.
---and Kaser, M. (eds), *The Soviet Union Since the Fall of Khrushchev*, second edition, London, 1978.
---*et al*., (eds), *The Cambridge Encyclopedia of Russia and the Soviet Union*, Cambridge, 1982.
Brown, E.C., *Soviet Trade Unions and Labor Relations*, Cambridge, Mass., 1966.
Brumberg, A. (ed), *Poland: Genesis of a Revolution*, New York, 1983.
Brzezinski, Z., "The Soviet Political System: Transformation or Degeneration?" *Problems of Communism*, January-February 1966.
Bush, K., "Major Decree on Private Plots and Livestock Holdings," Radio Liberty Research (hereafter RL) 38/81, 26 January 1981.
Clarke, M. (ed.), *Corruption: Causes, Consequences and Control*, London, 1983.
Cohen, S.F., *Rethinking the Soviet Experience: Politics and History since 1917*, New York, 1984.
Connor, W.D., "Social Policy under Gorbachev," *Problems of Communism*, July-August 1986.
--- *et al*., *Public Opinion in European Socialist Systems*, New York, 1977.
Conquest, R., "Immobilism and Decay," *Problems of*

Communism, September-October 1966.

Corti, M., "A *Samizdat* Work on the Events in Poland," RL 319/83, 24 August 1983.

De Weydenthal, J.B. *et al.*, *The Polish Drama: 1980-1982*, Lexington, Mass., 1983.

Di Franceisco, W. and Gitelman, Z., "Soviet Political Culture and 'Covert Participation' in Policy Implementation," *American Political Science Review*, No 3, 1984.

Doder, D., *Shadows and Whispers: Power Politics Inside the Kremlin from Brezhnev to Gorbachev*, New York, 1986.

Drewnowski, J. (ed), *Crisis in the East European Economy: The Spread of the Polish Disease*, New York, 1982.

Economist Intelligence Unit, *Quarterly Economic Review of the USSR*, Nos 2, 3 and 4, 1981.

Elliot, I., "Dissent, Opposition and Instability," in McCauley (ed), 1983 (see below).

Evans, A.B. Jr, "The Polish Crisis in the 1980s and Adaptation in Soviet Ideology," *Journal of Comunist Studies*, September 1986.

Fainsod, M., "Roads to the Future," *Problems of Communism*, July-August 1967.

Feifer, G., "Russian Disorders: The Sick Man of Europe," *Harper's Magazine*, February 1981.

Feshbach, M., "The Structure and Composition of the Industrial Labor Force," in Kahan and Ruble (eds), 1979 (see below).

Friedgut, T.H., *Political Participation in the USSR*, Princeton, 1979.

Garton Ash, T., *The Polish Revolution*, London, 1985.

Gelman, H., *The Brezhnev Politburo and the Decline of Detente*, Ithaca, NY, 1984.

Gidwitz, B., "Labor Unrest in the Soviet Union," *Problems of Communism*, November-December 1982.

Gloeckner, E., "Underemployment and Potential Unemployment of the Technical Intelligenstsia: Distortions Between Education and Occupation," in Lane (ed), 1986 (see below).

Hanson, P., "Economic Constraints on Soviet Policies in the 1980s," *International Affairs*, Winter 1980-81.

---"Labor Discipline and Production Stoppages in Soviet Industry," RL 200/83, 18 May 1983.

---"Discussion of Economic Reform in the USSR: The 'Novosibirsk Paper,'" RL 356/83, 23 September 1983.

---"On the Limitations of the Soviet Economic Reform Debate," Birmingham, 1985.

---"The Serendipitous Soviet Achievement of Full Employment: Labour Shortage and Labour Hoarding in the Soviet Economy," in Lane (ed), 1986 (see below).

Hauslohner, P., "Gorbachev's Social Contract," *Soviet Economy*, January-March 1987.

---"Reforming Social Policy: A Comment," in the 1987 US Congress Joint Economic Committee compendium on the Soviet economy.

Haynes, V. and Semyonova, O. (eds), *Workers Against the Gulag*, London, 1979.

Holloway, D. and Sharp, J.M.O. (eds), *The Warsaw Pact: Alliance in Transition*, Ithaca, NY, 1984.

Hough, J.F., "The Soviet System: Petrification or Pluralism?" *Problems of Communism*, March-April 1972.

---"Political Participation in the Soviet Union," *Soviet Studies*, January 1976.

---"Policy-Making and the Worker," in Kahan and Ruble (eds), 1979 (see below).

---"The Generation Gap and the Brezhnev Succession," *Problems of Communism*, July-August 1979.

Hvat, I., "Chronicle of the Catholic Church in the Ukraine," RL 3/85, 7 January 1985.

Kahan, A. and Ruble, B. (eds), *Industrial Labor in the U.S.S.R.*, New York, 1979.

Kaiser, R.G., *Russia: The People and the Power*, Harmondsworth, 1977.

---"The Soviet Union: A Time of Failure," *International Herald Tribune*, 26 September 1984.

Karatnycky, A. *et al*. (eds), *Workers' Rights, East and West*, New Brunswick, 1980.

Kaufman, R.F., "Soviet Defense Trends," study prepared for the Subcommittee on International Trade, Finance and Security Economics of the US Congress Joint Economic Committee, Washington DC, 1983.

Klose, K., *Russia and the Russians: Inside the Closed Society*, New York, 1984.

Kolankiewicz, G., "The Polish Question: Andropov's Answer?" in Schapiro and Godson (eds), 1984 (see below).

Kusin, V.V., "How the Soviet System is Studied," mimeo, 1984.

Kux, E., "Contradictions in Soviet Socialism," *Problems of Communism*, November-December 1984.

Lampert, N., "Law and Order in the USSR: The Case of Economic and Official Crime," *Soviet Studies*, July 1984.

---"Law, Order and Political Power in the USSR," paper delivered at the annual conference of the British National Association for Soviet and East European Studies, Cambridge, 1984.

---*Whistle-blowing in the Soviet Union: Complaints and Abuses under State Socialism*, London, 1985.

---"Job Security and the Law in the USSR," in Lane (ed), 1986 (see below).

Lane, D., *Soviet Economy and Society*, Oxford, 1985.

---(ed), *Labour and Employment in the USSR*, Brighton, 1986.

---and O'Dell, F., *The Soviet Industrial Worker: Social Class, Education and Control*, Oxford, 1978.

Laqueur, W., "What We Know About the Soviet Union," *Commentary*, February 1983.

---"Is There Now, or Has There Ever Been, Such a

Thing as Totalitarianism?" *Commentary*, October 1985.

Larrabee, F.S., "Instability and Change in Eastern Europe," *International Security*, Winter 1981-2.

---"Soviet Crisis Management in Eastern Europe," in Holloway and Sharp (eds), 1984 (see above).

Matthews, M. with Jones, T.A., *Soviet Sociology, 1964-75: A Bibliography*, New York, 1975.

McAuley, M., *Labour Disputes in Soviet Russia: 1957-65*, Oxford, 1969.

McCauley, M. (ed.), *The Soviet Union After Brezhnev*, London, 1983.

McNeill, T. "Images of the Soviet Future: The Western Scholarly Debate," paper presented at the Second International Congress of Professors World Peace Academy, Geneva, 1985.

Medvedev, Z., *Andropov*, New York, 1983.

Meiklejohn Terry, S. (ed), *Soviet Policy in Eastern Europe*, New Haven, Conn., 1984.

Michael, J.C., "The Independent Trade-Union Movement in the Soviet Union," RL 304/79, 11 October 1979.

Moreton, E., "The Soviet Union and Poland's Struggle for Self-Control," *International Security*, Summer 1982.

Morgenthau, H.J., "Alternatives to Change," *Problems of Communism*, September-October 1966.

Nagorski, A., *Reluctant Farewell*, New York, 1985.

Nahaylo, B., "Ukrainian Dissident Comments on Events in Poland," RL 472/83, 11 November 1983.

---"World War II: Moscow's Selective Memory," *Wall Street Journal*, 8 May 1985.

New Encylopaedia Britannica, fifteenth edition, Chicago, 1985.

Nove, A., *An Economic History of the USSR*, Harmondsworth, 1969.

---"Whither the Soviet Economy?" *Washington Quarterly*, Spring 1984.

Parta, R.E., "Listening to Radio Liberty in the

USSR, 1976-77," Radio Free Europe/Radio Liberty Soviet Area Audience and Opinion Research, June 1978.

Pipes, R., *Survival Is Not Enough*, New York, 1984.

Porter, B.D., "The USSR and Poland on the Way to Martial Law," in de Weydenthal *et al.*, 1983 (see above).

---"The Repercussions of Gdansk: Poland's Crisis and the Socialist Community," in de Weydenthal *et al.*, 1983 (see above).

Powell, D.E., "Labor Turnover in the Soviet Union," *Slavic Review*, June 1977.

Pravda, A., "Spontaneous Workers' Activity in the Soviet Union," in Kahan and Ruble (eds), 1979 (see above).

---"East-West Interdependence and the Social Compact in Eastern Europe," in Bornstein *et al.* (eds), 1981 (see above).

---"Is There A Soviet Working Class?" *Problems of Communism*, November-December 1982.

Radio Free Europe Research, *The Strikes in Poland*, Munich, 1980.

Radio Free Europe/Radio Liberty Soviet Area Audience Opinion Research:

---Analysis Report 1-81, "Attitudes in the USSR toward the Right to Strike," January 1981.

---Background Report 2-81, "Soviet Citizens Comment on Events in Poland," January 1981.

---Background Report 3-81, "Attitudes of Soviet Citizens to the Strike Movement in Poland," May 1981.

---Analysis Report 8-81, "Developing Soviet Citizen Attitudes toward Poland," October 1981.

---Analysis Report 5-82, "Attitudes of Some Soviet Citizens to the Solidarity Trade Union Movement," May 1982.

---Analysis Report 6-82, "Soviet Citizen Attitudes toward Poland since Martial Law," September 1982.

Reddaway, P., "Dissent in the Soviet Union," *Problems of Communism*, November-December 1983.

Ruble, B.A., "Factory Unions and Workers' Rights," in Kahan and Ruble (eds), 1979 (see above).

---*Soviet Trade Unions: Their Development in the 1970s*, Cambridge, 1981.

---"Labor Relations in a Period of Economic Constraints," mimeo, 1981.

---"Soviet Trade Unions and Labor Relations After 'Solidarity,'" in US Congress Joint Economic Committee, Part 2, 1982 (see below).

---"Industrial Trade Unions in the USSR: The Soviet Model of Dual Functioning Trade Unions," mimeo, 1983.

Rutland, P., "Productivity Campaigns in Soviet Industry," in Lane (ed), 1986 (see above).

Scanlan, J.P., *Marxism in the USSR: A Critical Survey of Current Soviet Thought*, Ithaca, NY, 1985.

Schapiro, L. and Godson, J. (eds), *The Soviet Worker: Illusions and Realities*, London, 1981; second, revised edition, London, 1984.

Schroeder, G.E., "Managing Labour Shortages in the Soviet Union," in Adam (ed), 1982 (see above).

Sharlet, R., "Law and Discipline in the USSR: The Early 1980s Under Brezhnev, Andropov, and Chernenko," paper presented at the Annual Convention of the American Association for the Advancement of Slavic Studies, New York, 1984.

Sheehy, A., "Blue-Collar Workers Elected to Central Committee Buros in Five Union Republics," RL 57/81, 5 February 1981.

Shipler, D.K., *Russia: Broken Idols, Solemn Dreams*, New York, 1983.

Simis, K.M., *USSR: The Corrupt Society*, New York, 1982.

Smith, H. *The Russians*, London, 1976.

Sochor, Z.A., "NEP Revisited: Current Soviet Interest in Alternative Strategies of Development," *Soviet Union/Union Sovietique*, No 9, Part 2, 1982.

Solchanyk, R., "Criticism of Local Trade-Union Organs in the Ukraine: Impact of Polish Developments?" RL 303/80, 27 August 1980.

---"Ukrainian Party Journal Raises the Specter of Poland," RL 70/81, 17 February 1981.

---"Ukrainian Party Shows Concern for Trade Unions and Workers," RL 303/81, 4 August 1981.

---"Poland's Impact Inside the USSR," *Soviet Analyst*, 9 September 1981.

---"Nervous Neighbors: The Soviets and Solidarity," *Workers under Communism*, No 1, 1982.

---"Poland and the 'Ukrainian Connection,'" RL 19/84, 11 January 1984.

---"Poland and the Soviet West," in Wimbush (ed), 1984 (see below).

Solzhenitsyn, A.I., *The Gulag Archipelago III*, New York, 1976.

Steele, J. and Abraham, E., *Andropov in Power*, Oxford, 1983.

Stephan, Paul B. III, "Comrades' Courts and Labor Discipline Since Brezhnev," University of Virginia School of Law, 1985.

Taras, R., "Official Etiologies of Polish Crises: Changing Historiographies and Factional Struggles," *Soviet Studies*, January 1986.

Teague, E., "The USSR Law on Work Collectives: Workers' Control or Workers Controlled?" in Lane (ed), 1986 (see above).

---"Gorbachev's 'Human Factor' Policies," in the 1987 US Congress Joint Economic Committee compendium on the Soviet economy.

Teckenberg, W., "Labour Turnover and Job Satisfaction: Indicators of Industrial Conflict in the USSR," *Soviet Studies*, August 1978.

Tenson, A., "Food Rationing in the Soviet Union," RL 321/82, 11 August 1982.

Treadgold, D.W., *Twentieth Century Russia*, fourth

edition, Chicago, 1976.

Trehub, A., "The Belorussian Railway Experiment: A New Shchekino?" RL 318/86, 20 August 1986.

---"Social and Economic Rights in the Soviet Union: Work, Health Care, Social Security, and Housing," RL Supplement No 3/86, 29 December 1986.

US Central Intelligence Agency, *Handbook of Economic Statistics 1982*, Washington DC, 1982.

---*Handbook of Economic Statistics 1984*, Washington DC, 1984.

US Congress Joint Economic Committee, *Soviet Economy in the 1980s: Problems and Prospects*, Parts 1 and 2, Washington DC, 1982.

US Department of State, *Human Rights in the USSR*, Washington DC, 1983.

Vardys, V.S., "Polish Echoes in the Baltic," *Problems of Communism*, July-August 1983.

Voronitsyn, S., "Growing Interest in the Study of Public Opinion," RL 142/78, 27 June 1978.

---"Latest Soviet Efforts to Counter the Influence of Foreign Radio Broadcasts," RL 272/82, 5 July 1982.

---"Campaign Against 'Parasitism' Likely to be Stepped up in RSFSR," RL 519/82, 27 December 1982.

---"Counterpropaganda: A 'New Weapon' of Soviet Ideologists," RL 124/85, 18 April 1985.

Waedekin, K.-E., "The Impact of Official Policy on the Number of Livestock in the Soviet Private Farming Sector," RL 224/83, 9 June 1983.

Wimbush, S.E. (ed), *Soviet Nationalities in Strategic Perspective*, Beckenham, 1984.

Wishnevsky, J., "More Details Emerge About 'Socialists' Arrested in USSR Earlier This Year," RL 341/82, 23 August 1982.

---"*Samizdat* Symposium *Sotsialist-82* Reaches the West," RL 41/83, 20 January 1983.

---"New Law on 'Malicious Disobedience' in Soviet

Camps," RL 430/83, 14 November 1983.

---"New Additions to the Law on Crimes against the State," RL 78/84, 16 February 1984.

---"The Fall of Khrushchev and the Birth of the Human Rights Movement in the Soviet Union," RL 382/84, 8 October 1984.

---"Dissent under Three Soviet Leaders: Suppression Continues, the Style Varies," RL 89/85, 21 March 1985.

Ziegler, C.E., "Worker Participation and Worker Discontent in the Soviet Union," *Political Science Quarterly*, Summer 1983.

Zinoviev, A., *Kommunizm kak real'nost'*, Lausanne, 1981.

INDEX